by Rod Laver

WITH
Bud Collins

The Education of a Tennis Player

A Fireside Book
Published by
Simon and Schuster

A Fireside Book
Published by Simon and Schuster
Rockefeller Center, 630 Fifth Avenue
New York, New York 10020
First Fireside paperback edition 1973
SBN 671-20902-7 Casebound
SBN 671-21533-7 Paperback
Library of Congress Catalog Card Number: 70-139639
Designed by Irving Perkins
Manufactured in the United States of America

2   3   4   5   6   7   8   9   10

ACKNOWLEDGMENTS

It didn't hurt to be born an Australian. Certainly I can't thank my Mum and Dad, Melba and Roy Laver, enough for their part in my tennis life—for always having a court wherever we lived, and thus making it possible for me to play a game all my life, for fun and a living. (I have long since forgiven Dad for his early judgment that my older brothers had the tennis talent in the family.)

I'd also like to thank:

Those same brothers, Trevor and Bob, who hit with me even when it was a bother.

Charlie Hollis, who showed me what the game was really about— and how to get where I had to go.

Harry Hopman, who made me and the rest of his dynasty, from Sedgman to Newcombe, realize that talent is nothing without fitness.

Peter Schwed, my publisher, whose forehand is nearly as incisive as his literary judgment, a rare editor who knows tennis thoroughly and whose ideas and suggestions were the basis of this book.

Mark McCormack and the others at International Management, who taught me how to make money without running a step.

Roy Emerson, good friend and remarkable doubles partner—strong enough to carry me.

Ken Rosewall and Lew Hoad, who finally convinced me to turn pro by offering to back the guarantee with their own money. (I hadn't realized anybody was that anxious to beat me.)

Bud Collins, who yanked the whole story out of me, and who suffers as much as I do when I lose. (After all, he shares in the royalties from this book.)

Palmer Collins, whose reading and editing pulled her husband's manuscript together, and whose understanding of the Australian stomach expressed itself humanely in servings of steak-and-eggs and Foster's Lager whenever I, a travel-worn Queenslander, landed on Beacon Hill.

R.L.

For Mary, who made it the grandest Slam

CONTENTS

ILLUSTRATIONS

INTRODUCTION

WHY AM I writing a book? Me, with no literary background, foreground, inclinations, or even interests.

One of the reasons might be that I have received an advance from a publisher with instructions: write a book. There is something about an advance that inspires almost anybody to thoughts of literary creation. Some take the money and run. Others pull up lame in the typing fingers (or finger). Publishers learn to adjust to those breaks of their game just as I do to bad bounces.

But most of us literary-set types, with an eye to supplementing the advance with further royalties, press on and deliver a manuscript which in time becomes a tome to be peddled in bookstores. In this case, this one.

Sports personalities have been doing this for a long time. First to appear in the English language was Dame Juliana Berners in 1486, whose *Book of St. Albans* was about hunting and fishing. Dame Juliana liked to hunt and fish, and so do I. I hope we prove to have something else in common. Her book is still selling. If mine is four centuries from now my heirs will be extremely pleased.

After Dame Juliana came a deluge of boxers, football, basketball and baseball players, cricketers, horsemen, golfers and tennis players putting their stories in print. Football players in America have done quite well in recent years, but Joe Namath I'm not. I don't think I'm getting better looking every day, and since I'm over thirty I can wait for tomorrow. Johnny Walker Red would thrill me only if I owned the distillery. I suppose I would settle for a Carling's Red Cap ale if Australian beer is unavailable.

My story, focusing particularly on the year 1969, is part of what I want to tell you. In winning the singles championships of Australia, France, England and the United States to register the first open Grand Slam in tennis history, I owned 1969 as much as any athlete can own a year. There were other major championships, too, and $124,000 in prize money, and the honor of being selected not only Player of the Year but No. 3 in the all-time rankings behind Bill Tilden and Don Budge.

I don't think any athlete has had such far-flung success as I enjoyed in 1969, winning tournaments on four continents. I wonder if a tennis player will ever have a season like that again? I rather doubt it. Even though I won more money in 1970 (cash is pouring into the game at ever increasing rates), I couldn't equal the achievements of 1969. That was my special year, and I wanted to set it all down.

But there was more to 1969 than winning, and more that I want to tell you apart from my story. Even though I've been playing tennis for more than twenty years, I was still learning in 1969, and I want to pass the things I learned then and in other years on to you.

Because you need help. Yes, you—standing there with your racket dragging. You aren't keeping your eye on the ball for one thing. I know because when I watch movies of myself I notice that I'm guilty of that sin. If I'm caught with wandering eyes—and not only when there's a blonde in the first row—I'll assume that you are, too.

It's funny how the most simple tenets of the game, like keeping your eye on the ball, are overlooked at times by even the top players. You can be the best player in the world and still butcher a lot of routine points and situations, just as I have done—and still do. When I blow an easy smash at the net you can see that the hacker within me is still alive and well. I'm sure this must comfort those who are the backbone of the game—the hackers everywhere.

Well, hacker, I'd like to help you out by showing you some

things that should pick up your game. I don't want you challenging me for first-prize money at Forest Hills, understand, but there's no reason why you can't improve. Or why you can't take up the game, if you're not a hacker yet, and play respectably and have fun.

And if you're really serious about tennis, and care to invest about 22,000 hours on the court, you stand a fine chance of overtaking and beating me. By that time I'll be around seventy.

I've put in my 22,000 or so, and there are more to come I hope. I don't know if the first million strokes were the hardest, but I do know they were fun, and that's what tennis is all about—even if you make your living from it as I do.

This book is part of that living, and I hope it's fun as well as instructive. While there is some doubt that an Australian, collaborating with an American, could actually write a book in English, I felt it was worth giving a try.

1 TURN OFF THE RAIN

THE NIGHT Mary hung up on me the year nearly went sour.

I was almost through the biggest year any tennis player—and maybe any athlete—ever had when the pressure that suddenly grabbed me was one that almost every man has felt: domestic. I had an unhappy, angry wife who wanted me home when I had to be somewhere else 3,000 miles away, and who ended the argument strongly—she stopped talking to me. Although numerous husbands would consider that a lucky break, I did not. There's no way I can play or feel well if there's something wrong between me and Mary.

For a while I worried that it would stay wrong, just when I was within reach of everything. If it had, I couldn't have joined those exceptional athletes who made 1969 such an extraordinary year in sports.

So many wonderfully improbable things happened in 1969: The Jets ruled football. Those magnificent antiques, the Celtics, came to life one more time to conquer basketball. The Mets climbed out of the trashcan to glitter atop baseball. Arnold Palmer, who had begun to be regarded as a monument to past glories, began to win golf tournaments again. And in tennis, where I had labored practically underground since becoming a professional in 1963, I won the first open Grand Slam and became something of a household name—at least more of one than Spiro was prior to the Republican convention in 1968.

This was my year, 1969, and people were becoming aware of me and my sport. I realized this when Americans began asking me for my autograph—on the street and in other public places away from tournaments. This had been going on for a number of years in England and Australia, where there is a substantial tennis public. In *Time* magazine an article referred to British talk-show host David Frost as "the Rod Laver of television . . . [who] would consider success in the U.S. the culmination of his own grand slam." A couple of years before, my name would never have been used for that sort of comparison in *Time*. Sporting references are common but tennis is never the sport cited. Not in America. In his memoirs Field Marshal Montgomery could talk about breaking Rommel's serve, but that was for British consumption.

It meant more to me than just seeing Laver's face and name more frequently, in wider pictures and taller type. It meant that the game I've devoted my life to was beginning to catch on big and that more and more people were becoming aware of it and recognizing that it was the best game for them.

Life had been very different seven years before, in 1962, the first time I made the Grand Slam—the singles championships of Australia, France, England, and the United States all in the same year. Then the Slam was an affair for amateurs only. Open tennis —the integration of amateurs and professionals in competition— was a long way off, and seemed unlikely to arrive during my career. I was an amateur making a comfortable living from play- ing. Twenty-four years old without a worry. Single. Free. Hitting a tennis ball. Seeing every bit of the world I could. Having a few beers. Partying a bit. That was all that was on my mind. Most people felt that was about all my mind could hold: another bland, efficient Australian tennis champion. A countrywoman of mine, Lemeau Watt, once remarked at a tennis party: "Rod does his job extremely competently and thoroughly. No show, no emo- tion. Like a good plumber. A plumber doesn't put on a show down there alone in the basement, does he? On the court Rod is totally oblivious to his surroundings."

I don't think of myself as just another Australian, though I'll agree we aren't the most flamboyant breed. I do have some distinguishing marks, although hardly any that would make you single me out as a big-time athlete. Red hair, scrawny, 49,000 freckles, a crook in my nose and a bow in my legs. Maybe I have a certain appeal to the spectators because I seem ordinary enough to be one of them. Maybe, but are they looking for the ordinary, even if they can identify with it?

There's one thing: my unimpressive body hangs from King Kong's left arm. Of course, it probably doesn't seem that unusual from the grandstand. I was stunned myself when Dave Anderson of *The New York Times* tape-measured me one afternoon in 1968 and reported that my left forearm is twelve inches around—as big as Rocky Marciano's was. And my left wrist is seven inches around. Floyd Patterson, another former heavyweight champion, has a six-inch wrist.

I guess I hit tennis balls more times than Rocky and Floyd hit people, although not as damagingly. The balls still had some bounce when I got through with them. You couldn't say that for many of Rocky's opponents.

I imagine throwing a good punch is as satisfying as punching a winning volley. A lot of things changed for me in the seven years between Slams, but not the indescribably joyful sensation of hitting a tennis ball well. The hacker has to do this only once to sense what I'm talking about, and then he goes in pursuit of a repeat. It may take him ten minutes to find it again, but it's worth it. I'm lucky because I've been hitting the ball well for years. It's still an obsession. I suppose the same is true for a batter in baseball. I know it is for a golfer. I love golf, and shoot in the eighties whenever I can find time to play. The trouble with baseball and golf is you don't get to hit the ball enough. The better you hit the golf ball, the fewer opportunities per round you have to experience that great feeling.

Boxing and tennis, however, give you as much swinging and hitting as you want. Strangely, although they may seem worlds apart, boxing and tennis have a certain kinship. Two individuals head-to-head, probing for weakness and attacking it. Footwork, timing and stamina are essential. Just you and your opponent in there until one of you is beaten.

The element of inflicting physical harm is meant to be absent in tennis, but it isn't unheard of. This isn't the garden party game that originated among Victorian gentlemen in England. It's not hockey by any means, but players get "toey," as we say at home—edgy, annoyed—and punches get thrown. Probably the stroke-of-the-year for 1969 was the left hook with which an Englishman, Roger Taylor, gashed and flattened an Australian, Bob Hewitt, following their acrimonious match in West Berlin. Taylor won the match and the fight, but lost money because his hand broke against Hewitt's head and he couldn't play for a while. Even though he won, Roger was embarrassed. Antagonisms can develop during a match, but they don't often blossom so violently. Hewitt was embarrassed, too. We Aussies regard the English—we call them Pommies (for pomegranate eaters)—as below us in sport. In fist fighting the English are the ones who get knocked down. But Roger Taylor made up for all those hopeless English heavyweights in boxing history, and you won't catch me badgering Roger the way Bob did.

Nor was I going to badger Mary when she boxed my ear by dropping the receiver resoundingly to end our conversation.

Nothing could bother me the last time around the Slam. Now I was bothered. Then I didn't understand the workings of mortgages or wives. I didn't have either. Now I had one of each.

I don't know that my understanding is much greater, but I have learned that they take some thought and concern and effort, particularly the wife.

I had put through this call from Boston to our home in Corona-del-Mar, California, on a July night only eight days after I'd won Wimbledon, the tournament that is synonymous with the English championship—and the world singles title. With Australia and France already in the sack I was at the three-quarter pole on the run for the Slam and only a few weeks away from the finish at Forest Hills.

The conversation with Mary wasn't good. It was the worst of my life, and though I could see why she was furious, there wasn't much I could do about it. If you know how to stop the rain in

Boston, let me know and we'll make a lot more money in that line than in tennis.

Rain. That was what had put me and Mary in such a long-distance bind. I've heard about that Spanish plain, but it can't be as wet as Longwood Cricket Club during a tennis tournament. When O. C. Smith, the country singer, went on about the summertime rain in Indianapolis, he should have checked out Boston to really find out about rain.

Like India, Boston has a predictable monsoon season: it arrives when I arrive.

It was my sixth visit to Boston for the U.S. Pro Championships, and I was trying to win the title for the fifth time. Only once in all those years was the tournament not in danger of floating away.

Pancho Gonzales and I played the 1964 final, the first year I won, in a driving northeaster. In 1968 there was so much rain that we had to abandon the tournament and return two months later to complete it.

At the end of the summer of 1969, when I completed the Slam at swampy Forest Hills—Boston weather had gone South—the reporters marveled at the way I played in the muck, particularly the British journalists. They'd never seen such good tennis under such bad conditions, they wrote following my victory over Tony Roche. But that's only because they'd never covered tennis in Boston where I had trained well to become a bog-runner.

Nobody has drowned yet playing at Longwood, but I've fallen into enough puddles to worry about the possibility. I'm always pleased whenever Dix Walker, the club lifeguard, attends the matches.

I don't know what it is with Longwood, but in 1965 it seemed to be the only place rain fell during a New England drought. The club president then, the late John Bottomley, felt a little guilty in church on our semifinals Sunday. The priest led a prayer for rain— "for the farmers"—and John said he was praying for dry weather for the tennis players. "Actually," he said, "it was a split prayer, because I was with the farmers, too. But I knew I'd lose. We'd get drenched and the farmers would parch."

That's what happened. Mary was well aware of Boston's record, and she was worried that the tournament would drag on, eating into the last time we'd have together before our baby came at the end of the summer.

Pregnancy didn't help her disposition. She hadn't had a baby for seventeen years—there were three of them in her first marriage —and she was getting cumbersome and uncomfortable.

We'd had a marvelous time at Wimbledon, living in a quiet flat at Dolphin Square, a large block of apartments near the Thames. I'd spent very little time with my American wife during a year jammed with frantic traveling. London was pleasant even though I had to concentrate on the tournament. At least we were together.

After Boston we were going to have nine more days, and then she'd be alone the rest of the summer, alone when the baby was due to come on finals day at Forest Hills.

That was the obstetrician's prediction: September 7. If everything went well for the Laver family that would be the day of the Grand Slam for me and the Grand Slim for her.

We parted at London airport. I flew to Boston. She went over the Pole to Los Angeles, which is fifty miles from our home that hangs over the Pacific at Corona-del-Mar. Her flight was delayed, and arrived several hours late. By the time she got home the glow of London was gone and she was nervous and tired. How else should she have felt?

In the back of my mind I thought I might be joining her in a couple of days. Everybody has a letdown after Wimbledon, and I wouldn't have been startled if somebody had beaten me in Boston. After I won the tournament, Arthur Ashe commented: "Laver has to be inhuman to play that well after Wimbledon. You just have to have a letdown, but he didn't!"

That summer I was inhuman, I guess. Mary probably thought so for a while even more than my opponents.

While I've been complaining about Boston weather, I have nothing but good feeling about the place and the people. It's where pro tennis finally began to grow up, and maybe where the entire game started to turn around and head toward a boom.

The U.S. Pro Championships have been played since 1927, the

year after competitive professional tennis began. In 1926 C. C. (Cash-and-Carry) Pyle launched a new spectator sport by signing Suzanne Lenglen, Mary K. Browne, Vincent Richards, Harvey Snodgrass, Paul Feret, and Howard Kinsey to go on tour. Richards won the first U.S. title over Kinsey at a place called Notlek Tennis Courts, a site in Manhattan long since buried beneath a building.

The tournament had good days and mostly bad days in the years that followed, but it hardly became one of the great events. In 1963, my first year as a pro, Ken Rosewall beat me in the final, and the payoff was zero. Attendance at Forest Hills was poor, the promoters went broke, and all they could present us with was "sorry, fellows." Even on toast it wouldn't taste good.

There were no plans to continue the staggering tradition until Ed Hickey, a public relations man for the New England Merchants National Bank—and a tennis nut—talked his bosses into sponsoring us. The bank put up $10,000 in prize money, and Longwood, the oldest club in America, took us in. Just when it appeared that the pros wouldn't even appear in America in 1964, Boston rescued us, and due to the good name of the bank we were able to line up sponsors in a few other cities and get a small circuit going. Despite the weather, Boston was a success. We were in business unexpectedly in the United States.

That summer on the eight-city American circuit Kenny Rosewall was our leading money winner with $8800, while I was third with $6900. At Longwood alone in 1969 I won $8600, and in 1970 first prize went up to $12,000. The financial advances in pro tennis have been pretty substantial.

Because of this, we pros have felt an obligation to Boston, the bank and the club and their tournament. They meant new life. That's one reason, I think, that I always play well there. No letdowns in Boston, although, as I said, it wouldn't have surprised me to do badly.

There was more than the $8600 first prize on my mind. There was Mary and my first child.

Still, with luck, I told her in London, we'd be seeing each other in a week's time and have those nine days together, to fix up the nursery, to relax in the lovely home I seldom live in.

"See you next Monday," she smiled, "and tell them to turn off the rain this time."

For five days it was perfect. Then on Saturday the inevitable downpour began. "We'll play the final Monday. See you Tuesday," I told Mary over the phone confidently. I was playing well and believed I'd be in the final.

"Look, it isn't fair," she said, "for them to keep you there if the rain goes on and on. Last year you came back later to finish it. They could do the same thing this year if it rains again Sunday."

And it did rain. And I had to call Mary. This call I dreaded. Now my arrival was pushed back to Wednesday—if the rain stopped, that is. Maybe later.

"They can't keep you there indefinitely," she reasoned. "Tell them you're leaving Tuesday regardless of what happens. I want you to leave Tuesday . . ."

"But I can't just walk out, Mary," I replied.

"It wouldn't be walking out if you tell them now. Tell them that you've made plans, and you're already staying over. Just explain that you have to leave Tuesday and they'll juggle the schedule or reschedule entirely."

We talked that over for a while, and her mood wasn't good. Then, abruptly she said, "Well, Rod, if you aren't home Tuesday, don't bother to come . . ."

Bang! went the receiver in California. The click went through me like a sonic boom. Mary is a strong girl. She slams a receiver as hard as I slam an overhead.

What did she mean? I wasn't about to redial and ask.

Was one more day away that big a deal? Before Mary begins to seem the villainness of this piece, I'd like to make it clear that she's the heroine. Without her and the sense of purpose she's brought to my wandering life, there'd have been no Grand Slam of 1969. I'd be a very good player if she weren't sharing my life, I'll concede that. But I'd be a very lonely one, and not so good as I became.

Our marriage is one thing we're sure of, but it hasn't been easy for either of us. It isn't easy for any athlete's wife, with all the traveling her man does and all the time he's away from home. But

I believe it's the worst for a tennis player's wife. The other sports stick to fixed schedules; tennis' schedule is often erratic, and the weather plays a greater part in altering it. A baseball player is gone, on the road, for at most two weeks. Football players are away a few weekends, and the trips for basketball and hockey players are brief. For the most part the golf circuit is within the United States, and the players can often drive between tournaments. A golfer can even take his family along in a trailer when the kids are young.

With me it's Sydney one day and Philadelphia two days later. My season is the entire year, my places every time zone, every continent. I may be gone six weeks or more at a time. This was my 1969 itinerary, between January 10 and December 4:

To Australia—Sydney for the New South Wales Open . . . up to Brisbane for the Australian Open . . . over to Auckland for the New Zealand Open . . . off to Philadelphia for an indoor open at the Spectrum . . . down to Florida for pro tournaments in Orlando and Miami . . . home for five days . . . up the coast to Oakland, Portland, and Seattle for small pro tournaments . . . home, commuting to the pro tourney in Los Angeles . . . and then our "vacation," nine days in Hawaii . . . from there to New York for the Madison Square Garden Open . . . a long flight to Johannesburg for the South African Open . . . back home for a few days, while commuting to a pro tournament in Anaheim . . . then to Tokyo for a pro tournament . . . home for two days en route to New York for the Madison Square Garden Pro tourney . . . on to London for the BBC-TV match . . . over the Channel for a pro tournament in Amsterdam . . . up to Paris for the French Open . . . rebounding over the Channel to Bristol for the West of England Open . . . then settling three weeks in London for the open at Queen's Club followed by the Wimbledon fortnight . . . a jump to Boston for the U.S. Pro Championships . . . home a few days prior to pro tournaments in St. Louis, Binghampton, N.Y., Ft. Worth, and Baltimore . . . now New York for two weeks and the Grand Slam climax at Forest Hills . . . back home to welcome the baby and play the Pacific Southwest Open at Los Angeles . . . a hop to Las Vegas for the Howard Hughes Open . . . a few days at home before revisiting Europe for pro tourneys at Cologne and Hamburg . . . home to change shirts, then once more to Europe (via business stops in Boston and New York) to play tournaments in Barcelona, London, Stockholm, Basel, and Madrid.

One season—on the road 259 days; nearly 200,000 miles.

Countless take-offs and landings, hotel rooms, packings, and unpackings. The beer labels, from Sapporo in Tokyo to Foster's in Sydney to Narragansett in Boston to Coors in Vegas, ran together in a blurred montage. Within a year's time, beginning with the Argentine Open in November of 1968, I played every continent except for Antarctica. The only reason I missed that is Admiral Byrd spoiled the commercial possibilities by not charging the penguins to watch a visiting attraction.

I spent more time over the Atlantic than under my own roof, and that isn't a good basis for a marriage. Sometimes Mary must think she's married to a left-handed yo-yo, and naturally we've had our fights.

But Mary wouldn't ask me to give up the game, even though we'd be all right financially if I did. She's a trained accountant, and I too could get some sort of job. But she realizes that I'd be miserable in a nine-to-five job, that I've got to be hitting that tennis ball for a while yet.

At first I thought she was being unreasonable when she gave me the ultimatum and hung up on me. But one of her statements kept coming back: "The year just gets whittled down to nothing."

She was right about that. My contract called for an annual guarantee of $90,000 from my boss. In 1969 that was National Tennis League, an organization of pros run by George MacCall and Fred Podesta. That's $10,000 a month for nine months with three months off. I went to play wherever they told me, and I got that money if I didn't win a match. The prize money I earned applied against the guarantee, and in 1969 I won $124,000. That meant I went $34,000 above the guarantee, which delighted the bosses. They had to pay me nothing, but they had to make up the differences between earnings and guarantees for a couple of other players.

In addition they paid my air fares or other travel, while I was responsible for all my living expenses. How does a promoter make any money? They haven't been too successful. The theory is that they'll be able to profit by charging management fees to various tournaments for supplying our bodies. Or by running their own tournaments. It has worked out well only for the players.

Now, three months off sounds nice until you begin breaking it down. If the average worker gets a three-week vacation, two days off a week plus seven legal holidays, he has 126 days free compared to my 93. Of course, I like the $90,000 guarantee, and I'm not moaning. But I am pointing out what it can do to your family life. My three months off are spaced in dribs and drabs of five days here and eight somewhere else.

Once in 1969, because of rain and flying difficulties and a medical problem with my elbow, an eight-day holiday was whittled to eight hours. Mary met an incoming plane, drove me to a doctor's office for treatment, and then back to the airport to catch another plane.

It's been like this from the start, when we even had trouble getting married. We were supposed to have a week's honeymoon after a tournament in St. Louis in June of 1966, and it turned out to be one day when another tournament was added to the schedule.

"Spare me from long honeymoons," was Mary's reaction. She took it pretty well, although only a day earlier she thought even that much was going to disappear.

Where was the groom, everybody wondered at the bridal dinner. I wasn't sure myself. I was in the singles and doubles finals at St. Louis and lost them both, being a little shakier than usual with the wedding set for the next day. Lew Hoad and I grabbed our rental car and headed for the airport to catch a plane for San Francisco. On the way to the airport the car gagged and quit. "I think we're out of gas," said Lew, reading the gauge astutely.

"I think we're out of one bridal dinner and wedding rehearsal in San Rafael, California," I said. "And maybe one wedding."

"With your footwork they'll never let you go through a wedding without a rehearsal," Lew said cheerfully. "Let's have a beer somewhere."

I thought we should try for gas first, and eventually both needs were filled, and later on there was a plane on which we flew all night, arriving about 3:00 A.M. Nobody to meet us at the airport then. We rented another car and were about to try and find where we were staying when, "For God's sake, Lew, I left my travel folder, air tickets . . . all my vital stuff on that plane." I was in tip-top shape for the biggest day of my life.

By that time the plane was in a hangar somewhere, but we tracked it down, found the folder and spent the next four hours driving around the San Rafael area, trying to discover where we were. At daybreak we got un-lost and found the house. We did get some breakfast and a shave en route to the church.

Graciously, after all that, Mary showed up, too, and we did get married. She got an idea of what it was going to be like, and she became reconciled to it.

But the whittling down of the time we're supposed to have together gets to her, and this was magnified—with everything else— by her pregnancy.

Her mood was not magnanimous, and all through that Monday I wondered, what kind of man am I? Wasn't my commitment to my wife and child as important as a tennis tournament? Shouldn't I explain my position to the tournament officials, excuse myself and leave?

Several times I thought of doing just that. I even made a plane reservation for Tuesday morning. If I defaulted early, the tournament wouldn't really be left in the lurch, I tried to tell myself. I was to play Rosewall in the semis Monday night. I could forfeit the match to him beforehand and be on my way. The crowd would get to see the other semi—John Newcombe against Fred Stolle—plus some doubles. They would feel cheated by my withdrawal, I suppose, but there would still be an excellent final on the Tuesday between Rosewall and the Newcombe-Stolle winner. I'd won the tournament four times in five years. It might be nice for somebody else to win. I didn't believe it, but you know how you can rationalize almost anything in those inner arguments— especially with those angry words of hers bouncing back and forth inside my brain like a long baseline rally.

I didn't think long about a default. I couldn't do that. I had to play Rosewall, but I was beginning to get fatalistic, which was something new for me. I started to tell myself that it was no disgrace losing to Kenny. He's often beaten me when I was playing splendidly. I would try, but my concentration would be broken and he'd probably beat me. Well . . . so what?

I was really building myself up for a loss, convincing myself that it was all for the best. Mary wanted me to walk out on the final. It wouldn't be necessary. In my state of mind I wasn't going to be in the final. The sound of that phone clicking was in my ear, and I was worried about Mary and the baby.

Kenny and I walked onto the court, and my head was buzzing like mission control. Our argument was being replayed along with a soliloquy of my own. I was saying why doesn't Mary understand, and replying that maybe it was me that didn't understand. What difference can one match make? None, but this might be our only baby, and weren't Mary and the little fellow everything?

As we began warming up I welcomed this inner conflict because I knew it would jam my concentration. There's no way you can play well with ruptured concentration. So Rosewall would beat me but I wouldn't be taking a dive. If you can't concentrate, you'll lose. It was comforting.

And it didn't work out. It was a lovely evening. The stands were full, more than 5000 people, which outside of London, Paris, or New York is a big tennis crowd. Well, we're all bloody ham actors. Put a crowd in the place and we haven't got time to worry about our wives running off with the milkman, or having a miscarriage, or spending the prize money before we've won it. We stop having soap operas in our brains—or at least I do.

Kenny and I were ready to go. There he was, Kenneth Robert (Muscles) Rosewall across the net. A friend, yet for seven years a deadly enemy. My most difficult opponent. And you know, everything bugging me just vanished. It's funny—and I don't understand why—but I just don't know how to play a match without trying. There was no way to keep myself from doing everything I could to beat Rosewall.

I was a winner before I was a husband. I'm a victim of a

wanting-to-win that has been inside me since the first time I hit a tennis ball nearly twenty-five years ago, and this wanting has more control over me than family, money, anything.

I won.

Then it started again, the cerebral soap opera . . . "Can Rodney the Rocket win the tennis tournament and the game of marriage, too? Or is it one or the other?"

As I walked to the clubhouse, the debate came along with and within me. The plane reservation is set for tomorrow morning, Tuesday, the day of the ultimatum. But so is the final. Walk out now? Would I be the first man to win the Grand Slam, welcome his firstborn and get a divorce all in the same day—while being sued by the New England Merchants Bank for betraying their tournament?

I had to talk it over with somebody. A friend, who knew me mostly as an athlete—a competitor—had a couple of beers with me, and I told him the whole thing. It felt better to talk it out. Finally he said, "You're not going to be on that plane tomorrow. You're going to be playing tennis tomorrow night."

"I guess you're right," I agreed. We had another beer, and I said good night. I slept well.

The next day I knocked off Newcombe, and in the doubles old Pancho Gonzales and I, playing our first tournament together, beat the Wimbledon champions, Newcombe and Roche. It was an $8600 evening for me. Vinnie Richards, the first U.S. Pro champ, won the tournament four times. Now I was one up on him, but still three singles titles behind Gonzales.

I was on the first plane to the West Coast the next morning, and Mary was waiting for me at the L.A. airport with a big kiss. I was apprehensive, a day late. She didn't mention it. Neither did I. She didn't mention the phone call, and never has.

LESSON 1
Mental Preparation

Pancho Gonzales has told me about the night before he played his first Davis Cup match, against Australia in 1949. He and Ted Schroeder, who were to be the singles players for the U.S., were terribly nervous. After dinner they settled into a bridge game with Alrick Man, their captain. "Alrick kept looking at his watch," Pancho said, "and around midnight he finally said, 'Aren't you fellows going to bed? You've got a big match tomorrow.' We told him to relax and enjoy his bridge. There was no sense going to bed when we were so keyed up that we knew we'd just lie there and think about the next day's matches. It would be anything but restful. Finally, at about three A.M., we got tired and quit playing cards. We were tired enough to sleep, and the few hours sleep we got were good ones."

I know the feeling. At Forest Hills in 1969 my semifinal with Arthur Ashe was halted by darkness with me leading. It's a tough situation when you have to come back the next day to finish. You could drive yourself bonkers thinking about it. So I stayed up a little later than usual, had an extra beer to make sure that when I got into bed I'd go right to sleep.

Otherwise you can get up more tired and psyched than when you turned out the lights.

A match played in your mind can be harder than one on the court. I know of club players so determined to be rested for a match that they'll go to bed at nine, planning to get about twelve hours sleep. Instead they think about the match and play it about five times and sleep fitfully, if at all. I'm not recommending that you stay out all night. It's an individual thing. But I do think it's silly to get in bed before you're tired and risk counting shots that don't bound over the net.

I try not to think about a match at all until a few minutes before

31

I go onto the court. Then I welcome the rush of nervousness. It tells me the adrenaline is pouring. If I'm not nervous I worry because my mind and body aren't getting me up for a match.

The mental and the physical are very close. If I'm not in tune physically I'm going to be lazy-minded. With the amount of tennis I play over nearly the entire year I never feel really unfit. Thus my daily practice sessions are pretty strenuous. I like to practice an hour and a half the day of a match—in the morning if I'm playing in the afternoon, or in the afternoon if I'm playing at night.

Obviously that's too much for the ordinary player, but I think the principle is important. By playing a fair bit the system wakes up, mentally and physically. For you it might be a ten- or fifteen-minute knock, but I think practice on a match day is vital.

It's easy to say don't think about a match until just before you play it, but how do I manage to avoid those thoughts? Well, I try to keep myself busy in other ways, doing errands and other things. If I can keep moving about, doing something—not strenuous—my mind will shut out the coming match. I also try not to arrive at the court much before my match is scheduled. If I did absolutely nothing during those hours preceding a match, I really would get fidgety and edgy.

2 SOMETHING CALLED THE GRAND SLAM

THERE WAS plenty to do in the few days I was home. A nursery to set up and decorate. Some golf for relaxation. Some tennis, too—with Mary—which was also relaxing. She played until she was seven and a half months pregnant, and tennis kept her feeling fit, and from going crazy when she was alone.

She hasn't been playing very long, but she's enthusiastic. Although she doesn't expect me to hit with her, I like to. Picasso shared his work with his roommates by using them for models, didn't he? Why shouldn't I share my talent at home, too? I don't know if Cassius Muhammad Ali Clay practices swings with his wife, but it all depends on your line of work. Tennis is fun and laughs we can have together. That's why it's such a good family game. More women are discovering that tennis is an agreeable way to keep trim, and gives them a nice, quick break away from the house. Golf can turn into a project that takes up most of the day, but you can get enough tennis in an hour.

After a week I was ready to go again. Corona-del-Mar restores me nicely. I like looking out at the ocean, watching the surf. From our house you have a good look at a great surfing area called the Wedge. You may have seen it in that movie, *The Endless Summer*. I love to body surf, but not in California. Too cold. I reckon the water back home in Queensland is just right for it, and it amazes me to see all those Californians in the water.

If I was that cold-blooded I'd never lose a match.

But I was pretty cold-blooded the rest of the summer after leaving home and heading East. This was the stretch run, the last quarter on the way to the winner's circle and the Slam at Forest Hills, and I didn't lose a match.

Grand Slam varies in meaning in the games of bridge, baseball, golf, and tennis. A sweep of the tricks, or a home run with the bases loaded, is unusual but not rare. The bridge table and the ball diamond offer the possibility daily.

In golf and tennis a series of triumphs make up a Slam. Golf's has been singular, celebrated only in 1930 when Bobby Jones, the phenomenal Georgian, won the amateur and open championships in both Britain and the United States. I can't imagine there'll ever be another just like that one, since only an amateur is eligible to enter all four tournaments, and the amateur who can compete evenly with pros in golf and tennis no longer exists. Today golf's Grand Slam is considered the winning of both the U.S. and British Opens plus the Masters and the PGA. No one has ever done it or even come very close.

The Slam in tennis is also an obstacle course of four national championships to be won in one year, though farther flung in time and location: the Australian in January, the French in May, the English in July, and the American in September.

I like to think the tennis Slam is the hardest of all because you have to get your game up to top level four times over an eight-month stretch, and of course you're playing other tournaments in between, too. Much travel and changing conditions are involved. In 1969, I started in the tropical summer heat of Brisbane and wound up in the autumn rain of New York.

I'm not sure when I first heard the term Grand Slam, but it was Don Budge—the original Slammer—who cleared up the meaning for me. Don explained that the only countries to win the Davis Cup—Australia, the U.S., France, and Britain—became known as the Big Four, the world's tennis powers, and when

Budge was the first to sweep the Big Four titles in 1938—the year I was born—his feat was called the Grand Slam.

Five years earlier an Australian, Jack Crawford, came very close. Jack won the Australian, French, and Wimbledon (which is the English or British—take your pick. The official name is the Lawn Tennis Championships, period, but everybody calls this event Wimbledon.) At Forest Hills for the U.S. Championship, Crawford led Fred Perry two sets to one, and it appeared that he would have a Slam.

Crawford hadn't set out specifically to win all four, as did Budge in 1938, and numerous others including myself later. He just won the first three, and that had never happened before. But there was little, if any, ballyhoo about a Slam preceding his bid to complete it.

In his column in *The New York Times*, John Kieran did write: "If Crawford wins, that would be something like scoring a grand slam on the courts, doubled and vulnerable."

And when Crawford fell short, Allison Danzig reported in paragraph three of his account in the *Times* that "Crawford's quest of the Grand Slam was frustrated."

With his 2–1 lead in sets Crawford may have looked the winner, but he was through, exhausted. He was having trouble with his asthma, and even occasional slugs of brandy taken during the fourth and fifth sets couldn't turn him back on. Jack won one more game, and Perry won the match.

The next year Perry, the dashing Englishman, took three of the titles, but he was cut off early, losing in the fourth round of the French. But he won the French in 1935 and became the first to win all four Slam titles, though not within a calendar year.

Budge not only made the first Slam, he says he invented it. "I take certain whimsical pride in . . . creating it [the Slam]," he wrote in his autobiography. "Crawford almost won something that didn't exist. There was only passing notice at the time that I had won all four titles, but with time and publicity the stature of the Grand Slam grew. The expression became popular and it was what I came to be best known for.

"In 1938 I had set my goal to win these four titles, but only my good friend and doubles partner, Gene Mako, was aware of it.

"The fact that there was no such acknowledged entity as the Grand Slam made it somewhat easier for me because I wasn't bothered by the cumulative pressure of the press and fans that Laver and Lew Hoad [in 1956] had forced on them. But the pressure from within was no less intense for me than for them."

The *Times'* "passing notice," as Budge calls it, was just that after he beat Mako in the Forest Hills final. "Feat Sets a Precedent" was the fourth deck in the headline, and well down in his story Danzig noted: ". . . a grand slam that invites comparison with the accomplishment of Bobby Jones in golf."

Budge relates that his biggest goal had been attained in 1937 when he led the United States to its first Davis Cup success in ten years. He was clearly the master of the amateur world, and he wanted another goal to keep his interest high in 1938 before he helped in the defense of the Cup and then turned pro.

He set out to make a Slam, an original contribution to sporting lore, and a target for those who followed.

Thanks to his pioneering, the Slam received plenty of ballyhoo thereafter, and was uppermost when I made the rounds.

In Budge's time, obviously, few non-Australians made the twenty-one-day haul Down Under to play in our championship. The boat trip was forbidding and expensive. In 1938 only Budge, Mako, and three or four Australians even played all four Slam tournaments. By my day the jets opened up the world to everyone and squeezed it together, making it relatively easy for a squad of tourists to hit all the major stops. The same tough crowd was everywhere—there was no avoiding them.

In Budge's Slam, 6 of his 24 victories were over men ranked along with him in the world's top ten. In mine of 1969, I won 26 matches, 12 of them against others in the top ten. I also won the South African championship, the British Indoor, the U.S. Pro, and 11 other tournaments, a total of 18 titles in 33 tournaments. The pace had accelerated. We were playing every month of the year, probably too much for our own good. But the money was there, and we went after it.

Tennis wasn't a year-round occupation in the Budge era. It is now. I think it's more demanding, flitting between time zones, and there's more pressure with so much money being pumped into the game. But I like it this way, the money and the constant movement.

When I make comparisons between today and the more leisurely Budge period, I'm certainly not trying to make my triumphs sound any grander than his, just pointing up differences. At the end of 1969 a panel of the most respected tennis writers drew up an all-time ranking. It was headed by Bill Tilden. Second was Budge, followed by me. I don't think anybody can really say who was the greatest, but I am happy to accept that ranking. Moreover, I consider Don a friend, and I'll always be grateful to him for the way he treated me in 1962 when I was on the verge of my first Slam.

Another man might have been resentful of my claiming a piece of the property that had been his alone for twenty-four years. Not Don. He had been through the tension, and knew what it could be like. He helped me relax by spiriting me away for a day in the country before Forest Hills began that year. We drove to the Grossinger's resort in the Catskills where I could take it easy. Nobody asking questions, no phones ringing. We even played a couple of nonchalant sets. He was great.

In Don's year he was unquestionably the best player in the world, though an amateur. I couldn't very well consider myself the best when I won the amateur Slam in 1962 so long as such splendid pros as Pancho Gonzales, Ken Rosewall, and Lew Hoad were at large. Plus Butch Buchholz, Alex Olmedo, Andres Gimeno, Barry MacKay, and Mal Anderson. I was excited and tremendously pleased at making the Slam in 1962. The collection of titles raised my asking price when I turned pro a few months later—but I knew I wasn't the best.

Probably Rosewall was then. Knowing that took something out of my satisfaction at dominating amateur tennis. I had my Slam; now I wanted a shot at Rosewall, Gonzales, and the others. To get it I had to drop into limbo with them on the pro circuit and give up any thought of ever repeating the Slam.

It was either glory or money in those days prior to open tennis. You took your choice: glory (and, of course, enough money to get by on) with the amateurs; or very good money and anonymity with the pros. It was time for me to make the good money, and to satisfy my competitive urge against the blokes I knew were the strongest. But no more Slams . . . I thought then.

I'd heard about Budge's Slam, and Maureen Connolly's, too. Until Margaret Smith Court did it in 1970, Maureen had won the only women's Slam in 1953. My first year away from Australia, 1956, I was a witness to a near-thing. Lew Hoad was the world's No. 1 amateur then, one of my early heroes, and I was able to watch almost all of his matches as he took the Australian, French, Wimbledon, and came into the final at Forest Hills. One match away, but across the net was Kenny Rosewall.

I sat there marveling at Rosewall, along with the rest of the crowd, as he destroyed Lew's bid in four sets. I marvel at him now. Thirteen years later he was still around trying to break up my second Slam. He had his shot at me in the final of the French, but I played the clay court match of my life and avoided the treatment he gave Lew.

But in 1956 it was exciting enough just to be at Forest Hills and follow Lew's progress. I was eighteen, awed, and unknown. A few aficionados recognized my name because I'd won the U.S. junior title a month before, but I could wander around getting the feel of the place completely unnoticed.

I was out of that tournament fast. Ham Richardson, then the No. 1 American, was my first-round opponent, and by virtue of the company I was keeping I played for the first time in the Forest Hills Stadium. Ham got me out of there before you could say one-two-three: 6–1, 6–2, 6–3. My Queensland mate, Roy Emerson, got to the quarters, and I was glad for him. It was fun for a young Australian to watch as his countrymen dominated the championship of their great rival, America, with Hoad, Rosewall, and Neale Fraser surrounding a solitary Yank, Vic Seixas, in the semis.

I didn't mind the passive role of spectator at the final. I figured I'd be there in one of the starring roles one day, but the thought of a Grand Slam for Laver didn't occur to me until four years later.

In 1960 I won the Australian title for the first time, and since that's the only way you can begin a Slam, I wondered: Why not me? After beating Neale Fraser—coming from two sets down—I had that feeling that it was going to be a big Laver year. Hadn't I been Wimbledon finalist to Alex Olmedo in 1959? So why couldn't I make a Slam?

Manolo Santana, the gifted Spaniard, showed me why. He and that slow clay in Paris abruptly brought me back to the real world. Parisian clay may look harmless, but it's quicksand for us outsiders from Australia and America, a trap that clogs our power and swallows us.

Europeans are like kids snapping up peanut butter sandwiches when they operate on the home ground against big hitters. My visions of a Slam were almost blacked out in the first round of the French by a Pole named Andrzej Licis, who pushed me all over for five sets. Weird luck was the only way I beat him—with a no-hope shot made up on the run, a backhand topspin lob at match point that floated over his head, plunked on the baseline and left the ball stained with a big white chalkspot. I had never heard of Licis before, and seldom after, but that afternoon I thought he was one of the greatest players in the world. I doubt he felt the same respect for me.

I wasn't thinking Slam anymore, just wondering how much longer I could last. Not another round. Santana, who really was one of the best, and plays a clay court as artistically as Isaac Stern plays the violin, put me out with little trouble.

I had to learn to play on clay, to firm up my patience and prepare my way to the net better. The Slam is three-quarters grass, and I wasn't worried about myself there. The other quarter, the French, is something else, more challenging than the others, more difficult to win, more satisfying from the standpoint of having survived a terrific test.

There isn't as much pressure, perhaps, because it's early in the season and the prestige isn't as great as Wimbledon or Forest Hills. But in Paris you know you've been in a fight. You come off the court exhausted, looking battle-stained, your clothes and body smudged with red clay.

I promised myself that in 1961 it would be different for me in Paris. It was to the extent that I got to the semifinals before running into Santana, who was the No. 1 seed. And I gave him a better match. After four sets we were even—in the score anyway, two sets each, and I'd had a fine chance to win in four, leading 4–1. But I was through, and Manolo wrapped me in a lovely web of shotmaking, 6–0 in the fifth. I believe that's the only time it's happened to me since I've been a world-class player. It happened so fast it was almost painless.

In the second set Manolo sprained his left ankle. He took off his shoe and hobbled around, testing, to see if he could go on. I followed him to commiserate, but not to step on his bare foot as I should have. I missed my chance. Still, it didn't seem to matter when I had that 4–1 lead in the fourth set.

Then Manolo exploded. He was sure of his ankle again, and he rang up eleven straight games and the match. I never got close until we shook hands.

Five weeks later I won Wimbledon and was considered No. 1 in the world. Was that a nice thing to do to your leader, Manolo —blitz me in Paris with all those people watching? The next time I'll jump on your foot with both of mine.

LESSON 2
The Killer Instinct

When I was a kid, and beginning to play well, a little better than the ordinary, I first experienced the enjoyment of playing to a crowd. It was a good feeling to have my strokes admired, and I was in no hurry to get off the court. As a result I let too many opponents off the hook. I found out that you have to play with the intention of making it a short day, of doing the job quickly and thoroughly.

I don't mean rush it. Anything but that. But when you have the opportunity you strike then, and you realize that no lead is as big as it looks. If your opponent is serving at 1–4, you feel pretty good: three games ahead. But that's only one service break, and you want to keep the pressure on, or you're going to be in trouble. It's no time to experiment with new shots or to show off for the sheilas in the crowd.

I've heard it said that you're either born with the killer instinct or you're not. I don't agree with that. I feel I had to develop that killer outlook which, to me, means making the shot called for to win the point and resisting certain temptations. You don't try to blast a ball 200 mph crosscourt into a corner when you have an easy sitter and your opponent is way out of position. If a soft, unimpressive-looking dink is called for, you hit it and make the point.

The good chances don't come that frequently, and the killer knocks them off surely when presented with them. The killer doesn't let up or ease off when he gets a good lead. This can be learned. Make sure of the easy shots—concentrate extra hard on those. Everybody has problems with difficult shots, but the killer gets his edge because he is meticulous with the setups.

Don't compose eulogies to yourself when you get ahead. Concentrate on staying there. When Charlie Hollis, my coach, decided that I wasn't homicidal enough, he sent me out with the intent of win-

41

ning every match 6–0, 6–0. That seems grim for the usual player, but Charlie's theme was good and clear: run scared and don't let anybody up.

3 CHARLIE HOLLIS

THERE WERE decided similarities between the Grand Slammers Budge and Laver. Both redheads, freckled, a bit shy and reticent. Conscientious about learning to hit a tennis ball harder and better. Conscientious about winning.

Although Don came along first, conditions where I grew up were a good deal more primitive out in the never-never land of the Queensland cow country. I'll bet Don never sat in the rain to watch a movie. The moviehouses in Oakland undoubtedly had roofs, but not the one in Rockhampton where I saw my first cowboy film—and became permanently hooked on John Wayne and others of that celluloid style. It was just an outdoor screen with folding chairs set up in rows. If it rained the movie kept going, and I stayed. You don't walk out on John Wayne, do you? And risk getting shot in the back?

I think we got started on roughly similar courts though. Don describes the public park court where he took his first swings as gravel. I would take that to mean a gritty surface, unlike the cement more common to California on which he really developed and refined his game. My first court was antbed, homemade by my Dad and the boys in the family. It's common stuff in the Australian Outback. You knock over an anthill, which has become quite hard, crush it and spread the grit on a level piece of ground where the grass has been skinned off. It plays a lot like clay.

About a month before Don, who was then twenty-two, concluded his Slam, I was born at the Tamachy Hospital in Rock-hampton, August 9, 1938. As far as I know there is no plaque on the wall of the hospital to mark the occasion. A lot of people are surprised to learn that there were even walls, but Queensland isn't quite that rugged. And we weren't that far out in the Out-back. It was far enough that we boys could hunt kangaroos, though; and when we built a tennis court we had to clear quite a determined scrub growth.

It was a thoroughly outdoor life, but I didn't shoot up majestically as Budge did. I was a midget, five feet four, the first time I played at Wimbledon. I'm glad I grew a little more as I left my teens, to my present height of five feet eight and a half inches.

We Lavers aren't big people, but we're sturdy and athletic, as were the Roffeys, my mother's people. My grandmother, Mrs. Alice Roffey, was still riding horseback in 1967, the year she died. She was ninety. Uncle Frank Laver made a name as captain of an Australian national cricket side, but then a fellow should be pretty good if he is brought up on a team. There were eleven boys—my Dad, Roy Laver, the youngest—and that was just right for cricket. They were known as the Laver family side around Gipsland, the cattle country in Victoria where dad comes from.

Dad was raised in the cattle business. He went north, to Queensland, to go on his own, and he did well with various properties—what Americans call ranches. He met Melba Roffey, my mother (like many Australian girls named for Dame Nellie Melba, the great opera singer of the time), married her, and they settled in the Rockhampton area. We moved around a bit in those parts. Rocky is on the coast, above Brisbane, tropical coun-try, a town of about 30,000 then.

Until I was nine we were on a property called Langdale. Then we were in a tiny town called Marlborough, where Dad ran the butcher shop. He was fifty now, and easing out of the cattle business where he'd done well. After his brief stint as a butcher we moved into Rocky. Dad wanted us closer to school and closer to organized tennis.

We'd had a court on the Langdale property, and on the weekends the "neighbors" from properties in the area—sometimes from miles away—would gather at our place to play. When there was a tournament in Rockhampton, Mum and Dad would gather us up and we'd all go in. They'd play all the events, mixed doubles together.

They were keen on the game, and Dad was very ambitious for us three boys. Trevor is six years older than I, and Bob four years. Lois, the only girl, is a good deal younger. She was born when I was nine, and didn't figure much in the family tennis. Dad wanted us to be good at tennis, and he felt Trevor could be a fine tournament player.

He didn't think much of my chances because I was so small, but soon after Charlie Hollis took over coaching us in Rocky, Charlie told Dad that I'd be the best. "They're like you, Roy," was the appraisal of Trevor and Bob that Charlie Hollis gave my Dad. "Quick-tempered. They blow up too fast. Rodney has the more easygoing manner of his mother. If we can build the killer instinct in him, then it'll be the perfect blend."

Charlie was always after me to beat my opponent as badly as I could. "Your job is to go out there and win as quickly as possible, Rodney. If you can beat him 6–0, 6–0, do it. Give them no chance to come back at you."

In Rocky, where Dad was semiretired, working a little in contracting business, we cleared trees and scrub and built ourselves another court. Lighted, too, although the five 1500-watt bulbs we strung overhead were about as strong as candles in a London fog. We were eager, though, and our sharp young eyes could have sighted a ball in a coal mine.

It was one of those nights I sneaked out of bed for my introduction to Charlie Hollis. I was a little over ten. He was having a knock with Dad, Trev, and Bob, and when he spied me in my pajamas, my nose sticking through the chicken wire, he said, "Let the little bugger have a hit." Pajamas and barefeet may be the costume for some pretty good games, but not tennis. I went out there anyway and kept the ball going with Charlie.

Later he advised Dad, "Rodney's got the eye of a hawk. I believe we can make a champion out of him."

They were determined to do it. Dad drove me everywhere to play tournaments, even as far as Brisbane, which was 450 shaky, dusty miles over dirt roads. He had started me off, and he made sure I paid attention to Charlie, whose ability as a teacher he respected.

When we boys began a daily program under Hollis, we'd get up at five in the morning, ride our bicycles five miles to the town courts and play by ourselves until Charlie woke up and supervised us before we had to go to school. After school it was more tennis, and then some more at night with Dad when we finished our homework.

The fences on the town courts didn't last long after Hollis got himself established as the coach in Rocky. He had his class practice serving by knocking the ball at the fence from six feet away. We didn't waste time chasing balls, and a lot of kids could use one court. It was a good way to get grooved in our motion before we actually began playing.

Charlie was a great one for a complete approach. Tennis was more than just hitting a ball if you were going to go someplace in the game. He was a bachelor and he often ate with us. He'd scold me if he thought my table manners were off. "You have to know which fork to use when you go abroad to play Wimbledon," he'd say.

He was always talking about the great players, holding them up as examples. He'd been a good amateur himself, and had seen Budge when Don toured Australia in 1938. He would describe Budge's wonderful backhand, and he'd quiz us frequently.

"Who was Gentleman Jack?"

"Jack Crawford," I'd answer.

"Why was he called Gentleman Jack?"

"Because he was a fine sportsman, and he always was well groomed, on and off the court."

My brothers still like tennis, but they prefer fishing and skin diving from their boat that they take out to the Barrier Reef. That's my favorite vacation, going out to the Reef to fish, away from everything in marvelous hot weather.

Charlie would come fishing with us—Trevor and I both won

local fishing championships—but his mind never left tennis. We'd be reeling in a big one, excited at the catch, and Charlie might remark, "You know, that Fred Perry certainly had a marvelous forehand. . . ."

No amount of work on your game was enough to satisfy Charlie, and he was a good man to coach me because I thrived on work. For the same reason, I enjoyed the tough training and drills Harry Hopman put us through, first when I attended his clinics in Brisbane and later when he was my Davis Cup captain and I was playing for Australia. This wanting within me to be the best drove me to do any amount of work. If Charlie had directed me to walk to the top of the Toowoomba Range on my hands, I would have done it.

He's still teaching, and he continues to take a critical interest in me. After I'd made the second Slam I received a terse cable from him: "Congratulations. Do it again."

Twice around the Slam isn't enough for Charlie. Nothing ever is.

Conditioning and Equipment

As Australians we pride ourselves on being very fit. Harry Hopman, our Davis Cup captain, pushed us hard, and I think conditioning is sometimes more important than ability. You can have the greatest strokes in the world, but you won't be able to hit them very well if you're tired.

I went to a gym as a youngster to build myself up, punched a bag and followed the rest of the strenuous routines of boxers. It depends on how serious you are about the game. Running is a must. After you practice you go for a run. Once you're tired I reckon the next five or ten minutes—when you really push yourself—is the real benefit you get out of that day, as far as making yourself stronger. You've got to go beyond the limit. If you run four laps, and feel like you've had it—then you'd better run a couple more. Quicker. This is to get in top shape. By staying this way I find I have not only second wind in a match but third and fourth wind. It's a great feeling to know that you have more in reserve when you're playing a tough match. The running and the exercises, the feeling of fitness, are an important part of my enjoyment of tennis.

For the older player, who isn't particularly keen on being able to go five sets with Ken Rosewall on a clay court, tennis itself is a nice conditioner. You go along at your own speed, and you're not going to kill yourself, maybe. But there is this to remember in a match: if you're tired, maybe your opponent is exhausted. By sticking with it just a little longer instead of saying, oh, the hell with it, you'll often come through in a match you thought was lost.

You've got to play at your own pace, however, and maybe that means doubles as you get a little older. You're not covering as much court, but often doubles is more satisfying because the ball stays in play longer—and you pick a spry partner to run down the lobs. Selection of partner—one who can carry you—is the chief consideration in doubles. Why do you think I play with that pillar of fitness, Roy Emerson?

Don't give up the game just because you've slowed down at singles. Jean Borotra, the old French Davis Cup ace who's over seventy, says, "Never give up singles. If you play one hour per day without fail you can go on forever." And that's just what he does.

One of my most thrilling experiences was being on the same court with Pieter Smith during an exhibition in Johannesburg. Smith was the beneficiary of a heart transplant, and is back playing tennis. Doubles. Sensibly—which means not taking an unnecessary step. This rule doesn't apply to heart patients alone. As you edge into the over-45 senior league (a senior is a person who believes that every day in every way he is getting better—even though his legs aren't), you should learn that it's silly to chase down every ball. I do because it's my living. But unless you have a real play at a ball—forget it.

You should give some thought to preparation for a match. Loosen up the muscles. A few sit-ups, bending and stretching exercises. Run in place for a minute or so. Unless you're warm, you risk pulling a muscle or straining something. I've noticed that few people take enough practice serves. It's very easy to injure your arm or shoulder if you aren't properly warmed up. Don't be one of those "first one in" guys. Take your time and hit a dozen practice serves, easily at first. Pamper that arm and shoulder.

If it's cold, wear a sweater, maybe even a sweat suit at first until you're functioning smoothly. If it's hot, take salt pills, about a half-hour before the match. It's too late once the match has begun. Wear a hat. One of our floppy Aussie fishing hats is best. On the depressingly torrid Australian days I would wear wet cabbage leaves inside my hat. Honestly. It helped. I sometimes wear a dampened handkerchief around my neck in extreme heat. It's refreshing, and keeps sun off the neck.

During a match it's all right to sip water. I might have a total of five glasses during a long match, which includes some used for just rinsing my mouth out. After a match I take Gatorade or one of the other drinks that replenish mineral losses. I don't think they help much during a match. For instant energy I take glucose tablets during a match. I don't think carbonated drinks are good.

Naturally you don't stuff yourself before a match. I eat three or four hours prior to a match, although that's an individual thing. I don't believe you should eat less than two hours before playing. Your diet is up to you. About the only thing I avoid is potatoes the day of a match.

Now, let's say you're an ordinary player. You aren't going to do backbreaking calisthenics or run as though you were getting ready for the Boston Marathon. Your fitness will come mainly from playing two or three times a week, and the thought of punching a bag is fatiguing. Well, I'd say you could help your condition, without making a project out of it, by walking as much as possible, using the stairs instead of an elevator—unless you work near the top of the Empire State Building—and carrying a tennis ball around with you. Squeeze it on that odd moment you have nothing else to do. You'll be amazed at how this will build up the strength in your racket wrist and arm. A tennis ball can take the place of worry beads. I imagine if Captain Queeg had fiddled with a tennis ball instead of those ball bearings he might have fattened up his forehand instead of his neuroses.

My Life
and
Times
in
Pictures

A promising junior player from Australia (1956)

Mom and Dad

53

LES WA

My first big prize

and my latest ones. This is the Wimbledon Trophy

and this is the U.S. cup that completed the Grand Slam.

*Along the way
I ran into
some mighty
good ones,
fellow Australians*

Ken Rosewall

Tony Roche

Roy Emerson

John Newcombe

*And a bunch of
tough Americans*

Pancho Gonzales

Arthur Ashe

Stan Smith and Bob Lutz

Dennis Ralston

*And a lot of others
whom you meet
in the pages
of this book
if not in this
photo section.*

59

WIDE WORLD PHOTOS

MADISON SQUARE GARDEN CENTER

Professional tennis has come a long way since this day in St. Louis in 1964 when Pancho Gonzales, Ken Rosewall, Butch Buchholz, and I had to have traffic stopped downtown in order to let anyone know we were alive and playing

A good example of how far, this check, the largest in more senses than one ever offered up to that time, which was presented to me by Alvin Cooperman after I won the Madison Square Garden Invitational Tournament in May 1969.

Sometimes you belt one . . .

Sometimes you s-t-r-e-t-c-h for one . . .

Sometimes you just scramble

*Some
funny things
happened
on the way
to the tennis
courts . . .*

*Torben Ulrich during his five-set lo
to Gonzales at Forest Hil*

Cliff Drysdale

Cliff Richey

Guess who?

Martin Mulligan losing to me in the all-Australian Wimbledon final of 1962, probably because he wasn't keeping his eye on the ball. Later he became Martino Mulligano, the mainstay of the Italian Davis Cup team.

April 1969 and my partner Pieter Smith, South Afric heart transplant patient, in exhibition match against Panc Gonzales and Ray Moc

*Another piece
of silver for
Mary to keep
polished*

Our best prize—Ricky

65

4 BRING A COAT AND TIE

BRISBANE WAS the first big city in my life, a huge place to me as a boy. Not anymore. In Sydney and Melbourne they think of Brisbane as a country town, and I suppose it is the least sophisticated of the five major Australian cities. Population about 850,000. Hot. And I hope you don't land there on a Sunday when it's closed up tighter than a drum. Centuries—the days when the temperature goes over 100—are common during the summer as the humidity encloses you like a wet shroud. The best thing to do in Brisbane in the summer is leave—head for the beach. There are so many beaches on the Queensland coast that you should be able to find one all for yourself, if you like solitude. Most people prefer Surfers Paradise on the Gold Coast below Brisbane. Surfers' style is early Ft. Lauderdale. It's a seaside town where the three B's harmonize sweetly—birds, bikinis, and beer. I don't think Australian birds will ever go for nudity, but considering the bikinis at Surfers, who'd know the difference?

Despite this, and other evidence of the generally relaxed nature of Australians, just try to dine out in Queensland without coat and tie, regardless of the temperature. Like a lot of things in Australia, such propriety is a hangover from the days when we looked to Britain for our customs. Without a coat and tie, you are a thug in the eyes of a headwaiter, who is usually encased in boiled shirt and tails. You approach him and it becomes a con-

67

frontation. You'd have an easier time getting past the Chicago police. An American friend of mine, stopping at Lennon's Hotel between planes, had left his luggage at the airport and strolled into the dining room in a neat sports shirt. It was Sunday. Lennon's had the only dining room open. Only after much pleading, arguing, and finally threatening to roll on the floor and die of hunger tremens did my friend persuade the maitre d' to relent. Although the room was practically empty he was seated in a distant corner where the waiters regarded him as though he were an Arab at the Tel Aviv Hilton.

Lew Hoad still giggles about getting that same treatment at a sleazy hotel in the bush, a town called Cloncurry where the heat—110 degrees, and no air conditioning—was only slightly less oppressive than the flies. The pros were on a tour. Cloncurry wasn't a glamor spot for them even in the vagabond days of 1958, but they'd been booked there.

"Get coats and ties or get out, you mugs," snarled the unshaven innkeeper. They couldn't believe it. But the man presided over the only beer tap in town. They complied.

So I had a coat and a tie in my bag when I returned to Brisbane to play the Australian Championship for the first time in seven years. It was finally an open tournament, the last of the Big Four to abandon its amateurs-only policy and welcome the pros in the new era of integrated tennis that began in 1968.

The Slam was totally open, and here I was to try to launch another one—this time a universal Grand Slam.

It was good to be back. This was home. Though I came from Rockhampton, I moved to Brisbane and went to work for the Dunlop Sporting Goods Company when I became really serious about a career in tennis and quit school. I was fifteen.

It was no country town to me. Brisbane had streetcars! Long gray things that looked like destroyers. And the lights were pretty bright for a kid off a cattle property. You didn't take a chance on getting rained on when you went to the movies. The theater had a roof.

Charlie Hollis decided I was ready to try on metropolitan life in 1951, and Dad drove me to Brisbane for the state championship for boys fourteen and under.

"Don't come back if you don't win," were Charlie's instructions. I think Dad would have brought me back, but I got the idea. Charlie didn't temporize. I won, and was pretty happy. Being a state champion was a very big thing to a thirteen-year-old.

The next year Dad took me down again to attend the clinics that Harry Hopman was giving as a promotion for the newspaper, the *Brisbane Courier-Mail*. That made me very nervous at first. Everybody in Australia—and, I thought, the world—knew and admired Harry Hopman. He'd been a fine player, then captained the Australian Davis Cup team of Frank Sedgman and Ken McGregor that broke America's postwar grip on the Cup in 1950. He was working with Hoad and Rosewall, who were about to burst forth as young world-beaters, and here I was, getting instruction from this important man who was respected everywhere—Wimbledon, Forest Hills, Paris, Rome.

He had a nice way with kids, though. Firm, but good-humored. He seemed to treat us as though we all had the potential of Hoad and Rosewall. He could explain everything clearly and make you work.

Charlie Hollis told Hop I was going to be a champion. I was embarrassed, but I appreciated Charlie's testimonial, knowing well that I looked like I'd been on a hunger strike most of my life. I was short, skinny, and not too quick either.

After a couple of days, Hop remarked, "You're the Rockhampton Rocket, aren't you?" "Rocket" stuck.

"He was the Rocket—because he wasn't. You know how those nicknames are," Hop has said. "Rocket was one of the slowest lads in the class. But his speed picked up as he grew stronger."

I became determined to build up my strength; if I couldn't grow much bigger—I weighed 143 when I finished the 1969 Slam—I would at least get stronger. One of the simple things I did to build up arm strength for my wristy game was to carry an old tennis ball around and squeeze it every time I had a chance. This would help any player.

One of our group at Hopman's clinic was a good little player, Brian Littleproud, from a cattle crossing called Chinchilla out west. Sometimes I wonder what became of him. Too bad he didn't become a champion. Wouldn't that have been a marvelous name for the sportswriters to play with: Brian Littleproud, the cowboy from Chinchilla?

There was tremendous interest in playing tennis in Brisbane, and in watching good tennis. Americans find it a dead town. They're amused by the numerous houses built on stilts, to allow air to circulate underneath. But never in populous America has there been a tennis crowd to equal the mob at Milton Grounds in 1958. Not anywhere else either, except Sydney and Melbourne.

Until 1958 Brisbane had been considered too small to support a Davis Cup Challenge Round, the grand final in the worldwide tournament. A Queenslander was on the team then, Mal Anderson, who'd also been coached by Charlie Hollis, and the local officials convinced the Australian Lawn Tennis Association that the support would be forthcoming.

Milton has seats for about 6500, which even today outdoes every tennis stadium in the U.S. but Forest Hills. Huge Bill Edwards, who wraps his 300 pounds in suit, vest, starched collar, and tie every day no matter what the weather, runs tennis in Brisbane and was determined the town would make a marvelous showing when the American team arrived to play for the Cup. Up went the temporary bleachers, up, up so high they could have used Sherpa guides for ushers. I'm glad I didn't have to sit on the top row because the stands seemed to quiver all the time. Each day for three days 17,886 people crowded themselves onto those precarious perches. With the exception of Wimbledon, no tennis event in the world comes close to those figures, and this was 1958 in a small city.

It was an exciting match with the Peruvian Alex Olmedo carrying the U.S. to a 3–2 win, one of the infrequent times that the Americans have been able to carry off the Cup from Australia.

Those were the days of tremendous U.S.-Australia rivalry in the Davis Cup, when attendances of 25,578 at Sydney and 22,000 at Melbourne were the largest in the game's history. Sadly, that day is over. The last time Brisbane was host to a Cup final, 1967, total attendance for three days was 14,500. Nobody seemed much interested. Spain was the opponent and the sporting public knew it would be no contest. Australians won't buy tickets for a lower grade product, and the Davis Cup, once the high spot of the season, has lost its glamor but may regain first-rate status if it becomes an open competition, as now seems likely. Australia's last good Davis Cup team was seen in that crushing of the Spaniards— John Newcombe, Roy Emerson, Tony Roche. All became pros and, like me, were barred.

Dominating the barroom of the Milton Club, covering practically one wall, is a gigantic photograph of that 1958 mob scene. It's almost a shrine now, and many a glass has been lifted wistfully to that portrait of another era, with the prayer that it might return. I hope it does. It doesn't seem likely for a while, even though I'm convinced the tennis is better today. Intelligent promotion is needed. We found that out when we arrived in Brisbane for Australia's first open championship. France, England, Germany, Ireland, the U.S., Argentina, and even Switzerland had staged national opens in 1968, all these after the Australian season had closed in January. Australian tennis officials had nearly a year to prepare for their first open and the experience of other countries to learn from. Nobody bothered to learn or prepare in Brisbane and the first Australian Open was a terrible flop.

It shouldn't have been held in Brisbane anyway. Sydney was the only place for the first big one, but it was Brisbane's turn since the nationals is shared in rotation with the other three eastern cities, Sydney, Melbourne, and Adelaide. It was understandable that the stands weren't filled in 1967 for the Davis Cup against Spain, but I for one thought Brisbane would reawaken for an open because the standard would be the highest again, and the Australians who hadn't played in the championships for one or more years—Rosewall, Stolle, Roche, Emerson, Newcombe, and myself—would be back. We weren't looking for the crowds of 1958. Those temporary bleachers had been taken down long ago, but we thought we could fill the permanent stadium of 6500. We didn't. The biggest crowd was 4500 when I beat Emerson in a match between the hometown boys. Other days it was lonely there. Thousands and thousands of people were watching all right, but they were at the beach, accompanied by TV sets. The tournament organizers had given away the TV rights, and they didn't have enough foresight to black out the Brisbane area. Why would a bloke pay for a seat in that bloody heat at Milton when he could sit in his bathing suit with a beer at Surfers Paradise and catch a wave or squeeze a bird during the lulls on the screen?

Brisbane was the last place I thought I'd encounter tennis apathy. It would have surprised me less to learn that Las Vegas had lost interest in blackjack.

The sporting climate in the No. 1 tennis nation had changed, no doubt about it. For one thing the press had soured on inept officials who persisted in maintaining the phony "amateur" game and ostracizing pros. These officials, backward in just about everything they did, felt they didn't have to promote tennis and compete for spectator dollars. They continued to live in the past, when tennis could command a huge following without any effort. In the postwar years there was great national pride in tennis and the fact that our small country—in terms of population—could defy the world and smash the mighty U.S., our idol. U.S.-Australia Davis Cup conflict guaranteed sellouts. Times changed. Listen to Fred Stolle:

"When I was a kid, tennis was a great future, a way to travel and represent your country. We worked our butts off for the chance and the competition was phenomenal. There were tennis courts everywhere. Now because of building demands a lot of courts have disappeared, and kids have more to occupy their minds as Australia grows up and becomes more like America. They have cars, there's surfing, golf, they have more money. They think of college, which we never did. They're just not as bloody hungry. The press has knocked tennis so much in recent years that the public has grown to regard it as inferior. In the old days the sports pages were packed with tennis. That's changed and it isn't going to come back overnight. The market has been hurt, and the officials are going to have to realize that nothing is automatic

anymore. You have to hustle your product, as they say in America.
Just announcing the open championship wasn't enough, but that's
all they did."

Fred and I and others feel that tennis can make a comeback
in Australia, but it will take much hard organizational work by
younger officials who realize that the game is now merely one of
many diversions for the public. In my day as an amateur you
could sell a youngster on the benefits of being a career "amateur"
athlete. That was the system. You can't anymore. If he's going to
devote himself to a game, he has to know there's a sound professional future so that he can support himself openly and well. You
won't get the best athletes to play tennis otherwise. America is an
example of that. Their best athletes play baseball, basketball, football, even golf.

Tennis always got its share of our top athletes, but not so many
in recent years. I hope that intelligent organizers will reverse the
trend and restore Australia's old interest, get the assembly line
running again. The way the game is improving all over the world
I'm not sure Australia could ever be in such a dominant position
again, and I'm not sure it would be a good thing. Too much
success did have something to do with spoiling the game. Winning
the Davis Cup year after year became boring to an extent, but
only, I think, because other countries—specifically the U.S.—
couldn't make a good match of the final. Many people, of course,
are glad to see Australia decline. "Break up the Aussies!" would
be the cry in baseball, but I can't agree with that.

I will agree with those who say that in its present state the
Australian championship shouldn't be considered a leg of the
Grand Slam. Undoubtedly the South African, Italian, and German
opens attract stronger fields. The Slam might be more balanced to
include another clay court event (Italy or Germany) or a cement
court event (South Africa). But as soon as the Lawn Tennis Association of Australia fattens its championship with sufficient prize
money, the players will be there, and nobody will have to apolo-
gize for Australia in the Slam.

I'm not apologizing now. There may not have been great depth to that 1969 tournament, but I had to beat Emerson, Stolle, Roche, and Gimeno in succession to win, and that's just about as tough a lineup as you can find.

There was some doubt that our pro group would play Australia at all. Prize money was low ($25,000), and the most I could win in singles was $5000. That's not much when you consider the expenses of that trip, and the boss, George MacCall, was having trouble negotiating with the tournament officials for the price he thought he should get for transporting his troupe to Brisbane.

Nevertheless the Slam was uppermost in my mind, and George sympathized. He agreed that I could enter on my own even if he held the rest of his group out of the tournament. In this case the title meant a lot more to me than the money.

I was relieved when George, along with Bob Briner of World Championship Tennis (the other pro group), was able to make a deal for all the pros. Without the rest of them there, trying to make life miserable for me, I would have been truly miserable. It would have been an easy, empty victory, no fun. I've never looked for tournaments I could steal.

LESSON 4

Tennis Anyone? Any Age?

Is there an ideal age to begin tennis? Depends on what you expect to accomplish. I'm convinced of this: you can start late in life and still learn to play respectably, so that you can have a lot of fun. And that's the most important aspect, isn't it? In California, the area I live in near Newport Beach, it's remarkable the number of people giving up golf in their forties and taking up tennis. They want the exercise which makes them feel better, and they don't have to devote the best part of the day to a game. My wife, Mary, was a late starter and now she bats the ball around fine. Not great. But she enjoys it as much as anybody. Mostly these people will play doubles. You don't have to be so accurate or cover so much court.

In regard to becoming quite good, the younger you start the better. But a kid shouldn't be pushed. I've seen five- and six-year-olds with wonderful coordination and ball sense who go right at it. But they were also strong enough to handle the racket comfortably. Usually a youngster isn't ready for it until eight or nine, and not then unless he has a genuine interest. The "tennis parent" who drags his youngster onto the court isn't doing the child a favor. There was a recent case of an American man who started his kids off with full-size rackets almost as soon as they could walk. His theory was that they would build a tennis sense immediately and increase their strength even if all they did was drag the rackets around the court. His kids did become very good at early ages, won national junior titles—and then became sick of the game before they were out of their teens.

There have been striking exceptions to the general rule of starting young. Orlando Sirola, the Italian, first played at twenty-two. He had strength, size, and aptitude, and four years later was a Davis Cupper. Stan Smith, one of America's best, hadn't been playing very long competitively before he won the U.S. junior title at age eighteen.

If a very young child shows an interest, but doesn't have the strength, you could saw off a racket for him, lower the net, and cut down the dimensions of the court. Some teachers have experimented successfully with smaller courts laid out specially for kids, the dimensions of the court and net reduced proportionately as in Little League baseball. The size of the racket and court and the height of the net can be very discouraging for young beginners. In fact, the height of the net is often very discouraging to me.

5 THE FIRST LEG ON THE SLAM: THE AUSTRALIAN

THREE YEARS had passed since I'd been home, and I was very anxious to see my parents. They're getting older—Dad's over seventy—and there won't be too many more times when we're all together. Tennis means a big sacrifice in family life. More so if you're an Australian because almost everything is happening somewhere else. I left when I was fifteen to make tennis my career and have spent precious little time at home since.

You wonder, quite a lot in the beginning, if the loneliness and the being away from the family is worth it. I've really been a gypsy more than half my life. I've made good friends and enjoyed seeing the world and I believed I was doing the right thing to secure my future. But, remember, I've done extremely well. That fact helps combat the loneliness. I've known young Australians who seemed to have as much promise as I, who were my friends, but couldn't fight the homesickness. This kept them from being outstanding, and they had to find something else to go into.

During the open, I learned that Mary was going to have the baby. Only that, and seeing my folks, made Brisbane bearable. The tournament was the most discouraging I've ever played in. There have been worse conditions while barnstorming as a pro, and fewer spectators. But when you come into Milton Courts, where your memories are so good, and then this long-awaited open turns out as a terribly bush league production—well, it hurt.

Bill Edwards and several of his fellow officials snubbed the tournament one day to go to the races. We know Bill doesn't care for the pros and the idea of open tennis, but did he have to insult us by acting that way—to the detriment of an event that could have made money for Milton, his club? Australia's tennis old guard needs to be excused from the scene.

I arrived at Milton and walked out onto the stadium grass to look around and I thought back nine years. My first major title was the Australian in 1960, when I got that premature notion I could keep going through a Slam. It was a marvelous win for everybody, not just me, because by beating Neale Fraser of Melbourne in the five-set final I became only the second Queenslander to win the national championship since 1905.

Eight thousand were in the stands, among them a good-sized gathering of friends from Rockhampton, crowing for me every chance they got. Of course it was my crowd, considering the circumstances. Fraser was the No. 1 amateur in the world then and he had a match point on me in the fourth set. I slipped away and had seven of them on him at 7–6 in the fifth on my serve. He busted loose every time, but finally I held serve for the title.

A lot of people thought it was the most exciting match they'd ever seen. That was how I remembered Milton, for that struggling, unexpected triumph which had Australia talking, and started my collection of major championships. Others may have remembered it, too, but few bought tickets to witness the hero's return. Neale Fraser showed up, only as a spectator. And he was in on a free ticket.

A young Italian named Massimo di Domenico gets a mention as the first of twenty-six victims on the Slam. The grass wasn't as fast as usual at Milton, and I could experiment and get the feel in beating him, 6–2, 6–3, 6–3. Brisbane is always hot, but the heat seemed more blistering to me, though I'd grown up in the area. I wasn't used to it after years away from Queensland.

I knew it in my next match against Roy Emerson, and I'm happy we played at night. Dew makes night tennis on grass a bad, slippery idea. But we didn't miss the sun at all, and the crowds improved a little.

If there was one match that did revive some of the old tennis feeling in the town it was Emerson and Laver.

We were the local boys who had made it better than any Queenslanders. We'd played so many times that sometimes our matches seemed as familiar as summertime reruns on TV. No matter what happened, though, we became better and better friends. We're doubles partners now, very close, but Emmo would cut out his heart to beat me. He's a tremendous competitor, unbelievable when it comes to fitness. I think he's the hardest-working athlete I've ever seen.

Emmo and I come from the same kind of background, out in the bush. He was brought up on a cattle ranch at a little place called Black Butt, and he got those really strong wrists by milking cows. I don't know whether he used the continental grip on the cows, but they knew he was going to hang on until they produced their daily quota. He must have milked thousands of them. When Emmo began to show a high aptitude for tennis, his family sold the place and moved to Brisbane. They had a court on their ranch, but his father wanted Emmo to be able to get the best competition and instruction.

At first, in Brisbane, Emmo couldn't get used to taking a bath whenever he felt like it. "Out on the station, water was scarce and precious. It was almost rationed," he told his new friends. "I thought we were going to run out in Brisbane, and I never used much until I was certain we could have as much as we wanted."

Emmo has a very rigid code for himself, and we like to think this is the way of a dinkum (honest-to-God) Aussie. Although he has had numerous injuries during his career, one of them costing him his fourth Wimbledon title and the other possibly costing him a fifth—and making it easier on my Slam in 1962—he never, never talks about them or implies that an injury was the cause for defeat.

"Once you walk onto that court," says Emmo, "you're signifying that you're in perfect shape. Otherwise don't go on. Only two things happen. You win, or your opponent beats you. Injuries have nothing to do with it." Any talk of injury, as an excuse, grates on Emmo. He once snorted about the chronic moaner, Niki Pilic: "I never beat Niki when he was well." You'll never hear Emmo complain, but you will hear his footsteps all through a match as he charges the net incessantly, and sometimes you'll hear that piercing laugh of his, and be glad. That's Emmo's way of releasing the tension when he's bungled a shot he should have had.

Emmo gleams on a court, the sun or the lights glistening off his patent-leather hair and the gold fillings so prominent in his front teeth.

The sight of him is as much with me as anything else in the game because we've played each other so often in important matches. He has been my downfall, and I his. Titles of our own nation and numerous others have been at stake often when we've met, and we've meant a lot of disappointment for each other. During the two Slams, in eight tournaments, I've had to get past Emmo five times.

By 1960 Emmo and I were the rising players in Australia while Neale Fraser was briefly at the top. In the semis of the nationals at Brisbane, I somehow pulled up from 2–5 in the fifth to win five straight games and beat Emmo. Then I knocked off Fraser in that wild final. That delayed Emmo's winning his first Australian title, which he got a year later by going through me in the final. Later, in 1961, after winning Wimbledon, I was favored to win my first American championship. But there was Emmo in the final, winning his first instead, and me shaking his hand and saying, "Well played, Emmo."

Although Emerson has never won the Grand Slam, he's won more of the Slam titles than anybody else, a total of twelve—six Australian, two U.S., English, and French. At the close of 1969, I was one behind him with eleven, ready to pass. Emmo has lost just enough of his edge so that he's not likely to win one of the Big Four again, but he'll always be dangerous.

The grass was slick when we went on. Because of the slipshod scheduling it was after 9:00 P.M. Emmo's a slow starter. So am I, but he was slower and I got the first set pretty quickly. And the second. But he took the third, and he had a break and was serving at 7–6 in the fourth, looking like he'd catch up. It was just about midnight now, the crowd excited. The year would be marked by patches like the one I struck then. I began hitting my returns harder, and they were buzzing with topspin. Emmo was charging in, but he missed a couple of volleys. I broke back, and kept going for a run of three straight games and the match, 6–2, 6–3, 3–6, 9–7.

There wasn't much time to have a beer and relax because after I'd showered and talked to the reporters it was one in the morning and I was due back to play Fred Stolle in ten hours. Hardly time for breakfast.

Stolle, a tall, slim blond, probably would have been a basketball player if he'd grown up in America instead of Sydney. He was quite a good cricketer, a wicket keeper, which corresponds to catcher in baseball, but he was always getting his hands banged up and his mother didn't like that. She encouraged him to play more tennis, and he had a talent for it. We're the same age, but Fred was a late developer and first made a name as a doubles player. I didn't consider him a rival when we were both amateurs but with his rifling serve, good volleys and backhand, he came along strongly in 1964 and won Forest Hills in 1966.

We had a terribly long second set, and I had to serve well to stave off a set point, but Fred couldn't get into the match after that and I won 6–4, 18–16, 6–2.

Like Emmo and me, Tony Roche is a country boy. He grew up in Tarcutta, a tiny New South Wales settlement surrounded by nothing and sheep, about 200 miles from Sydney. His father, Andy Roche, is the town butcher, as my Dad had been briefly in Marlborough, and Tony has the strokes to do a splendid job with a cleaver. He prefers a racket, and is as threatening with that.

After pounding a ball against the side of his house so much that he nearly knocked it off the foundation, Tony decided he'd have to get out of Tarcutta if he was going to be a serious tennis player. He was missed. His departure cut the population noticeably, by almost one per cent. Moving on to Sydney, he was quick to be noticed as an exceptional prospect.

All through 1969 Tony was trouble for me. The main trouble. He beat me five out of nine times, giving me my own medicine— a lot of left-handed spin—and making it clear that he thought my time was over and his had come. It seems strange with all the millions of tennis players in the world that two left-handers from the Australian Outback, from places called Rockhampton and Tarcutta, would be one-two for 1969.

One reason Tony got a jump on me, I think, is that he had more opportunity to play against left-handers. For years I was the only lefty among the touring pros. This was a decided edge for me because the only time my opponents encountered left-handed spin was against me, while I was well accustomed to the right-handed spin.

When Roche went pro with Dave Dixon's Handsome Eight, two other lefties went with him, Taylor and Pilic, so that he became well grooved in opposing his own kind. The abundance of left-handers in their troupe probably was a reason that Newcombe, Drysdale, and Ralston were able to give me exceptional trouble.

I wish I had more time during a match to watch Tony, but I'm pretty busy following the ball. When he signed with the World Championship Tennis pro troupe, with seven others, they were called the Handsome Eight. Roger Taylor, John Newcombe, Niki Pilic, Pierre Barthes, Butch Buchholz, Cliff Drysdale, all have movie star looks, or what we used to think of that way, in the pre-anti-hero days. Denny Ralston has an All-American appearance, but Tony? Ask him where he ranked in beauty among the Handsome Eight, and he replies "fourteenth." The movie star he resembles is Victor McLaglen. He has a plastic face that he's always trying to rearrange with his right hand when he makes a bad shot. Tony's facial expressions are fantastic. He may not be pretty, but he does have a rugged Aussie look about him with his shocks of blond hair, his heavy jaw and sturdy chest. He could have been a fine boxer or football player, I think. Tennis was lucky to get him.

Just before we got to Brisbane, Tony beat me in the New South Wales final in Sydney, which was our country's first actual open.

He took a lead on me that he never gave up over the year, but he couldn't beat me in the matches that mattered most—and paid best.

I brought three sunhats to the court that Saturday to play Tony in the semifinals, and each one was thoroughly soaked when we finished over four hours later. We started at noon. My brother Trevor was coming down from Rocky for the weekend, and since he keeps his sports goods shop open a half-day, he phoned me: "I won't be there till two. Try to keep it going so I can see something of it." We laughed about that later. Trevor got to see more than enough of me and Tony struggling away with the temperature at 105 and no shade anywhere. We kept towels in an icebox beside the court and draped ourselves with them every change game. It was only momentary relief. I kept taking glucose and salt pills, but I got groggy. It turned out to be the longest match I ever played—90 games—and by far the hardest. Ten years back, at Wimbledon, I got by big Barry MacKay in 87 games at Wimbledon, also a semifinal. But the London climate was a lot easier to take than Brisbane.

There wasn't much to choose between us after Tony got into the match. It looked like I had him when I won the first two sets, 7–5, 22–20, but I was getting tired. At that point of the season Tony was fitter than I, and when he grabbed the third set 11–9, you could see him begin to puff up with confidence. That brought merciful intermission with a shower in the dressing room, one of those showers you never want to leave. Too quickly we returned to the oven, and Tony came back eagerly to resume with the same heavy serves and stiff volleys. I was in a daze as he ran off five games. The set was gone. I conceded that much as I served the sixth game, but I wanted badly to hold serve so that I could lead off in the fifth set. It was hard to do because Tony was playing full-tilt now and felt he had me. He'd already beaten me in Sydney and he was going to do it again.

Confidence is the thing in tennis, as I'm sure it is in any sport. I hear other athletes talk that way. Confidence separates athletes of similar ability.

Tony had it . . . and in an instant during the decisive set he lost it, through no fault of his own, on what may have been a very bad break. I'll never be certain, but Tony Roche will go through life thinking he was bad-lucked out of that victory by a linesman's decision. Maybe he was.

We went to deuce in the sixth game of the fourth set but I worked to make sure I got the game. It was important to me, even though Tony and I both saw that the set would be his. Maybe he didn't sense the importance. He served out in the next game for 6–1. We were even, and the momentum was his.

But serving first in the fifth set picked me up a bit. It's a psychological help to go into the lead every time you win your serve in a close match, and that's why I tried so hard for a seemingly meaningless game when I was down 0–5 in the fourth. I wanted to serve that leadoff game.

Naturally, now I had to hold my serve, and I hadn't been serving too well. Tony'd broken me three of the last four times. He was returning serve better than I was, and returning was tricky business on that court. It was freshly resodded and playing badly. Any time a ball landed on the court, hitting it was guesswork. That's unusual for Australian grass, but this was Brisbane '69, with everything schemozzled. Bad courts were just one more factor in a general screw-up.

Now I knew I had to get my first serves in because Tony would be jumping all over the second ball. I tried to pull myself together and make sure the first serve was a good one and that I was up to the net in position to make a good volley. I figured one break of serve would decide the match, the condition we were in. Tony was stronger, but he'd never been in a fifth set with me, and he'd have just a little more pressure on him, serving second.

Every time I held, the situation would be just a little dicier for him. My serve began to work all right. His continued too. One love for me, but he tied it. Two–one, and then 2–2. Three–two. I was feeling a little better. He wasn't blasting me off the court the way he had in the fourth set, and my confidence was beginning to come back. I've lost five-set matches, but not many, and I'd have to think hard to remember one. Three-all as Tony held, but his volleys didn't have quite the zip. I served to 4–3 and we changed courts. Slowly. The wet towels from the icebox felt good on my head. I wrung out my sun hat and it was like squeezing a sponge. One of the things I used to do on hot days was put a piece of wet cabbage inside my hat. That was a pretty good trick for keeping cool. Nothing like a green salad on your head, although I don't know if oil and vinegar does much for your scalp. I was tennis' answer to Mrs. Wiggs of the Cabbage Patch. But I had no greens this day, and Tony and I felt like the cabbage that lies alongside boiled corned beef.

It was his turn to serve and I screwed my mind into working for every point as though it were the last. If you do that when you come down the stretch in a tight match you'll be surprised how often a superhuman effort will come out of you. "It's 3–4 in the last set, and I'm going to hack and grub," I told myself. "Just do anything to get the ball over the net. It doesn't matter how you look. Form won't win this one."

You learn to hack, as we call it, when you join the pros. Get balls back, and the hell with trying to slap a winning shot that doesn't have too much chance. It looks great if you make it, but at this stage you can't give away points.

A big shot may look lovely, but anything that goes over the net now will look lovely. You still win matches by getting the ball over the net one more time than your opponent.

You face up to that when you leave the amateurs. You settle down. You can slam away when your opponent isn't too sound, or you clearly dominate him, but I was in with Tony Roche in the decisive set, and it was no time for pride and flamboyance. I was going to scratch and dig and bloop the ball over any way I could.

I was chipping my returns now, trying to squib them onto his feet. With the ball skipping erratically on those courts, the opportunities to hit full out were limited, and the best thing was just to meet the ball.

So Tony was serving at 3–4, and this was the place for me to do my utmost. He knew it; everybody who hadn't passed out from the heat in the stands knew it. Win this one and I'd be serving for the match at 5–3. This had to make it even a little more tense for Tony. We split the first two points: 15-all. Then he missed a volley. The 15–30 point is an awfully big one in this spot. He came in with a good serve, down the middle, spinning into my body. I sliced under it with my backhand to chip the ball crosscourt with underspin. Tony looked relieved because he thought the ball was going out. He was sure it was out, but there was no sound. Tony turned around and looked at the sidelines-man sitting behind the court. The official held out his hands, parallel to the ground, like a baseball umpire signaling "safe." It meant my shot was good, and the umpire called: "Fifteen–forty!"

Tony was furious, and I can hold his hand and sympathize . . . now. It was such a big point, and the ball may have been out. I didn't have a good view, but I had the feeling when I hit the ball that it might be going wide. I wouldn't have been surprised if it had been called out because it was terribly close.

It was a judgment call. Nobody—and I know Tony agrees—can blame a linesman if he misses one on a day like that. He'd been sitting there broiling for more than four hours, trying to stay sharp and alert. And maybe the ball was good and the man was correct. No matter. It stands as good forever because the lines-man said so.

"Fifteen–forty" was the best thing I'd heard all day. Two break points, and Tony was riled. Tony swung hard on his serve, and I knocked the ball back to him. He was at the net to make a backhand volley and sent the ball crosscourt to my backhand. Now this was a shot I love—the backhand down the line. Tony realized it and began moving to his left to cover it. But in this situation—two points to break—I was going for it with every-thing. I got the racket back and drove at the ball, snapping my wrist to load the ball with topspin. Tony and I have been through all this before. But even though he anticipates me, he's going to have a hard time volleying that topspinning ball down his sideline whenever I hit it that well. Out went his arm in the reach that failed. His racket probed for the ball and found it, but he couldn't control it. One of the most beautiful sights of 1969 was that ball clunking into the net.

Tony's game was knocked apart by that line call, and he

couldn't get himself to function in the last game. He was mad
and frustrated. He hadn't quit, but it all seemed so unfair to
him. In that moment of his anguish I served through the game
promptly, getting only token opposition.

Ninety games, the eighth longest singles match ever played:
7–5, 22–20, 9–11, 1–6, 6–3. It's a good thing that players cus-
tomarily shake hands at the end of a match. It was an effective
way of holding each other up.

Even though Roche has been around, and at the highest level,
he let himself get flapped out of that match like a novice, forgetting that you have to play the calls, as we say. Let's assume the
decision that upset Tony was outrageously wrong, and everybody
thought so.

You can ask the linesman if he's sure of his call. Sometimes
he'll change it or ask the umpire's advice. But if he won't there's
nothing you can do. You have to forget it, and make yourself
work harder for the next point.

Serving on grass at 15–40, Tony still had something like an
even chance of winning that game. When he didn't, he still had
a shot at my serve. But by the time he pulled himself together
the match was over. You mustn't let the worst call in the world
fluster you. I'm glad to offer this advice to Tony today.

Physically, that was the toughest match of the year, certainly
of the Slam. But the element of pressure wasn't there. Not for
me. The Slam hadn't even begun. I'd won nothing, and there was
nothing to be concerned about. It was only the second tournament of the year, and though I wanted the Slam, I really had no
idea the year would turn out so incredibly well.

It could all have ended there as easily as not, on the center
court at Milton. How many thousands of shots did I need to
make the Slam? I don't know. Nobody counted. This isn't baseball. But that one shot, the questionable call, could have changed
the whole thing. Roche, of course, is convinced that it did, and
I can't argue with him. It's funny, the hours and hours you practice, the miles and time you put in, and maybe the whole thing
hinged on a bloke sitting in a chair, looking down the sideline,
whose job it was to decide whether a ball was out or in. I like

to think he was right, that he was wide awake and decisive and that my shot was a deftly hit winner. It reads better that way. But it doesn't matter. Over the years the calls even up, Tony, but that one will hurt even a century from now when you're playing mixed doubles against Bonnie and Clyde at the River Styx Sauna and Racket Club, won't it?

But it may have been more than just a point—15–40 instead of 30–all—for both of us. If Tony had won the game, he might have won the match. That would have given him three straight victories over me, and a substantial heightening of his confidence. It wouldn't have helped mine. I can still see that backhand return of mine streaking for the sideline. Was a season for two men riding on that shot? That's one way to look at it, but maybe I'm getting too dramatic.

Nevertheless it's weird how a simple mistake can change not only a match but perhaps a career. To my mind the most fantastic example occurred in Brisbane during the Queensland Championships of 1955. Nineteen-year-old Ashley Cooper, just out of the junior ranks, was playing and losing a first-round match to a local entry, tall Les Flanders. At match point, Flanders stood at the net about to crush a sitter. It was all over, Cooper was reconciled to that, and he didn't much care where Les put the ball. He was astonished when Les butchered the smash, knocking the ball way out of court.

The reprieve turned Coop into a tiger, and he went on to win the match. His confidence soared and he was the sensation of the tournament, beating Mal Anderson and Merv Rose (then No. 10 in the world) on the way to the final where he played well in losing to Rosewall.

Cooper never should have gotten to the second round, Flanders' carelessness let him live one more point, and somehow the spark he needed was kindled. Less than three years later Coop was Wimbledon champion, No. 1 man in the amateur world. Those wins over Anderson and Rose gave him faith in himself, put him in a position to battle Rosewall impressively. But I wonder if Coop would have gone to the top if Les Flanders had finished off that easy shot properly.

The championship match in which I met Andres Gimeno was an anticlimax. Andres wasn't spirited, not strutting the way he usually does. He dislikes grass and extreme heat. Few Spaniards brought up on clay, care for grass, and for Andres, bad grass is more agonizing than eating dinner before 10:00 P.M. Nevertheless he'd had a good tournament, beating Kenny Rosewell, Butch Buchholz, and the amateur Ray Ruffels, without losing a set.

I think he felt he'd done enough, and he seemed pretty much resigned to defeat when he played me. I hadn't lost to Andres in a long time, and though he had several chances to break my serve in the third set, I took him pretty much as I knew I should, 6–3, 6–4, 7–5. I got my $5000 although the tournament went broke, and now the Slam was a definite possibility. I hoped my troublesome elbow would hold up, and I was pretty sure that there'd be no more 100-degree days along the way. Emerson and I won the doubles over Rosewall and Stolle, so we had a chance for a Slam there, too. One doubles Slam has been made, by Aussies Frank Sedgman and Ken McGregor in 1951.

I was so disgusted with the mismanagement of the tournament that I wanted to get out of Brisbane before I said some things I'd regret. The best part of it was seeing my family. We stayed together in a motel. Though it was pleasant, a reunion like that is spent mostly in talking about old times. You're not really a part of the family anymore, and you aren't planning any future as a group. You talk about things you've done together, a lot of good times, but you know there won't be a lot of time together in the future. My life just isn't built that way. Maybe someday I'll go back to Australia to settle, but I don't know.

LESSON 5

Confidence and Shrugging off Bad Luck

Amnesia, that's what a tennis player needs. Well, maybe not quite a total loss of memory, but I can't stress too much the importance of shoving the last point right out of your mind. Forget it. A point won't come back no matter how much you think about it. If you played it badly there's no way you can reverse it; if you played it well, it won't help you on the next point.

The next point—that's all you must think about. "Gotta get the next point!" is what you tell yourself. "Gotta get the next point."

Sure, it hurts when you get a bad call or you blow an easy shot. Worse still is brooding about it. I've seen this sulking about what-might-have-been tear players apart and cost them matches.

You beat yourself by thinking about your bad luck. It's unfortunate for a fine player like Dennis Ralston that he can throw himself off for two or three games by getting upset at something that you have to regard as ancient history and beyond your control. This is something, I guess, you have to start early. But maybe it's a mark of maturing.

You can't change the last point—forget it.

Get the next one.

6 LIVING WITH PAIN

TONY ROCHE wasn't by any means destroyed by that semifinal in Brisbane. The next week in Auckland he handled me in four sets to take the New Zealand Open. My left elbow was aching again. A cortisone shot prior to the Australian had quelled the pain and I was able to play as I wanted. But in Auckland I was hurting.

The long hauls were beginning. Two days out of Auckland we were back in snow country, in Philadelphia for the indoor open at the Spectrum. En route I stopped in Los Angeles for a quick visit to Dr. Robert Kerlan, an orthopedic specialist well-known to athletes, who had helped another left-hander with his aches, Sandy Koufax of the Dodgers.

I suppose anybody who's played tennis for any length of time has had a sore arm or elbow. Dr. Kerlan told me that the way I flick the ball he's surprised the elbow was functioning at all.

He gave me another injection, and I was okay in Philadelphia, beating Tony in the final. But by March the arm was seizing up so that I could hardly straighten it. If I played more than an hour the pain was terrific.

The injury went back to June of 1968 when I fell on my wrist going for a ball in Boston. With the wrist weakened, I think I put too much strain on the elbow. I won Wimbledon all right, but then everything gave way and I was beaten at Forest Hills.

91

Now six months later it still wasn't right, but I had to keep playing. You do that in tennis when you're a pro. It's not a team game. There's nobody to take your place. Pancho Gonzales found that out fast in his rookie year, 1949. He'd twisted his ankle badly and didn't think he'd be able to play against Jack Kramer on the tour. Kramer was also the promoter, thus Pancho's boss. "I don't think I can make it tonight, Jack," said Pancho, sincerely regretful. "Don't be silly," said Kramer. They taped the ankle, shot it with novocaine and Pancho went on. He and all the rest have played with injuries often. The way we travel and play you can't expect to be 100 percent all the time, but if you can get onto the court, you play.

When my cortisone wore off there were decagesic pills. Those worked for a while, but when I got to New York for the Madison Square Garden Open my arm hurt so much I couldn't bear to practice. I figured the adrenaline flow during a match and the usual competitive flame would keep me heated up.

Dr. Kerlan had given me something to think about: "There may come a time, and nobody can predict when, that you hit one tennis ball too many. When a bathtub is filled to the top, it only takes an eyedropper to make it overflow. Your elbow could be near the point when just one little swing will finish it."

Cheery observation. Sandy Koufax reached that point with his elbow and decided against going any farther.

Was I there? I began to wonder in New York on the most ironic day of my life as I went from hero to zero within hours. At a luncheon in my honor I was presented with the 1968 Player of the Year trophy, the top award in the game, sponsored by the Martini & Rossi distillers and selected by the foremost tennis writers. It was very nice. Free lunch. Roast beef. And then a scrappy Young Texan, Cliff Richey, roasted me. To a turn.

I won the first set, had good leads in the second and third sets of the best-of-three match, and came completely apart. When I seemed to have the match won at 3–1 in the third set, I started double faulting all over the place. I was a public spectacle, a perfect example of how a good player can lose his cool in an instant and play the game he usually owns like an outsider. Sure, the pain was fierce, but it shouldn't have made me stop thinking so completely that I lost five straight games, all but giving them away. You can't do that against anybody, least of all a tiger like Richey.

I began to rush my serve. That's fatal. You lose your rhythm. As a result I wasn't throwing the ball high enough. That's common when you get anxious and speed up. You have to slow yourself down and make yourself go through the phases of your serve carefully. The first phase is throwing the ball up properly.

Even when I didn't double fault, I usually missed the first serve. But I came storming into the net behind the second, as though I were serving beautifully. I should have noticed that Cliff was knocking the ball by me. Didn't I have the best view in the house? Racing to the net is a wonderful tactic—if you prepare your way. I was like one of those Polish cavalrymen in World War II, gallantly charging a Nazi tank on horseback.

Unless you're playing an unseasoned opponent that you can disconcert merely by showing yourself at the net, you've got no business up there on less than forcing strokes. Richey wasn't disconcerted by a close-up of my freckled face. He kept passing me. I didn't seem to notice. Panic—your magic spell was everywhere.

The Player of the Year had panicked, forgetting all the fundamentals. Cliff Richey, playing his first prize money event, came off with a first-round victory, an unexpected check ($900), and a scalp (Laver's).

Not since my first visit in 1956 when I ran into top-seeded Ham Richardson at Forest Hills, had I lost an opening-round match in New York. It was embarrassing, particularly the timing. In the papers the next day: photo of Player of the Year receiving his Tiffany trophy . . . and below, the story about him receiving his Richey thrashing.

My humility was high that morning. And my confidence was lower than the Grand Central subway station. I wondered if I'd ever be able to play well again. Confidence is that flighty. Even when you're not playing particularly badly. Arthur Ashe says, "Before a Davis Cup match I'm so gripped with self-doubt that I actually wonder if I'll be able to hit the ball over the net. Suppose I never get one ball back? That's what I wonder." I know what he means.

I had a long time to wonder and worry, a flight from New York to Johannesburg. Would the elbow be any good for anything but bartending? I've known Australian bartenders who got tennis elbow from working too hard during the maelstrom of the Six O'clock Swill—those last desperate minutes before closing time. It didn't affect their careers, but my line of work was different. I thought about it, and Dr. Kerlan's advice that I would have to learn to live with some pain. A lot of people do.

He'd also given me another decagesic prescription, and suggested a stronger dose. The pain had started on the outside of the elbow and moved inside. Needing more than pills, I became the pots-and-pans man of tennis as Kerlan recommended equipment as vital to me as my rackets: a hydroculator and a pot to heat it in. A hydroculator is a canvas pad which retains steam heat after being boiled.

He instructed me to wrap the elbow in the hydroculator for twenty minutes before I played and to pack it in ice afterward. I felt like a frozen daiquiri every night. The pots were too cumbersome to pack, so I bought one every place I went.

"I'd like to see your pots," was my line to the dime store salesgirls.

"What do you want to cook?" she'd inquire.

"Elbow," I'd answer.

"Oh . . . " she'd say, as though I were some kind of nut, or a cannibal.

Mine got well cooked, and I have to say I couldn't have won the Grand Slam without my dear hydroculator. And the pots. Plus thousands of ice cubes. Ice cubes meant more to me than they did to W. C. Fields—and he kept a refrigerator in every bedroom for emergency use.

Those treatments, combined with the pills, allowed me to regain my customary rhythm. I was determined not to become a pill-gobbler, and took them only a couple of other times during the year, prior to the biggest tournaments.

LESSON 6
Handling Injuries, and Other Props

It seems to me that people can put up with more pain than they tend to. I don't think you can hurt yourself that drastically by playing with slight muscle pulls. Doctors may disagree with me, but I think you can work these things out by playing. It's like stiffness. They'll stay with you twice as long if you don't run them out.

I guess I feel that the average player tends to pamper himself, but it may seem that way to me because we can't do it as pros. We frequently play with injuries. It's the way our business is.

Stretching exercises before you begin playing will reduce the possibilities of muscle pulls and will get a pulled muscle ready for play.

Blisters on the feet and racket hand can be bothersome. The best way to prevent them on the feet is to wear two pairs of socks, to cut down on friction. It's common to wear a light pair under a heavy wool pair. I generally wear two reasonably heavy wool pairs because I change directions so quickly and for me two pairs of wool are more comfortable. Pancho Gonzales still has trouble with blisters on his fingers. He tapes his fingers very carefully before he plays. There are gloves on the market, similar to golf gloves, that protect the racket hand and also help keep a firm grip if your hands are sweaty.

Wristlets, or sweatbands, are available to prevent sweat from running down the arms onto the racket handle. On scorching days it can still be difficult to keep your hand from slipping. I think an old-fashioned answer to that is as good as anything I've seen: sawdust. You can keep a supply in your shorts pocket and beside the court, and sawdust will take care of the moisture and keep the handle dry.

It's also worth shopping for other grips for your racket if you're having trouble holding it the way you want. Many players don't realize that they can buy the leather stripping in a variety of grips —welted grips, for instance—and it's a simple matter to wind a new grip on your racket, or have it done in a tennis shop.

95

Shoes should be lightweight, durable and comfortable, and there are plenty of brands that fit the description, although I feel that the Adidas is the best. Don't forget to put on two pairs of socks when fitting shoes.

Dead is the rigid idea that white is the only suitable shade for tennis clothing. We pros have led the way in breaking the textile color bar, and many clubs are relaxing their white-only rules of apparel. Once I became used to wearing colors, white seemed bland. Color peps up our appearance as it does in other forms of athletics.

In the days of Tilden, players used to feel unequipped without polo coats in which they swathed themselves after matches. The idea was good. You need a cover-up costume to ward off chills. Today a tailored track suit is what most of us use. We don't look so dapper as they did in the 1920s, but a track suit is more useful, easier to warm up in, and easier to launder.

Most tennis clothes are drip-dry and quickly cared for. A quick way we itinerants sometimes do our washing is to wear our tennis clothes right into the shower and soap them down.

I travel with several changes, but Tony Roche, for one, limits himself to one pair of tennis shorts. "It saves space in packing," says Tony, "and I haven't met a tennis player yet who wears more than one pair at a time."

7 SOUTH AFRICA

SLOW CEMENT is the surface for the South African champion-ships. You have to be able to keep the ball going, hit ground-strokes and play patiently. It's the kind of game people like to watch, and the stands at Ellis Park are always crowded. Good tennis is one reason; the other is shrewd promotion by Owen Williams, the man in charge. Owen's management has raised the South African Open to a high position in Johannesburg, as a leading sporting and social event. Johannesburg is comparable to London during Wimbledon: everybody is aware of the tour-nament and the players, and wants to go watch the tennis.

Well, maybe not everybody. The blacks, of course, are not part of the mainstream, and it is their exclusion—the policy of apartheid—which may lead to the breakdown of this tournament as one of the world's best. Now Johannesburg is a major stop on the world circuit. Owen Williams attracts most of the first-class players, and certainly his entry list is heavier with talent than the Australian Open. But apartheid is making it more and more difficult for South Africa to be accepted in the scheme of interna-tional sport.

South Africa was kicked out of the Davis Cup competition in early 1970, following the refusal of the Vorster government to issue a visa to Arthur Ashe. Owen Williams and other South African officials had invited Ashe to enter the 1970 Open where, Arthur had hoped, he would be the first Negro to play any game

97

amongst whites. Alf Chalmers, president of the South African Tennis Union, pleaded with the government to be moderate in this case. Chalmers knew that the U.S. would react by joining Sweden and the Communist nations who had been trying to expel South Africa for years on the grounds of racism.

Ashe became a cause célèbre. Many within the tennis community felt that all players should stand up for Ashe and boycott South African tournaments. There is something reasonable to the thought that tennis players make up an international brotherhood, and that if one is not permitted to go somewhere in our world, then the others should not go. It made all of us conscious of this mixing of politics and sport, which was distressing. I don't think any of us approves of the South African government. I was disappointed by the barring of Ashe. Everybody was. But I couldn't see what good a boycott would do, and I considered it futile to join those players who did refuse to play in South Africa. I wouldn't be hurting the South African government, whose line is hard and firm, but by not fulfilling my commitment I would be harming the tennis community in Johannesburg, which has been very good to me over the years.

It's sad to see what has happened because the South Africans may very well be the most enthusiastic sportsmen in the world. They're very much like us Australians in outlook, but their governmental policies are pushing them into a bleak corner in the sports world. If Ashe had gotten in, it would have been a wonderful breakthrough, and he may yet. There was a breakthrough in 1971 when the first Black was invited to play at Johannesburg, a countrywoman of mine, aboriginal Evonne Goolagong. Then in 1972 an American Black, Bonnie Logan, received an invitation and played. But even more hopeful was when Dan Beuke, a Black local schoolteacher, was permitted to enter.

South Africa was reassuring because my arm didn't fall off. It didn't even come loose through six rounds of singles. The tournament was a good test—Frew McMillan in the fourth round, Bob Hewitt in the quarters, Cliff Drysdale in the semis, and Tom Okker in the final. Drysdale, who has been troublesome for me with his deceptive, two-handed backhand, was the only one of them to take a set in a match of strangely one-sided sets: 6–1, 1–6, 6–1, 6–2.

Only for one set did Okker press me in the final, 6–3, 10–8, 6–3. It was a long way to go to win $2800, my smallest first prize of the year, but right then I would have gone to the South Pole for nothing to get the same result—to know that the elbow would hold up. The way I packed it in ice after every match, the South Pole wouldn't have been a bad place for me to play.

Although I was the winner, a guy named Gonzales stole the show from me as he has so many times. When I first came with the pros I was annoyed that the only man in the troupe who got much attention from the public was Pancho Gonzales. I guess Kenny Rosewall and I resented it because we knew we were now consistently better players than Pancho, and yet in the public's mind—especially the American public—Pancho was the champion. Always was and always would be. I've heard about Americans who still regard Jack Dempsey as the heavyweight champion, and are oblivious to anyone who has followed. That's the way many American sports fans seem to be about Pancho. To them he's the only tennis player worth discussing, and I will say that at least until my second Grand Slam I had to acknowledge the fact that, in the U.S., Gonzales was the only tennis name immediately recognizable to any group of sports nuts. Rosewall and I have as much pride as anybody else. We were bothered by the general feeling that Pancho was the only name who could sell tickets in the U.S.

"Without Pancho you guys would be out of business." We heard that over and over, and it cheesed us off. We reckoned that people wanted to see us, too, especially since we were the big winners. It was disheartening even to consider that Pancho was holding the pro game together through the force of his fiery personality. Could our game be so shaky that its success depended on a player who was past his prime?

This bothered us, and so did Pancho's attitude in the mid-1960s. He was ungracious to say the least, a loner, and an absolute jerk on the court. He tried to take every advantage.

Various Gonzales incidents widened the affection gap between him and his competitive colleagues. But here we were in Johannesburg, shortly before Pancho's forty-first birthday, and I found my old distaste for him gone. He was still a bastard in a match. Off-duty he'd mellowed. We all used to secretly, and openly, cheer against him, but now I was finding myself enthralled to watch him, just like any other spectator.

He captivated Johannesburg completely by outlasting Fred Stolle, 11-9, in the fifth set after losing the fourth, 12-14, in the longest match of the tournament, 73 games. Next, in the quarters, he showed no signs of wear until the end of another five-setter. He grabbed the first two sets from Drysdale, barely lost the third, 8-10 and the fifth, 5-7.

In 1968, the first year of open tennis, Pancho had a few bright moments, but he really wasn't ready for the transition from the shorter matches and tournaments of the pro tour to the week and two-week major events involving best-of-five-set matches. He faltered badly in England, the first pro to lose to an amateur (Mark Cox) at the British Hard Court Open, and wilted at Wimbledon against the Russian Metreveli.

But 1969 found Richard Alonzo Gonzales, one of the world's more resilient grandfathers, ready. South Africa was important to both of us. Pancho showed he was going to be a factor, not just a relic worth watching out of curiosity. He was really playing better tennis at forty-one than he did when I first encountered him at thirty-five. Much better. There were times when I wished he'd just give it up and disappear, but now he's showing us that if a man takes care of himself and is determined he can play this game productively for longer than I'd thought. Pancho's ten years older than I am, and I'm pleased he's around as an inspiration.

When he was out of the singles at Johannesburg, Pancho kept going with the young hipster of the courts, South African Ray Moore, to win the doubles. This was one of the beautiful combinations—Moore, the Wolfman, and Pancho, the Old Wolf. Moore's now-generation coiffure—the frizzy blond hair that made his head seem a sunburst—and his mustache and headband identified him as a freaky son of staid South Africa. Ray is such a pleasant, kind guy that he's a favorite everywhere. At home they don't know quite what to make of him except that he ought to get a haircut. It's only a matter of time before Ray will be wearing mod tennis outfits off Carnaby Street, or perhaps off Pierre Cardin's racks. He does cover himself with psychedelic T-shirts on occasion, although these were a bit much for the tournament officials in Johannesburg who insisted on all-nice-and-white. Deviation from white is just that—deviation—in South Africa. Ray didn't make much fuss. He just played good tennis with the man eighteen years his senior, permitting no generation gap to form down the middle which they covered with sharp volleying. Ray and Pancho had never played together before, but they got it together, as Ray would say, for a few days, and soon had the crowd backing their improbable run to the title. "Pancho's really all right for a man his age," Ray enjoyed saying. "He listens to my Led Zeppelin records and I can communicate with him. He's a nice man." I guess I'd agree although I wouldn't have five years ago.

Moore seems to be an odd character in his hippie style, but there is depth to him. While it is easy to condemn South Africa from a distance, Ray has done it where the heat is—at home—and one of the results is that he has been barred from playing in the Eastern Province. He has been outspoken on the racial question, and has even campaigned on behalf of the Progressive Party, which opposes apartheid. This has brought public criticism down on him in South Africa, but he hasn't been afraid to speak up.

Ray considered boycotting the 1970 Open as his protest of the Ashe case, but decided that he could do more good by appearing in his country and working however he could for a change. He is the only South African athlete to oppose his government so vigorously.

I took a title out of Johannesburg, and so did Pancho. We were going to do all right this year, even though we probably didn't imagine how well. I was glad my elbow responded, but I still had my doubts about its going the distance through Forest Hills, which was five months off.

Changing Your Game as You Grow Older

In 1963 at Adelaide, when the American team of Chuck McKinley and Denny Ralston took the Davis Cup away from Australia, the pivotal victory was the doubles match. The Yanks beat Neale Fraser and Roy Emerson largely because Fraser couldn't hit his overheads. McKinley and Ralston obliged by feeding him lobs whenever they could, and Fraser's failure caused an astute observer, Jack Kramer, to say: "The first thing that goes in an aging tennis player is not his legs—but his overhead."

Now Fraser was by no means an antique. He was thirty, but he hadn't been playing quite as much as the others. It was a good lesson to remember. The overhead is the most tiring stroke to hit, and if you can make older opponents hit a lot of them, you're going to cause a breakdown. (Unless the older opponent you have in mind is Pancho Gonzales—although Pancho can be wearied a bit by good lobs, too.)

Pancho, by the way, is a good example of a prudent change by a man over forty. He uses a much lighter racket than he did years ago, barely 13 ounces. Red Hoehn, the teaching pro at the Badminton and Tennis Club in Boston who has done stringing for Pancho, was jolted a few years ago when he weighed Pancho's rackets. "This is the same weight my twelve-year-old daughter uses," said Hoehn.

The lighter racket is easier to whip around, causing less strain. Pancho is now a devotee of the metal racket. Again, it can be swished easily, offering less resistance with the split shaft. Serving with the metal rackets is not as tiring.

On the serve it's doubly important for the older player to get the first ball in, for this is a fatiguing stroke, too, and you want to hit as few serves as possible.

Elderly players—and there are people in their nineties who continue to play—might consider using VASSS (Van Alen Streamlined Scoring System) rules, in either single-point or no-ad form. Single-point is similar to table tennis scoring, with the serve changing every five points. No-ad eliminates deuce; thus the first to reach four points wins the game. Both reduce the strain of serving long deuce games or sets. Van Alen also invented the sudden death tie-breaker which was a revolutionary introduction at Forest Hills in 1970. This prevents deuce sets, going into force at 6–6 in games. Sudden death is a best-of-nine sequence of points ending the set. The first server serves points 1–2 and 5–6. His opponent serves points 3–4 and, if necessary, 7–8–9. In doubles one player of the first team serves points 1–2 and his partner serves points 5–6. One player from the other side serves points 3–4 and his partner serves 7–8–9 if necessary. Complete rules of VASSS are available on request from the Tennis Hall of Fame, Newport, Rhode Island.

The older player may be surprised at finding himself a better player in many ways than he was as a youth. He will if he learns that he can't blast away all the time with the gusto of bygone days, and that he must play more thoughtfully, mixing up his strokes, hitting the ball on the rise to take advantage of the pace his opponent puts on the ball and using less energy of his own. He won't run for a ball that is obviously out of reach, or on a point that probably doesn't mean much, say at 40–0 or 0–40.

Gonzales is a good example. He musters his energy, saving the big serve for when he really needs it. He keeps his returns low and soft, and uses the lob often and well. When he does come to the net he makes sure it's behind a worthwhile shot. He feels that his eyes and reflexes have gone just a little and has trouble with balls hit directly at him at net. This is always a good tactic to use with a volleyer—bang it right at him—and it pays off more against an older opponent.

Older players are more likely to pull muscles, so they should be sure to be warmed up properly, and should take it easy if they haven't been playing regularly.

It's a great game at any age. So take it easy and enjoy it.

8 THE DAVIS CUP JITTERS

EVEN IN the jet age, Australia is a long way from any place. Getting out to any place takes time and money, and there aren't very many opportunities. Tennis is one of them, a good one. A privilege as well as an opportunity. And an honor because anybody sent away by the Lawn Tennis Association represents Australia. Playing ability is important, but so is behavior. A few Australians have made fools of themselves with temper displays and have been caught with their sportsmanship down. Very few. That doesn't mean that Australia doesn't breed racket-throwers and whiners. It's just that those types don't get sent away.

When we went away on a team headed by Harry Hopman—or any other captain during a non-Davis Cup tour—the man in charge had our parents' blessing to lay on the discipline. We'd get no sympathy at home if we complained, because this was a great opportunity for us. Travel came much harder for us than for Americans.

We're an easygoing people, but we're very competitive, too, somehow different from the Americans whom we consider our best friends and hottest rivals. Australians have handled the pressure of tight situations in tennis better than Americans. We don't blow up. That's not 100 percent true but it does seem that way, and when our players collapse or choke they don't rave and fume like Americans. I think it's because of the difference in the societies. We're competitive in sports all right, as much as anybody in the world, but the Americans are competitive in everything, every waking minute.

The pressures are much greater on American tennis players, and it's no wonder they explode. A young Californian isn't much different from a young Aussie. They grow up in tennis climates and tennis atmospheres. At fifteen the American may even be ahead of the Australian, but life is much more complex for the American. There is the pressure of school: he has to be thinking about his marks so that he'll qualify for a good college. At the same age the Australian with a future in tennis quits school and goes headlong into tennis.

There's no stigma attached to leaving school at that age in Australia. By fifteen you complete a segment of education that is nearly the equivalent of high school in America, and it is as much education as most Australians get, although more emphasis is now being placed on completion of high school and entering university than in my day. We're still a very young country and higher education is for only a few. I didn't even have the usual amount of schooling. When I was fourteen, I lost a year when I came down with hepatitis. My father took me away to a farm where I could recover my strength, and when I was ready for school, they said I'd have to repeat the entire year.

I was never that crazy about school anyway. I was sure tennis was going to be my life, so I wanted to get into it. Charlie Hollis, my coach, helped me get a job with a sporting goods company, the usual thing for a boy who wanted a career playing, but he had trouble doing that. Finally Dunlop took me on to do odd jobs around their plant in Brisbane, but Charlie had several turndowns before that. I was too scrawny and didn't look like much for the long haul as an athlete.

With that kind of job it was understood that I'd have time to practice and to go away to tournaments. I'd be giving clinics and exhibitions on behalf of the firm wherever they wanted to send me, and I'd be kept in equipment. The pay was nothing to speak of, but my parents found me a place to lodge, and I didn't need much money. What I needed was pretty clear to me: to hit thousands of tennis balls, get stronger and more accurate, and to accumulate tournament experience.

This is the way it was and is. Many times I regret my lack of education. At a party or with nontennis friends, occasionally I feel uncomfortable as the conversation swirls about me. I've always been shy, but well-educated people can make me feel shyer, at first, if I don't know them. It's a matter of gaining confidence, and since I've been married and met a wider circle of people, through Mary and living in California, I've begun to enjoy getting to know people outside of tennis. I've been reading more, and I guess have become more aware.

I can't say I'd stay in school if I had it to do again, or that I'd think about college. I had to get on in tennis, and the way I did it was the best way. This is where the Americans go "wrong," and I've purposely put the word in quotes because it depends on the surroundings you grow up in and what you want out of life.

In American tennis Cliff Richey is the closest thing to an Australian in outlook. For Cliff tennis was everything, and to his parents it was, too. They encouraged him in his desire to hit a tennis ball to the exclusion of just about everything else. Cliff did get a high school diploma somehow, although his original class graduated a couple of years before he did. He still shudders when he thinks about biology, which he had to hit a few times before getting the credit. Cliff is dedicated to tennis, and although he doesn't have the talent to be a great champion, Cliff's determination will make him a good living as an independent pro.

But Cliff is an odd-man-out in America. All his contemporaries in tennis have gone to college—gone "wrong" as I said—and that slowed their tennis development. While I was hitting tennis balls in Italy, learning the slow court game against a tenacious opponent and feeling the tensions of an alien environment and a hostile crowd, Ronnie Holmberg—who beat me in the Junior Wimbledon final of 1956—was juggling tennis with classes at Tulane.

There is plenty of tennis for American college players, but they're essentially part-timers fitting the sport into education. That's the right way for Americans, a fortunate way. But how could Holmberg keep up with me? From the age of fifteen I was a tennis professional. I didn't sign a contract until much later, but obviously I was a pro. Tennis was my life; it supported me. Holmberg and I were equals at eighteen, but thereafter I shot far ahead. We Aussies were on subsidies from sporting goods firms, an advantage not permitted then by U.S. amateur rules.

Frank Froehling, who gave me a good match at Forest Hills when I completed my first Grand Slam in 1962, was one of the Americans who tried to have it both ways by attending college and filling in the spare hours with big-time tennis. "It's pretty funny that we Americans would always be criticized for our Davis Cup failures," says Frank, "when to be a Davis Cup player on the Australian level you have to play tennis full time. So then when you'd play full time, somebody would call you a tennis bum, or say, how come you're not in college. They never asked Laver or Emerson why they weren't in college. Everybody accepted them as career amateurs. That wasn't nice for American boys, yet we were expected to rise up on the big occasions and beat them. People would say what's wrong with American tennis?

"After four or five years of tennis and college, a guy would graduate and decide he'd give the game a couple of all-out years. For all but the exceptional players this was too late, but many would try. They'd have to put up with this comment from their friends: 'Are you still playing tennis? When are you going to get a job?'

"How could you win?

"Things are better now, though, with more realistic rules, and the opportunities to make prize money from tournaments. It's honorable for a college graduate to go into pro football, basketball and baseball, and now at last there are the same legitimate career opportunities on the tennis circuit as there are in golf."

That's the pressure in America that has never been felt by an Australian. The background of the game in America, as a rich man's sport, made a career of playing tennis seem improper. A player had to seem to be doing something else as his principal occupation. It was ridiculous. We had the amateur hangup in Australia too, but a career as an amateur tennis player was perfectly acceptable. In fact it was choice, with all the travel, glory and privileges involved. Nobody asked when are you going to get a job, because we all had connections with sporting goods firms and because playing tennis was considered a very nice job. In America, with wider economic opportunities, a tennis player was expected to get educated and really go to work.

Occasionally a player would come along who, for a brief time, could blend college with tennis and play at the top. Chuck McKinley did that in 1963 when he won Wimbledon and spurred America to one of its then rare Davis Cup wins. Arthur Ashe had his big five-month drive in 1968 when he won the National Amateur, the U.S. Open, and led the Davis Cup charge, but Arthur's five years at UCLA and two years in the army may be time that he'll never make up in the game. And Arthur is a very diversified guy. His life is broader than a game. His uniqueness as the only black in big-time tennis has opened many business and social opportunities to him, each reducing the time available to hit balls and concentrate on the game.

Undoubtedly the time will come in Australia when higher education is as sought after as in America. Then tennis players will be like other professional athletes. They'll mix college with their game and wait until after graduation to specialize. But for years the Aussies have had the jump, and they've made the most of it.

I settled into my career young, and I think that helped my temperament. I knew what I was doing; I was beginning my adult role at fifteen. The American kid is bewildered about what he wants to do then, and he's got so many options.

When I was twenty-one, I was a seasoned pro and ready for my role in the cooker at Wimbledon and in the Davis Cup. American kids usually aren't.

In Davis Cup matches Americans feel strongly about playing for their country, just like everybody else. Ashe has said, "Maybe it can get too nationalistic. The Olympics do, but you can't escape the fact and feeling that your country is depending on you and your game. Too much can be made of it, and that's where the pressure comes from. It's built up by the press media.

It makes Davis Cup an altogether different competitive experience."

Although I played on four Cup-winning teams in four years, I regret that the competition wasn't too keen after the first year, 1959. Then it was as tense as anything I've been through. We had to battle in the early rounds as well as the final when we took the Cup away from the U.S. I lost to Mario Llamas of Mexico and Ramanathan Krishnan of India on the first day of those meetings to keep us in trouble in the best-of-five-match series.

In the Challenge Round, the grand final at Forest Hills, we took the Cup only because Neale Fraser was so sensational, winning both his singles over Alex Olmedo and Barry MacKay, and the doubles with Roy Emerson.

My contribution was mainly applause for Neale and Emmo. It stands as the biggest disappointment of my career that I lost to Olmedo on the third day with Australia ahead, 2–1. I could have clinched the Cup right there. I had set points in every set, but won only one as Alex beat me, 9–7, 4–6, 10–8, 12–10. Fortunately for us, Fraser came through against MacKay in the last match. Neale made me feel doubly glad—to be part of a victorious Australian team, and to be taken off the hook for my failure. All through his struggle with MacKay, which ran over two days because of bad weather, I hated myself for blowing the match with Olmedo.

After that, the Davis Cup wasn't much of a thrill. We were the defenders and had to play only the final against the survivor of the preliminary rounds. It was a letdown that the Americans never made it, and we weren't pushed by the teams that beat them, Italy in 1960–61 and Mexico in 1962. In the six singles and one doubles matches I played I lost a total of two sets. That was dull. Harry Hopman trained us in his usual thorough manner, as though we were going to run across Simpson's Desert. It was overkill, but Harry believed in running scared—or running any way as long as you kept running.

With the kind of backing he got at home, Hopman could be a "martinet," as the newspapers called him. I felt he was petty at times with his fines for minor training infractions, and failing to pay us the daily allowance if we lost a day crossing the dateline. His harshness probably prevented a few fellows, like Merv Rose and Bob Mark, from realizing their potential. They soured on him early. And his role as a strategist was overvalued. His usual advice during a Cup match: "Relax and hit for the lines."

But I have nothing but gratitude for Hop because his program of working our guts out made me a winner. Conditioning is often the deciding factor in a match between players of similar ability, and at the top there isn't much to choose between individuals in the matter of talent.

Hop showed us how to be the fittest. Running and strenuous exercises and drills were stressed. Fitness means more to you than strategy in a tight Davis Cup match. Hop got us readier than our opponents. That was his strength, getting us up physically and mentally, bringing us to the peak at the right moment. After that he could sit beside the court, mutter "hit for the lines" and appear a genius.

It's easier to bear down and get really fit when you're a member of a team. When you're out on your own as a pro, and have to discipline yourself, that's when it's a test of how much desire you have to get on. Will you make yourself get up early and run? Will you do those double knee jumps faithfully, and work as hard in practice as you would in a Wimbledon final, stretching for every ball in the two-on-one drill? Those of us who have been through the Hopman mill have been molded into these habits, and I reckon the conditioning of four of us in our thirties —Emmo, Stolle, Rosewall, and I—stacks up pretty well against any athlete.

Tennis is an individual game, and it is a game of individualists. The team aspect of Davis Cup competition gives tennis another dimension, a very satisfying one. It was Donald Dell's ability as captain in uniting a group of extreme individualists— Arthur Ashe, Clark Graebner, Bob Lutz, Charlie Pasarell, and Stan Smith—that enabled America to gain control of the Davis Cup in 1968 and possibly establish a long reign. Of that group,

Stan Smith was the only one who could be described as a self-sacrificing team man before Dell took over.

The desire to win for your country is common enough, but I had more than that going for me in 1956 when I went on tour for the first time. I wanted to win for the people at home, in Rockhampton. I felt I was playing for them and I didn't want to let down these friends and neighbors. Maybe you feel more that way when you come from a small town. Everybody knows you, and if you do well you'll actually be able to put the town on the map. I guess I did that, in a way, for Rockhampton. It sounds corny, but I played with the feeling that I'd let Rocky down if I lost. Nobody else from the town had ever gone abroad to play. This feeling was strong at first, then, of course, it subsided. But it was a part of me, it was always there. Frequently in Australia townspeople will take up a collection to help send a promising young player away. They did that for Jan Lehane in a little town called Kingsbury, and she felt that her friends were riding with her. "It made me try twice as hard as I thought I could," she said.

It's likely an Australian will feel a special allegiance to his or her hometown because tennis is so prominent a sport in Australia, and all your results are followed closely in the local papers. Dennis Ralston had something of this feeling for Bakersfield, California, an isolated community where tennis was important and he was a leading personality. After he and Chuck McKinley won the Davis Cup for the U.S. in 1963, in Adelaide, Ralston instructed the American correspondents to "tell 'em in Bakersfield that I won it for them." This is the way a small-town boy feels, and I was that boy.

My first world tour was paid for by an industrialist named Arthur Drysdale. It was common in those days for young Aussies to make trips subsidized by wealthy countrymen. Drysdale didn't choose me in particular. He gave the money to Harry Hopman for the purpose of helping develop two promising juniors. Hop chose Bob Mark and me, a pleasant jolt when I learned about it.

When Charlie Hollis was coaching me, he was concerned about

the whole picture of life as a tennis player—not just the strokes that supported that life. He drilled me on etiquette and dress, on whatever customs he knew of the countries where I'd be playing, and in the histories and personalities of the great players of the present and the past.

"We want to be proud of you when you're becoming a champion," he'd say over and over. "You have to know how to act the part. You're representing the people of Rockhampton and Queensland and Australia." My parents were with him wholeheartedly.

That might not make much of an impression with kids of today. They seem more sophisticated, but it sank into me.

I feel that I represented Australia pretty well, but there was a summer night in 1958 when I was scared I'd be going home in disgrace. I pictured the headlines in the Rockhampton paper: "Laver Jailed, Deported After Wild Boston Party. Tennis Stars Arrested for Peace Disturbance."

The entire Australian traveling team had been invited to a party at a penthouse in Boston's Back Bay section. Normally, on a night before the finals of the National Doubles, we'd have stayed home because some of us would be playing. That was an unusual tournament. All the Aussies had been knocked out in the quarters or semis, and our manager, Esca Stephens, said we might as well enjoy ourselves.

That we did until a group of policemen suddenly appeared on the roof. "You can hear this party all over Boston," growled the sergeant in charge. "We've had complaints from six blocks away. I'm backing the wagon up to the door, and taking everybody in."

I was terrified, even through my one-beer glow. This was my first trip away with the team, and I was going to jail. It had seemed like such a good party. A bit boisterous, perhaps, when Ashley Cooper defeated the rest of the crowd in a standing broad jump event on the living room floor.

"All right, you're all going in to Station 16," bellowed that cop. That is one precinct number that stays with me: Boston 16. I thought of jumping off the roof, but it was five floors up.

Could I escape like a cat burglar? No, we were a team and we'd go to jail as a team.

"Please, officer," one of our hosts, Charlie Cronin, pleaded. "These athletic fellows here are the Australian Davis Cup team. You wouldn't want to cause an international incident, would you?"

The cop, a burly Irishman, paused, looked us over, and replied: "Now what in hell is the Australian Davis Cup team?"

I never felt farther away from home.

But Cronin had enough Irish in him to somehow talk the cops off the roof, promising that the music would be turned off and that everybody would go straight home.

Something else I didn't want to let down was the Australian tradition. This is the way the Green Bay Packers and the old Yankees and Cleveland Browns and Boston Celtics felt, I think. As an Australian I was in a very illustrious line that began in 1950 with Frank Sedgman and Ken McGregor. There had been excellent Aussies before that—Crawford, Jack Bromwich, Adrian Quist, and even earlier, Sir Norman Brookes, Gerald Patterson, and J. O. Anderson. But beginning with Sedge and McGregor, Australia took over the tennis world and began a domination that hasn't ended. Between 1950 and 1968 Australia won the Davis Cup 15 times, and in 1952 Sedgman won Wimbledon (19 years after the last Australian victory by Crawford). Beginning then Aussies won 14 of 21 Wimbledon men's singles titles, 10 of 20 French and 13 of 21 U.S.

I didn't want to be the one to let the dynasty down. Sedgman, McGregor, Hoad, Rosewall, Rose, Hartwig, Cooper, Anderson, Fraser, Emerson, Laver, Stolle, Newcombe, Roche. That's quite a tradition, and I think you have to play better being a part of it. More is expected of Australians on a tennis court. Even an itinerant like Bob Carmichael. They call him "Nails" because he used to be a coffin maker, and he's a bloke who's seen the world through tennis. He lives in Paris now, and isn't really a great player, but when somebody beats him they feel good because they've beaten an Aussie. They'd even feel good beating

Jack Crawford, and Gentleman Jack is nearly seventy now, but a win over an Aussie is something to be treasured.

I think the lesser Aussies like Carmichael and Terry Addison (two-faced Terry, who wears a beard when he's abroad and shaves when he comes home to Brisbane because his mother wouldn't let a beard into the house) also play better merely trying to hold up their end of the tradition. We've got great pride in this tennis mastery. We like being the islanders from the bottom of the world who sit on top in the most international game. We probably are a bit boorish about it, too, but—and this is a bit odd—we also like to get beaten once in a while. We cheered for the Spanish and the Italians, the Mexicans, and the Americans each time when they came down to try to take away the Davis Cup, because we thrive on competition, and we want the feeling of a stiff challenge. But when the competition gets too tough, we'll cheer double faults and other mistakes by the enemy and we'll shout three times as loud for our own good shots.

We're sensitive to the fact that wherever we go people groan, "No, not another all-Australian final." Wimbledon had had ten of those in the twenty-one postwar years, and where once the British loved us madly because we broke an American monopoly and won a few titles for the Commonwealth, they now regard us as automatons. We don't show enough emotion. We don't hug everybody in sight when we win like Manolo Santana, the Spaniard. Nor do we throw our rackets and curse so that we can be lectured, like expatriate Bob Hewitt, all-time Aussie rascal, whose bad manners kept him off our Davis Cup team. (You can afford to discipline the bad actors when you have so many good players available). We are dull victors, they complain. I guess we are, but we are victors. And we do show emotion and glee—when we're doing our banking.

LESSON 8
Pressure

Harry Hopman, our Davis Cup captain, used to say to us during a tense match: "Relax and hit for the lines."

Easy enough to say, isn't it? But how do you do it when you're serving at 15–40 and the match is at stake? At our level this was where all those hours of training and drills came into play. We could pull our concentration together, tell ourselves to hit through the ball, and remind ourselves that the best way to turn the pressure on the other guy is to get the ball over the net. Then it's in his court—and points are usually lost on errors and not won on outright placements.

It's this way at every level. You won't have practiced so much as I have so that you can hit out on all occasions—well, almost all occasions—without clutching a little. But if the situation is tense, chances are the tension is on both sides of the net, and if you can keep hustling and putting balls back, you'll be piling the pressure up on your rival.

Scrambling and running have won more matches than great shotmaking.

Determination has a lot to do with dispelling pressure. You've got to go onto the court thinking you're going to win. Be positive. Screw in your concentration. This is the hardest part of tennis. Concentration separates players of equal ability. Ron Holmberg could hit the ball as well as anyone in the game, but he allowed himself to get distracted or bothered by little things.

In concentrating you have to wipe everything out of your mind but the match, particularly the ball. Nothing but the ball. Glue your eyes on it. Marry it. Don't let it out of your sight. Never mind your opponent, the weather, people watching, or anything. Nothing but the ball. Make that ball an obsession. If you can get yourself into that trance, pressure won't intrude. It's just you and the ball.

I'm not saying it's easy.

115

If your opponent is playing too fast, slow the match down. Or speed it up. Change courts quicker or slower. Try to throw his tempo off if things are going badly for you. This is all part of changing a losing game.

There are times when you can get so choked up on serve that your elbow feels like it's in a cast. The net seems a million miles away, and the balls are unresponsive lumps.

Stop.

Take a few deep breaths. Take the racket in your other hand and let your racket hand hang out and release its death grip. Try to smile and consider how silly this is. It's only a game. If your motion has deserted you, just hold the ball up and pat it toward the service court. Forget style. Just remember that to get the first ball in—any way—gives you a heck of a chance to win the point. The ball is on the other side now. A double fault gives you no chance.

Above all, don't give up. Hang in. Nobody is immune to the choke. It can leave you and grip your opponent just as strangely. Keep trying.

Maybe it won't be much consolation, but you ought to know this: I've choked, still do sometimes, and most likely always will. And I haven't met anybody who hasn't.

9 PARIS IN THE SPRING, 1962

THREE OF the Grand Slam tournaments are held in English-speaking countries, and an Australian gets along all right. The fourth is on alien ground—Parisian clay. The first time I saw Paris, in 1956, I had a few phrases ready in my atrocious French, so that I could eat and get to my hotel room. Bob Mark, who was my doubles partner, and I got taken for a few elaborate rides by the cab drivers, and we had trouble with the money, our pockets stuffed with francs that didn't mean much. This was when the exchange rate was 350 to the dollar. The French seem less sympathetic to foreigners than other people, and the master-pieces of French cooking don't do much for me, since I'm a typical Aussie, a steak-and-eggs man. You don't need Maxim's to fix that for you.

So Paris, as such, isn't one of my favorite places, but I look forward to it because the French Championships is the tourna-ment I enjoy the most from the standpoint of emotional involve-ment. I love to watch matches in Paris, grim struggles on that slow clay, beauties for the spectators.

When an Australian's playing, the rest of the Aussies show up for moral support because you know, if the opponent is Euro-pean, and especially if he's French, the gallery will be very anti-Australian. That's Europe. The crowds make more noise, they take it to heart, they cheer and boo. My introduction to Roland Garros, the tennis complex in the Bois de Boulogne, was a shaky experience in 1956. Bob Mark and I were playing a Davis Cup style junior match against a French team of Christian Viron and Mustapha Belkodja. In the doubles the crowd went all out for their countrymen, hissing us and even throwing small stones. They weren't angry at us, but they didn't leave any doubt about their sentiments. They really psyched us out, but you get used to that in Paris and Rome and Barcelona and Mexico City where the national pride seems to ride with every shot.

When you realize this, the French tournament becomes great fun. I've seen some fantastic matches at Roland Garros. Probably the most fantastic was in 1958 when a Frenchman named Robert Haillet was so far gone in a match with the stylish American, Budge Patty, that he needed extreme unction. Patty was serving and he led 5–0, 40–0 in the fifth set. Triple match point, and two service breaks up. There was no way Haillet could win, so he figured he'd drop dead with a flourish and he swung spectacularly on a return. The ball landed on a line for his point. Nice, but so what? Still match point and that tremendous lead for a Wimbledon champion and one of the world's finest clay court players. Haillet, as loose as Marie Antoinette at the guillotine, thought what the hell and kept swinging at Patty's serves with all he had . . . and the winners poured from his racket. By the time he got to deuce and then won the game, the crowd began to come back to the center court. But Haillet was a long way behind. The chances of the Tour d'Argent serving Rice Krispies were much better than Robert Haillet's winning the match. But that mob was screaming for him as though he were de Gaulle liberating Paris, and Robert flew to victory on the wings of bedlam.

I've never seen anything like it, but on clay a comeback is much more possible than on a fast surface like grass. Grass is more risky. A couple of mistakes, you lose your serve and maybe you're out of it. The serve isn't such a destructive weapon on clay. You can return easier, and anybody willing to work and scramble can hang in there.

Of course, when somebody was working and scrambling and hanging in there against me, I wasn't so fond of the clay. I realized that this was the hardest championship for me to win, and because of that it probably meant more than the other three. It was certainly the toughest in 1962 when either Marty Mulligan, an Australian who revels on clay, or Roy Emerson should have beaten me, and Neale Fraser could have. Those were three straight five-set matches beginning in the quarters with Mulligan. Fraser in the semis went to 7–5 in the fifth, and Emmo in the final won the first two sets before I began to wear him down. Mulligan—or Martino Mulligano, as his pals sometimes call him now—had the best chance, leading me two sets to one and holding a match point in the fourth set.

How do you make an instant Italian out of an Australian? Add two o's and stir some remote Italian blood in the genealogical pot. We kidded Marty about his conversion to the Italian Davis Cup team in 1968, but he was only doing the best he could with his tennis talents and nobody blamed him. Marty came out of Sydney and was a mate of mine on the Australian Cup team of 1959.

He's a little fellow, very steady, and he took to the European clay better than he did to his native grass. His strokes were accurate and consistent, but he lacked the booming game that intrigued Harry Hopman, our captain. He also came along at the wrong time, in the midst of some of the best tennis players any country has developed. So Marty wisely moved to Italy to live. There he went on the payroll of a large club in Milan, becoming available for the interclub matches, very popular in Italy. The Italian clubs buy players from all over to compete in these "amateur" affairs.

Marty fitted well in Italy, learned a few words, fell in love with an Italian girl, and accepted a bid to play on the Italian Davis Cup team. Since he'd never competed for Australia he was eligible, after declaring himself a resident. This caused a furor in Italy. One faction, backing Marty, wanted only to win, like the Americans in 1958 who broadened the Good Neighbor Policy to include Alex Olmedo of Peru on the U.S. team. But an opposing faction was horrified to think that an Australian would take the place of an Italian boy in representing the homeland.

All Marty wanted to do was play tennis and make as much money as he could. Europe is the place to do that in the amateur game, and he could make even more by playing for Italy, probably as much as $30,000 a year all told, with very favorable living conditions too. Luckily, he discovered an Italian grandmother in his family tree. She had immigrated to Australia. That made it reasonably okay, and Martino Mulligano wore the insignia of Italy in 1968, for one year. Italy wasn't able to win the European Zone, so Marty was dumped. They figured they could lose just as easily with full-blooded Italians.

But this was in 1962 when we played. He was just plain Marty Mulligan, promising young Australian—and he was one point away from cancelling out that Slam. I was down two sets to one and serving at 4–5, 30–40, the only match point against me in either Slam.

It's hard to get a bunch of Frenchmen excited about two Australians playing tennis, but I was the favorite, the No. 1 seed, and here was this nice-looking nobody named Mulligan about to pull the big upset. Momentarily the customers adopted him as though he were St. Martin, the Patron Saint of France.

If Charlie Hollis had been there, he'd have screamed: "Get your first serve in!" It was the only thing to do in a tight spot, and I got mine in all right—into the net. So now I was down to the second serve. I spun the ball to his backhand and came sprinting in to the net behind it. Maybe I should have stayed back, but all through the match he'd been sending his backhand return down the line, and I wanted to move right to the spot and cut off the return. Sure enough, he stuck to the pattern, and I was there to bang a winning volley. It was deuce. The match point was gone, and I held serve for 5–5. I was still in there, but Marty was fighting hard to close it out in four sets, and the crowd let him know they felt that way too.

The set stretched to 8-all, and then a linesman's eyesight was questioned by Marty, and this quiet, polite Australian erupted uncharacteristically. He was serving and I hit an approach shot that sailed over the baseline. At least Marty thought so, and I'll take his word for it. His word didn't count, only the linesman's who said the ball was good. My point.

This was too much for Marty. He began screaming at the man on the line and the umpire. I was shocked. I'd never heard him raise his voice before. Then I was stunned as Marty picked up a ball and smacked a high-speed drive at the linesman. The fellow's eyes were definitely all right; he ducked, avoiding a headache at the least. The ball hit the grandstand loudly and rebounded across the court.

Marty wasn't the only one shouting now. The umpire was shouting back. Neither understood what the other was saying, but they didn't need an interpreter for most of the remarks. The referee marched out to try and stop the argument. You'd think I'd written the script, the way things worked out, but I stood by uncomfortably until Marty got it all out of his system.

When we resumed he'd stopped complaining, but he'd lost his concentration—and he'd lost his followers. Suddenly he was no longer St. Martin to the crowd, and they began jeering him. They had been carrying Marty but now they got on his back, and he couldn't resist that load. I won eight of the last ten games.

In 99 cases out of 100 it's beneficial for you when your opponent blows up over an annoyance like a line call. The 100th case is Pancho Gonzales. Anger and rage make him play better, but I didn't have to worry about him in those days.

Last in line at the French that year were two more countrymen, Neale Fraser and the ubiquitous Emmo. They were both victims of caution. I learned something extremely valuable from those victories: don't change a winning game.

Fraser had me deader than Custer. But I got away because after surrounding me he didn't finish the job properly. He was serving at 5–4 in the fifth set, and with the best serve in the game he was 100-to-1 to liquidate me. Strangely, he decided to be very careful. He stopped following his serve to the net, and his moment of indecisiveness was all I needed. I had more time to make my returns, and more room without him crowding the net. I could take the offensive now that he'd relinquished it, and

I shot through three straight games to grab a match he should have won.

A player who goes cautious after building up a lead takes a risk. Emerson, of all people, did just that when he led me 2–1 in sets and 3–0 in the fourth. He'd been sweeping me off my feet, but he got too careful and that gave me time to breathe. When you've got your hands around somebody's neck, keep squeezing, don't let up. Your victim might live to victimize you. That's what I did to Fraser and Emmo in winning France in 1962.

Bill Tilden used to say, "Never change a winning game." I used the words "Don't change," which I think is slightly different. "Never" is a bit too rigid. A tennis match is a very fickle proposition that can do a flip-flop with one swing. An opponent can catch on to your winning game, and if you persist in the same tactics he's going to be all over you.

As long as things are going your way, you don't change, but you have to be ready to adjust. There was no reason for Fraser and Emmo to make such abrupt changes, becoming hesitant when they were beating my head in.

LESSON 9
Don't Change a Winning Game
(and Always Change a Losing Game)

I suppose Bill Tilden was the first to harp on the dual commandments: Never change a winning game. Always change a losing game. He was right, but it's amazing how many players disregard this sound advice. They get ahead and neglect the methods that got them there. They fall behind and keep failing with the tactics that put them down.

Am I serving badly and getting passed? I'd better go to the net only when I can prepare the way with a good approach instead of rushing up there behind an unreliable serve. Am I butchering my overheads? Perhaps I should let them bounce until my timing returns.

Often you can size up your opponent in the warmup. Give him a variety of shots and see how he handles them. You may be able to discover weaknesses right away. Pound away at those weaknesses and inadequacies. Not necessarily to the exclusion of everything else. You must maintain a fair variety so that your opponent doesn't know that the ball is headed right for that suspect backhand every time. That's one way to build up a guy's backhand, unless it's absolutely hopeless.

There are a couple of tactics you never want to change. Always go hard for the first point of a game and the first two games of a set. I don't mean that you can coast if you win them, but getting in those first licks can frequently strike a big psychological blow.

Roy Emerson says, "I try like anything for those first two points. Get those and you're going to win almost every game." If you can get that first break of serve, either in the opening game or in the second game, you can crack some players right there.

Tilden gloried in a radical method of breaking up the enemy—playing his opponent's strength until he got through it. "This," Tilden said, "is an exception to the rule of not giving an opponent a shot he likes to play. But, believe me, once a player finds his favorite shot won't work for him, his whole game collapses."

Bill found that exciting. I think of it as risky business. But he was a genius. And he didn't have to play Pancho Gonzales or Ken Rosewall.

10 THE YEAR OF THE REVOLUTION

I WASN'T to return to the French Championships until 1968 when it was the first big open. Open tennis came in officially, however, a month before on a rainy morning in Bournemouth, England, April 21, 1968, the first day of the British Hard Court Championships. This is always confusing to Americans, the term "hard court," by which they mean cement or asphalt. In Australia, Britain, and Europe a hard court is what the Americans call clay.

Some confusion was fitting after all the trouble and chaos progressive tennis officials had gone through to bring about the sensible blending of amateurs and pros in competition that has proved to be tremendously appealing.

It wasn't very appealing that first morning at the West Hants Club in Bournemouth, but it was history when John Clifton, amateur, served to Owen Davidson, professional, to begin this mixed contest. The traditionalists considered it mongrelization, a mixing of champagne and milk of magnesia. Clifton won the first point, on a smash, but Davidson won the match. Hurrah for the milk of magnesiacs.

The crowd numbered 100—99 people and one dog—but the weather was wet and dreary. Later it got better, and so did the crowds, and there was no room for the dog. Too bad for him, because he missed those epics created by Mark Cox, a British left-hander with tight blond curls who looked like an athletic Harpo Marx.

125

Cox went into the second round against a man as legendary and congenial as the Loch Ness Monster, Pancho Gonzales (referred to as Ricardo Gonzalez by the British sportswriters, who, in the matter of Christian names, either perplex you by using only an initial, or overwhelm you with the utterly correct baptismal name of someone who has been known as Pancho for thirty-five years). The first set went as Cox had expected: six straight games for Pancho. A blitz. "I could picture myself losing 6–0, 6–0, 6–0," Mark said, "and I was terribly worried."

His worries began to diminish as he hit out, convinced that within an hour he would be stacked in the monumental pile of Pancho's victims. But an hour later Cox was moving the ball—and Gonzales—around nicely; and Pancho, who hadn't played a five-set match in years, was feeling it in his forty-year-old legs. Cox eventually survived a last charge by the Old Wolf and a couple of Pancho's nerve-shaking rages to win in five sets.

It was lovely. A tennis player was on the front page of every newspaper in Britain and a good number elsewhere. Mark Cox hasn't been knighted, yet, but he has his niche in sporting history: he was the first amateur to beat a pro. And what a pro! Gonzales startled everyone by leaving the clubhouse as he had found it—standing on its foundation. The expected postmatch tantrum did not develop.

"Somebody had to be the first to lose, so it might as well be me," shrugged a weary Pancho. "This open tennis is a whole new world, and I'm glad I could still be a part of it."

It was indeed a new world, a better one, but a stranger one for us pros, whose existence had been narrow and ingrown. We'd become used to playing one another, and only occasionally did we have a tournament with as many as twelve players. We almost never played best-of-five-set matches, and we knew one another's moves better than a guy at Sing Sing knows his cellmate's. Rosewall and I were the bosses. Gonzales had his moments, and the rest were aware of their limitations, although the tennis was first rate—"superplayers," Allison Danzig of *The New York Times* called us. We played hard, no doubt about it, but there was an air of exhibition about it in the public mind, and there was nothing we could do to change that feeling. But opens did.

Immediately the pressure was on us pros. We were the ones who had to prove ourselves after all these years of living in the underworld, away from the customary events. We had derided the amateurs and had talked about ourselves so much as a super-class that everybody thought we'd walk right through the poor amateurs.

It didn't happen that way. On the first day at Bournemouth a shaky Fred Stolle was almost beaten by a young Englishman named Peter Curtis. The next day he had an even harder time with a lesser Briton, Keith Wooldridge. "We're the ones with the bloody reputations to lose," wailed Fred. "The amateurs can be loose. They're playing for expenses, and they're sure of those. If they lose it means nothing. But if I lose it disgraces my profession."

That was the kind of talk you heard in the early days of the unknown. Cox beat Gonzales, then kept going to beat Emerson, who was in his first year as a pro. He gave Emmo one of the worst lickings of his life. This was the same Emmo who had no trouble with Cox a few months before when both were amateurs. But wearing the pro label, Emmo choked badly.

We pros were shaken psychologically at Bournemouth, although I beat Cox and got to the final. There Kenny Rosewall, loving the slow, salmon-colored clay courts, knocked me apart in four sets. I didn't play badly. Once in a while I missed a shot; he never did.

That was the beginning of the most revolutionary year in tennis. More shocks—for us, the acknowledged pros—were to come. In the opening rounds of the first open Wimbledon, we toppled all over the place, and the amateurs were gleeful. "I always said they were overrated," chortled Marty Riessen, "and that amateur competition was a lot tougher."

He was right in some respects. Many of the amateurs were in better physical condition than some of the pros, and their competition was more varied. They weren't playing against the same guys all the time. They were also more accustomed to conditions outdoors. So a lot of strange things happened. Outwardly strange. We took our bumps at Bournemouth and the best amateurs weren't even there. Except for us pros, the field was second-rate. The top-money amateurs like Manolo Santana and Tom Okker were ducking us for the moment. They did have reputations to guard.

Things were a little better in Paris, following Bournemouth. A lot of good amateurs were there, and we were really finding out about new faces and different styles. It was almost like beginning all over again. I ran into a hulking Romanian named Ion Tiriac in the quarterfinals, completely new to me, but a real clay court operator. Europeans feel as hopeless as polar bears in Miami Beach when they go to Australia, England, or the U.S. and have to play on grass. But in Europe, on their clay, their outlook changes. Their competitive spirit goes up and they feel they can beat anybody. That's the way it was with this Tiriac. His strokes weren't much, but he lobbed well and he battled. He won the first two sets, and I had to make up my mind that I'd just stay out there three or four hours and keep running and hitting. Finally I wore him down, but that kind of match makes you know you've been in a fight. You're covered with that red dirt and look like you've fallen in a mudhole. You've been running and reaching—up and back, across court—and every point has seemed like a war. It has to be better for the crowd, and more satisfying for an athlete.

The crowds in Paris in 1968 were incredible. We were amazed that the tournament was even held because that was the spring of the student riots, the general strike. It was an exciting time to be in Paris, exasperating, too, and we thought sure the tournament would be called off. Paris seemed absorbed in more pressing matters than tennis. The students were throwing paving stones around on the Left Bank, and the only reason they weren't really dangerous, according to Buddy Weiss, editor of the *International Herald Tribune,* was "they didn't have a childhood background in baseball. Can you imagine the damage American college kids would have done throwing those rocks?" Later those skills were to be demonstrated to greater—sometimes tragic—effect on American campuses.

Public transportation was shut down and there was little gasoline for private cars. So people walked out to Roland Garros, the place named for a gallant French pilot of World War I, and the crowds were immense. Lance Tingay, who writes for the *London Telegraph*, remarked, "Well, demonstrations can get to be a bit of a bore after a while, you know. People would just as soon watch Laver crack a tennis ball for a change after weeks of the gendarmes cracking student heads."

They certainly knew how to do that. Those Paris cops were efficient and rough, and we stayed out of their way when we got caught in a mob.

Nobody went to work during the strike, and I guess that was a break for us, because for several days Roland Garros wasn't big enough. For years the French Championships had been going downhill, losing money. In 1968 the tournament rebounded with a huge profit. Our presence and the fact that it was France's first open had a lot to do with it. But the general strike didn't hurt.

Fifteen years before, as a teen-ager, Rosewall had won the French title to mark himself as the best clay court player in the world. Kenny is the doomsday stroking machine. His groundstrokes never end, and his volleying is bitingly sure. On the clay he has plenty of time to set himself for that magnificent backhand, and you'd better not come to the net on him behind anything that isn't shot out of a 16-inch gun. It was a long time between French Championships for Rosewall, who had signed his first pro contract in 1956, but he made the most of the wait, cutting me up in four sets.

Despite the early sabotage by amateurs in the first year of opens, Rosewall and I were in our second straight open final at Paris, and Tony Roche and I played the all-pro Wimbledon final.

Amateurs beating pros provided good copy, created debates, and drew welcome attention to the game. Form took a battering in 1968 and that is always newsworthy, but any realist knew that opens were something of an illusion. In effect you were putting one group of pros in with another, a group of wolves in amateurs' clothing clawing at the professed wolves. The difference was labels. Nevertheless, it was stimulating. All the players were together, as they should be, scratching for the top dollars in prize money. Some, like the Iron Curtain delegates, still called themselves amateurs because their countries chose to maintain the fiction, and some were going under the ridiculous guise of "players." The official definition of "player" was a tournament competitor over age eighteen who supports himself from the game and accepts prize money but is not a professional. Tennis officials have ever been capable of splitting hairs on Yul Brynner's head, and the nonsense continued. The end of it is in sight, and soon all competitors will be just true-blue amateurs or true-gold pros.

LESSON 10
Playing on Clay

Patience and legs. You'll go a long way with those assets on clay. The stronger the longer. This is always impressed on me when I play in Europe, especially Paris, where the slow clay courts dictate an entirely different game from the grass of Australia, Wimbledon and Forest Hills, or the cement of other areas.

If there is a universal surface it is clay, found almost everywhere, and won on by those players who can control the ball and their impulses to overhit.

The defensive player has an edge because of the slower, higher bounce of the ball, giving him more time and a better chance to reach a forcing shot and make a good return.

Clay blunts the force of a powerful serve and favors those who can play steadily and accurately from the backcourt.

In their perceptive analysis of singles, Bill Talbert and Bruce Old discovered in charting matches between two big hitters, Lew Hoad and Pancho Gonzales, that Lew and Pancho won 75 percent of their points at the net on grass and 40 percent at the net on clay. Yes, they are different games.

Ability to keep the ball in play, move it around with changes of speed and spin, will pay dividends on clay. This doesn't mean that you should forget about attacking. Far from it. Against a persistent and sure baseliner whom you can't outrally you have to get up to the net and break up his pattern with angled volleys. But you can't be impatient in going up there; your way must be well paved with a strong deep approach shot.

Most baseliners like it back there, and you've got to draw them up with soft shots and angles, make them play a few shots near the net where they're uncomfortable.

Since the huskiest serve in the business isn't going to be overly oppressive on clay, you'd better forget about blasting your serve and concentrate on placing the ball and getting the first one in. Naturally you'll let fly with a hard one just to keep the foe honest if he creeps closer on you.

Doubles on clay is about the same as doubles anywhere else—an attacking game. There will be more retrieving, longer points, but you have to get up to the net fast.

But in singles you may as well face the fact that you have to be fit and favorably inclined toward running. You're going to be on the court a while, most likely.

Bring your lunch.

11 THE SECOND LEG ON THE SLAM: THE FRENCH

PARIS IN the spring may mean love to some, chestnuts to others, but to me it signifies the toughest two weeks of the year. The French Championships are where I more often than not get my spring cleaning.

But I'm a masochist, and I approve wholeheartedly of this great test. Rex Bellamy of *The Times* of London tells it better than anybody in these six paragraphs that headed one of his accounts of the 1969 tournament:

"The French championships are the game's finest advertisement. The surface, clay, is gruelling to play on, yet provides the most exacting test of ability and the most satisfying spectacle. The entry is the best outside Wimbledon.

"All is grandeur and pathos. The grandeur is public—the protracted, absorbing exercises in tactics, technique, and physical and mental stamina. The pathos is private—the drained, exhausted bodies crumpled on the masseur's table or the dressing room benches.

"These are great but cruel championships. Nowhere else is the esthetic potential of the game so fully explored, or the physical cost of it so sadly apparent.

"The round of 16 in the men's singles summed it all up. We saw some superb tennis that day. But, at the end of it, the human wreckage of the men's dressing room was a pitiful sight. Manolo Santana, his head in his hands, was heaped on a bench. He was a broken man. John Newcombe, a superman at his physical peak, fell back onto the massage table like a crumbling pack of cards. He was so weary that he talked as if in some far-off dream.

"The bounding bundle of whipcord called Jan Kodes sat silently in a corner, looking as fragile as porcelain, hiding his pain behind an emotionless mask that told us nothing—but everything. There was hardly a murmur save for the birds outside, singing their evening chorus to the skies.

"All this after a day of crowded, colourful drama, booming applause, and smouldering heat . . . the contrast was as sharp as the thrust of a dagger."

By May of 1969 none of the "amateurs" or "players" or anybody of any other phony name were avoiding us pros and the big opens. The money was getting too good. Several had picked their spots in 1968, the year of the big mix, but anybody who meant anything in the game appeared at Roland Garros that spring for the second French Open.

This looked to be the roughest of the four Grand Slam legs. I'd squeaked by in 1962 as an amateur, with those clay court experts Rosewall and Gimeno outside the picture. Otherwise all I got from clay was grief and, literally, mud in my eye. Until I won in 1962 my won–lost record in Paris for five years was 6–5. Only once did I get past the second round.

Paris was relaxed, calm. No more riots. People were working again and the weather was bad, cold and chill. We pros played a small tournament in Amsterdam to get ready for the clay, but I was feeling pretty confident before that because I'd won the second biggest prize of the year, $15,000 in a Madison Square Garden Pro event two weeks before by beating Emmo on a slow, synthetic court, Uni-Turf. My groundstrokes were going well.

In my first days in Paris as a teen-ager I didn't care for the clay and the low-pressure balls. I was less patient, but now I was beginning to savor the clay game. I had my shots well under control, and I was as fit as I'd ever been in my life, so that I could run and hit hard all day.

Everything went beautifully. For one day. That's about all I can expect in Paris. Then it becomes work. After a quick brush with a Japanese, Koji Watanabe, I found myself looking up into a cheery Aussie face belonging to Dick Crealy. Dick is six feet five and loves to hit the hell out of the ball, especially with his forehand. I knew that, but I didn't think he could keep doing it as long as he did—which was long enough to win the first two sets. On clay the ball bounces high, and my topspinning shots bounce higher than most. This bothers a lot of people, trying to handle a groundstroke at shoulder level, but for a guy as big as Crealy it wasn't shoulder level. He was taking the ball right where he liked it, just above the waist and swinging through it with everything he had.

After the first set I felt I was just chasing balls. I wasn't getting very many of them, and I was sliding all over the place. Usually the footing is good on those courts, but 1969 was not a vintage year. They were dry, dusty and slippery, more beige than the customary red. Much of the top dressing was blown away by the difficult, eddying winds. I didn't like it, but should I complain about the best French Championships I ever played?

After you've played Paris once you realize that the whole operation is casual. Matches never start on time—a distinct contrast to Wimbledon—and not unlike the way Forest Hills has been run in the past. But where the Americans were merely disorganized, erratic timing seems to be a part of the French character. Don't worry—the matches will be played sometime, although it may not be the time you have in mind for producing your best tennis.

Crealy and I got started late in the afternoon, long after we were scheduled, and continued to play after dark under the lights. With Dick ahead two sets to one, a rainstorm stopped us for the night, a gloomy chilly night that matched my mood. He'd won the second set, 9–7, as I began to get into the match, and I took the third, 6–2. I felt I had him then, but the rain came and we had to sleep on it.

Sleeping is easy for me, luckily. It's meant a lot to my career, with our bloody wild traveling, that I can catch a nap anywhere and get some sleep no matter when I go to bed or what the circumstances. I was up at seven the next morning, because we were scheduled to resume at the silly hour of ten thirty. I hate morning matches. My reflexes are fuzzy at first, and I couldn't afford a bad start because here it would have been the finish. Some people can walk from bed to the court—and Crealy tried to. I can't. Emmo was up with me and we were at the courts a little before nine.

It was good of Emmo to help me out, but any Aussie would have done it. We stick together when we're away from home. When a bloke needs a hit, even at eight thirty in the bloody morning, he can find a compatriot who'll oblige. I wanted a long workout so I'd be good and warm. At most I'd only have to play two sets, and I couldn't afford my usual slow start being down two sets to one.

When the 12,000 seats in the stadium are filled and people are hanging from odd ledges, railings and the scoreboard, as they were for the final with Rosewall, it's a very lively, warm, emotional place. Those people give you a transfusion of elan and it's great joy to play for them—at least if you're playing well. It's not quite the same sensation as a filled Wimbledon Centre Court. Sometimes the stillness of Wimbledon can drive you crazy. You keep waiting for a noise, an indication that they're alive. In Paris there's no doubt. The buzz of humanity assures you this is combat as elemental to the people as a duel or a prizefight.

Although the better duels may have been held in the morning, when dueling was France's favorite sport, ten thirty is not really the French spectator's hour. I'll go along on that, and when you walk into that stadium and find yourself surrounded by nothing but cool, clammy cement tiers, it is the coldest place in the world. The stadium wasn't quite empty. I think there were four people there: the umpire and three linesmen he dug up somewhere.

The enclosure is larger than Centre at Wimbledon and much

deeper than Forest Hills, with great expanses behind the base-
lines. You feel very alone and small out there when the seats
are vacant. Maybe Dick felt smaller than I did, cut down in size
by seeming to play in a vacuum. I think it was much harder for
him, but my experience in all sorts of situations held me up. As
a pro I'd gotten used to odd hours and playing at my best even
though nobody showed up to watch, but the absence of people
seemed to hurt a twenty-three-year-old on the verge of the upset
of the year. No cheers would reward his good shots. People who
could be counted on to holler for his every point were somewhere
else at that hour. It probably seemed like a private practice
match to him, and he may have wondered if the result would
become known publicly even if he did win.

That's the way you can feel sometimes. He was a practically
anonymous Aussie, who had been reading about me all his tennis
life. Now he had a chance to make it all come true for himself,
and nobody dropped by to appreciate it.

I appreciated, and that's why I went through such an unusually
long prematch workout, forty-five minutes. In contrast, Dick's
was much briefer. I think he was afraid he'd leave something on
the practice court. That was a mistake, a lesson for Dick.

Ready to get right into it, I won the fourth set 6–2 to pull
up with him and took off on a 3–1 lead in the fifth. I'd won
nine of eleven games, and that should have broken his spirit. But
by that time some people were wandering in, and he was moving
back into his form of the day before, blasting his forehand again.

Right back into the match he came to win three games to 4–3.
I held serve for 4–4 and thought I'd better go all out to break
him. The wind was tricky, and I didn't want to be serving a
match game at 4–5 if I could help it.

Dick was thinking the same thing. "I'd like to have seen you
serve at 4–5 with the match on it," he needled me later. It
was his fault that I didn't, and only because he tried to make
a shot too good. It's a temptation that even the best have trouble
resisting.

He got to 40–30 and his next serve was a good one to my
forehand, pulling me out of the court. I was lucky to get the

ball back at all, but it didn't seem to matter. He was waiting at the net for it, ready to cream the ball and go to 5–4.

I shrugged mentally as he wound up, then watched resignedly as the ball streaked past me, crosscourt—and out. By two feet! Deuce.

I had to keep the ball down, make this big guy bend over. Once again he was eating up my high-bouncing topspin. I decided I'd try to slice it, get under the ball to make low returns. I played two good ones at his feet, and he volleyed badly. I had the game, the serve, and the wind at my back. There was no way I was going to lose that last game.

I put more spin on my serve to make sure the first ball was in and that I'd have added time to get to the net. I roared up there behind the serve, my nose practically hanging on his side of the court. I had the edge and I was going to push it. With the wind behind me I could afford to get closer to the net than usual. A deep lob would be tough for him into the wind. The pressure was on him to hit his best returns with me right up there. He couldn't, and it was over in four points.

Playing in a swirling wind like that is tricky. I lower my service toss a bit so the ball won't be bobbing around. And I shorten the backswing on my strokes to get better control.

Crealy will think about that missed volley in the ninth game occasionally and wince. He had the entire court, and he made the mistake of trying to keep the ball as far away from me as possible. He hit for the sideline and was wide. No need for it. Take your time on the sure volley, the easy sitter. You have more time than you think. Dick didn't need anything but firmness. There was no reason to try to put it close to the line. I was out of the point—but maybe my speed was on his mind.

That's an added benefit from hustling all the time, which you can and should do if you're fit. Your opponent has watched you chase down a lot of balls, and he may try too hard to put the ball beyond your reach. I think that's what Dick did.

If you consistently hit the ball well inside the court you won't get into trouble. I realize that sounds insultingly easy, but that's the way I play. I'm not a stickler for accuracy, but I do want to hit the ball hard on my groundstrokes.

So the answer for me most of the time is topspin. I can hit for a general area without cutting it fine. Topspin prevents the ball from going too deep, even when I bash it, and carries the ball higher over the net, putting me in less trouble with that bothersome obstacle.

The tournament committee was anxious to keep everybody playing and reduce the size of the field to eight, the quarter-finals, by the end of the first week. After a bite of lunch I returned to the court to fix an Italian, Pietro Marzano, in straight sets.

The next day, in the fourth round, I found tall Stan Smith to be a rapidly improving player. Stan was to give me a long, trying afternoon at Wimbledon a month later, but he still wasn't up to the clay court game. He's built like Crealy, six-four, and a hitter. Although 1969 began with America's highest hopes attached to Arthur Ashe, it was Smith, the less-publized Californian, who became the No. 1 player in the U.S. for the year. He had a cold and it didn't help him that we finished the match at night in a drizzle. Stan couldn't get a set. I worked hard on that third set. I didn't want any more serialized matches continued to the morning after.

One match in the tournament that every player anticipated as eagerly as a tax refund was Andres Gimeno vs. Manolo Santana. It may have been only a fourth-round match, but this was for the spiritual championship of Spain. It was the prodigal (pro Gimeno) against the son who stayed home dutifully and did well ("amateur" Santana). It was Barcelona against Madrid, the outcast against the bemedaled national hero. Here were two men born to clay, artists whose strokes are pure brushwork, graceful, filled with *duende*, as the Spaniards say. They were old friends, once Davis Cup teammates. But a rivalry had been growing in their minds for nearly a decade, and in the minds of the rest of us who awaited the match so long.

At a formative stage, Andres, twenty-three, turned pro in 1960.

He was Spain's best then, a shade ahead of Santana, but the game wasn't all that big in their homeland. Santana made it big in 1965 by spearheading Spain's 4–1 victory over the United States in the Davis Cup quarterfinal at Barcelona, getting even with the Americans for the Spanish-American War. Then he won the U.S. Championship, led Spain to the Cup final (where they lost to Australia), and in 1966 he won Wimbledon. Generalissimo Franco awarded him the country's highest civilian decoration, the Medal of Isabella, and henceforth he might be addressed as "Ilustrissimo." Manolo became a wealthy amateur, one who could not afford to join Gimeno as a pro for both economic and patriotic reasons. Could he ever desert Espana's Davis Cup team?

Many of us felt that Andres was the better player, and it rankled Andres that with tennis' sudden popularity in Spain, he was virtually unknown, and certainly not considered by his countrymen to be in Manolo's class. The average Spaniard was convinced that nobody could beat El Ilustrissimo Manolo, el Gran Campeon. That was that.

In a season and a half of open tennis, Santana played few opens, never encountering Gimeno. Now they would meet, and we all felt like Spaniards, wrought up—and festive, too—as though headed for a bullfight as we squeezed into the mobbed stadium.

I think we pros were for Gimeno to a man. Maybe we weren't too understanding—since all of us had been in Santana's position once—but we resented those who hadn't followed us into honest professionalism and still clung to the amateur make-believe. It isn't logical, admittedly, because every man has to make his way as best he can. For Santana it was "amateurism."

Watching was awfully tough that day because Andres was awful. He was so nervous he could hardly hit a ball. Santana went through the first two sets with ease, hitting shots that would make me shout olé—if an Australian could shout olé unselfconsciously. Finally Andres shook his jitters and crawled into the match to win the third set. They were straining for every shot as though this were an exhibition that would go on display at the Prado. One of those straining lunges of Manolo's pulled a groin muscle. Andres won the fourth set, and after the first game of the fifth Manolo surrendered. He walked from the court, unable to continue, and he was saluted with everyone's heartfelt cheers like a gallant bull.

Victory for Andres was not altogether satisfactory, although he did fight until his opponent had to give in. It made Andres feel better, but it wasn't clear-cut. I hope they get other chances to play, preferably in Spain. I'll pay my way there to watch.

Gimeno had to feel buoyed by that win, and it carried him through his first set with me, but I've always had the feeling that he's fatalistic about playing me. He doesn't believe he can win, but he's going to make a good showing. Winning that set was the showing. He could be pleased with himself. In the second set I began slicing my backhand more to keep the ball low as I went into the net. This made it harder for him to hit passing shots, and I controlled the match from then on to win, 3–6, 6–3, 6–4, 6–3.

A slice is the best approach shot. While topsin speeds the flight of the ball, slice slows it, and you have more time to get to the net with the slice. Your opponent will have more trouble turning the low-bounding slice into a passing shot. This is not a hard-and-fast rule, because you should avoid stereotyped patterns. Of course, I approach with topspin shots at times, but the slice gets the best results overall.

When Ken Rosewall played Tom Okker in the semifinals of the U.S. Open in 1968, he must have had the uncomfortable sensation of encountering his own reincarnation. Both of them are short and unbelievably quick. They skitter around the court fascinatingly, like souped-up rats, getting everything back. Since they aren't hard hitters, that 1968 match wasn't dulled by patches of serve-and-volley. It was point and counterpoint with long, sensational exchanges that keep a crowd ecstatic.

You might say that Kenny, the elder by ten years, is an early-model Okker. Or that Okker is a late model Rosewall. Close, but not wholly accurate because Okker, though he's small, cannot resist lashing out with colorful topspinning forehands whereas Kenny is more conservative, and his forehand is flat.

Anyway, for the last two matches of the French I was getting early Okker and late Rosewall in person. On clay you might be better off with double pneumonia. Either one can make you feel rundown fast.

I think Tom is going to be a great player who can mean as much to the game as Kenny has. His phenomenal speed and reflexes would be enough to make him quite a good player even if his strokes weren't so sharp and his determination so firm. He's the best player ever to come out of Holland, faster than Hans Brinker on his silver skates, although he wouldn't know what I'm talking about. To Americans Hans Brinker may be the most famous character to come out of the Netherlands, but he was created for American readers and the Dutch never heard of him. Before Okker is through he'll be more celebrated than Brinker.

Tom's like me in that he can hit a big-bounding topspin shot on the run for a winner, or pitch a topspin lob over the head of a man hanging at the net. He has these absolutely dazzling stretches, a wild man who makes you want to cry because everything he does is so utterly beyond you. That's the way he was in our first set.

But I don't cry anymore when I lose the first set. It happens too often. I'm habitually slow to start, and even lightning wouldn't have saved that first set the way Tom was flying. "Well, you're going to be out here a while," I said to myself, which is what I generally say in Paris because there's no easy way through a match.

Ten games it took for him to win the first set, and by that time I was right. My anticipation was keen and I was picking off balls at my feet with slick half-volleys as I took the net away from him. The points began coming in an avalanche, and Okker wasn't winning any of them. "This is all right," I was grinning inside, and I just slid into magnificent form and began whacking everything and knocking them by him. He was fast but I was making the balls go faster. When somebody warned Sonny Liston that Floyd Patterson had very fast hands, Sonny answered haughtily: "Can he catch a bullet?" I was hitting bullets and Tom wasn't reaching them. The second set was a tennis version of Liston-Patterson: 6–0. Taking a love set from Tom Okker in the semifinal of a major tournament is almost inconceivable. You have to be doing more than something right; you have to be doing everything right, and I was. I was plugged in, comfortably and completely, to the clay game, and the struggle with gangling Dick Crealy seemed distant. Okker took only six games in the last two sets as I won, 4–6, 6–0, 6–2, 6–4.

Rosewall had been coming along nicely on his side of the tournament. No problems. Tony Roche, who had won the French in 1966 and knew how to behave on clay, went down in the semifinals fast after a difficult first set, 7–5, 6–2, 6–2, and here were Kenny and I again just where we'd been the year before.

LESSON 11
The Serve and Spin

Most of the time I use a sliced serve, and that seems to be the common delivery. I'm not tall enough to try many of the all-out cannonball flat serves. When I do they usually wind up in the net, but with slice I can be more sure of getting my first serve into play and that it has something on it to move the ball around.

My slice (a left-hander's) will move to a right-hander's backhand, and that's convenient.

The kicker, or American twist, is useful when you want variety or you think you can bother your opponent by making him go for a shoulder-high ball. My kicker, from the first (or right) court will pull a right-hander wide to his right, opening up the entire court for me. If I slice from the second (or left) court I can do the same thing. It's pretty hard for him to make a crosscourt return when he's wide of the sidelines, but he has a good shot at a down-the-line return. Therefore when I serve a man wide I edge that way to protect myself against the down-the-liners.

For a right-hander, to hit the slice you toss the ball slightly to the right of your head. The racket brushes across the right side of the ball and follows through across the body, putting a sidespin on the ball.

For the American twist, toss the ball slightly to the left. Hit the ball with a snap of the wrist as the arm moves from left to right with the follow-through finishing on the right side.

It's a good doubles serve because you have time to get to the net behind the high bounce. A sliced serve stays low.

The kicker is nice to have in your repertory. But as far as I'm concerned its use is confined to surprising an opponent—the high bound throws off his timing when he's been looking at a slice. Or for those rare occasions when you play on bad grass. Then a kicker is very important because it's liable to jump anywhere. It was a great help on the wet, rutted turf at Forest Hills in 1969.

144

One thing I've noticed about less experienced players is that they tend to practice their serves only from the first court where they'll be starting. Take practices from both right and left, and take plenty of them. It doesn't cost any extra.

12 THE FRENCH OPEN FINAL AND KENNY ROSEWALL

I suppose Ken Rosewall is the least appreciated great player in the history of tennis. Those old-timers can tell me—and they do all the time—that Bill Tilden would cut us all down with his groundstrokes, but there's no way I'll believe that Big Bill could bomb out little Kenny from the baseline. I hope they get a chance to go at each other on that great clay court in the sky. I'll be content to act as ball boy and watch Rosewall's backhands go by. I've watched plenty of them already, to my discomfort, and I'd like to see what Tilden would do with them—even if he got divine guidance.

Rosewall never got the credit he deserved because he spent his best years with the vagabond rugbeaters, the pros, after signing his first contract with Jack Kramer at the close of 1956. He was twenty-one then, had just wrecked Lew Hoad's bid for a Grand Slam by taking the title at Forest Hills, and was about to be devoured by Pancho Gonzales on a head-to-head tour. Pancho beat him, and Pancho was at his prime then, but Kenny, though devoured, was very tough to digest. Eventually he took over the leadership of the group, overcoming Gonzales, but the public never knew or believed. To them Gonzales was the once-and-forever king. Kenny was playing second racket to Pancho's personality, just as he had to Hoad's as an amateur. Pancho and Hoadie were stormy, handsome guys with terrific physiques. Kenny, like me, is a runt, but has there ever been a quicker, steadier player in tennis? He never said anything, he went to bed every night as soon as he could, sent his money home to his family. Somewhere in his home outside of Sydney, Kenny has his first five-dollar bill framed over the mantel. When Harry Hopman, the Australian Davis Cup captain, was his chaperone Kenny thought the largest bill minted was a five. Harry handed out the money. Jack Kramer let Rosewall in on a secret about those stirring portraits of Grover Cleveland on the thousands. You may enjoy the *Playboy* centerfold, but Grover Cleveland's picture is what really turns Kenny on. Nobody knows how many he has, but easily enough to paper his house.

So as a quiet, clean-living little guy who kept his money in a buttoned hip pocket, Rosewall was not quite the colorful type to be built up by the sportswriters. Unfortunately for him—and for Gonzales—their best tennis was played before the game opened up in 1968 and we pros came out from under our rocks.

But some of Ken's and Pancho's best tennis is still evident. Every time I think either one of them has decided to be sensible and graciously step aside like gallant elders, I get stung. It happened as recently as the ultimate tournament of 1972, when he beat me by two points at the close of a three-and-one-half-hour struggle for the world pro title and a $50,000 cash prize for the winner. I'll tell you the sad details later.

In 1967 we were playing the final of a pro tournament at Berkeley, best of three sets, and I was ahead in the third set, 5-4, 40-0—triple match point. My serve. Muscles wasn't rattled. I can't rattle him—ever. Three unbelievable backhand returns he hit to get himself to deuce, and then two more for the game. I was stunned, and by the time I got with it again it was time to shake hands. He'd won the next two games and the match. As it turned out that was the minor stunning. The major occurred when the tournament promoter told us our pay was applause. He hadn't collected enough at the box office to meet expenses. This was the big league?

Suddenly the loss hurt even more, with no runnerup money to console me.

I thought about that match and was glad Charlie Hollis, my old teacher, hadn't been there. He'd have been mad as hell. You shouldn't let anybody, not even Kenny Rosewall, out of a trap like that—triple match point on your own serve. In thinking it over I realized that I'd fallen into a foolish routine that grips us all. I served every one of those five balls to the same place, and Muscles got grooved. I didn't mix it up at all. I'd been having success that day with serves to his backhand corner. But also, I'd put enough on the other side and down the middle to keep Muscles honest. He couldn't set himself for the backhand. But in that 5–4 game I guess I got stubborn and wouldn't believe that he could just keep smacking winners. I should have known better. If you give anybody enough chances at the same kind of ball, he's going to begin eating it up. If the guy is Rosewall, he'll have you for supper—and maybe you'll end up paying double. He got the win, and he got the dinner. Since there was no prize money, Kenny was quite right in expecting me to pick up the dinner check.

Maybe it was easy for me to get a little careless like that, to get mesmerized playing against him because we've faced each other so often. Somebody said we could play our matches by phone. There's something to that, but it wouldn't be on Kenny's dime.

We're like those two old welterweight champions, Jack Britton and Ted (Kid) Lewis, who fought each other so frequently and evenly between 1915 and 1921. Kenny knows what's coming and so do I. The only way I'm going to beat him is to have a very good day. He anticipates my shots so uncannily that I simply have to hit them bloody well enough that his anticipation and his legs are no use. I don't have too many days like that, but one of them was in that Paris final.

A year before he handled my case quite nicely, 6–3, 6–1, 2–6, 6–2. I spent the match retrieving as he dominated. It was the same in the Hard Court final at Bournemouth, the first open. I was hitting the ball into the corners, fine shots, but Kenny was right there to put his shots smack on the lines. I was quite good, which earned me second place.

Because of those two matches on clay in 1968, I both dreaded and looked forward to finals day at Roland Garros. I knew how impossible Rosewall could be on clay, but I also had something to prove. The Slam would mean that much more to me if my Paris victory was over Rosewall, on his kind of court.

I think the subject of Rosewall is one that the other players and I can agree on: he's the player we all have the most trouble with.

"No, Laver doesn't worry me," Fred Stolle says. "If the Rocket is hitting his shots there's no chance for me, true enough. But there's always the chance that he'll be a bit off and then you're right in the match. Rosewall is never off. The pressure is on you every second because you know when you hit a bad shot he'll make you pay for it without fail.

"He's got you crazy serving because his return is so good. You know if you miss the first serve you might as well forget the point because Muscles will murder the second ball. You're pressing so hard to serve well on the first ball that you usually miss it and you're at the mercy of what he'll do to the second. I'd rather play Laver any day than Rosewall."

Thanks, Fred. I don't think that shows the proper respect, does it?

But I know what Fred means better than most because I've had to play Kenny more than anybody else. Right after I'd turned pro in January of 1963, I played a series of matches in Australia against Lew Hoad and Rosewall. It was an inspiring indoctrination. Lew beat me seven out of seven. Kenny beat me four out of six, and he wasn't in very good shape at the time. I was two for thirteen in my first two weeks as a pro, and I felt like a midget batting against Vida Blue. I thought I would get him eventually, though, because we were sort of the same type. We were hitting big shots, and I thought I'd be able to keep it up longer than he would. He was getting past his peak.

But Rosewall, I could see, was going to be something else. He was closer with a point than a dollar, and he looked like he'd make about four mistakes a year, one for each season. That wasn't far off, although he began making more of them in 1969 because, I think, his nerves started to wear. He could still run as well and his reflexes stayed sharp, but the tensions seemed to eat at him a bit more, and he had some very sour patches, which wasn't like Kenny.

The first big win I had over him wasn't like Kenny either. It was in 1964 at the U.S. Pro Championships in Boston, the semifinal. Kenny was sick to his stomach, a bit of food poisoning. That is part of being a pro, of course. You play and nobody thinks anything about it, because we all go through these things. I had a very good day, and I was pleased to get through to the final where I beat Pancho Gonzales and won the title for the first time. Kenny was mad. This was one of the first decent pro tournaments in America and first prize was $2200, which was fantastic for us then.

As we came off the court, the reporters were all around me, and Kenny was off to one side, alone. A friend of his came up and asked him how he felt.

"Like a bastard on Father's Day," was Kenny's reply.

I suppose that says it nicely for everyone who has ever lost a tough match. I know the feeling, although in 1969 I kept it at such a distance that I almost forgot what it was like.

One or the other of us would know it that Saturday afternoon in Paris, though. No matter how many times I play Roland Garros, it's still startling to come into the stadium. You walk down through a tunnel. It's so dark that you're practically feeling your way, and then suddenly you're in the arena with 12,000 people surrounding you, responding excitedly to your appearance. Maybe it's like being the girl who pops out of a cake at a stag party.

From the minute we began, I couldn't miss. Usually I'm the one on the string, and Kenny plays me like a yo-yo. Not this time. I had perfect control, and everything I hit was going so deep that Kenny didn't have much chance to do anything but chase and scramble. I could get up to the net all the time, and I was moving quickly either way to cut off his passing shots. I don't know of any match I ever enjoyed more because I just kept getting better, and the points rolled in.

I never take Rosewall for granted. He's never gotten his due. I thought about it before the match. He'd won this title in 1953, at the time I was deciding tennis would be my career. I was fifteen. Fifteen years later he'd won it again. In 1971 he won the Australian title that he first won eighteen years earlier. There are no comparable feats of longevity in tennis history.

I wondered if, having won the French for the first time in 1962, I'd even be playing it in 1977. How many times would Kenny have won it if he hadn't turned pro, or if open tennis had come sooner?

Rosewall and Paris . . . they're linked forever in my mind like Sydney and oysters. In 1963, in the French Pro Indoor final I played the finest tennis I believe I've ever produced—and he beat me. It was a magnificent match on a whizzing wood floor and we hit groundstrokes as though we were on slow clay. I led 4–1 in the fifth, and just ran out of gas. We had both gone all out, hitting a million shots, and I couldn't keep up with him.

Kenny and I have brought the very best out of each other, but the day of the 1969 Open final was not one for sentimentality. Twelve thousand people wanted to see us do it again. After leading 3–1 in the first, I fell behind 3–4 as he won three games in a brisk streak. I held for 4–4 and broke him to take the first consequential step.

The first set was mine at 6–4 and my confidence was soaring. If I can't keep my shots near his baseline, I'm in trouble with Kenny because he takes anything short with his backhand, rams it into a corner while he dashes to the net. He may not be a heavy hitter, but when he gets position at the net his volleys are crisp and well angled.

But my groundstrokes were working so well and landing so deeply that he was having trouble getting to the position he likes. He couldn't swoop in on the short balls simply because I wasn't offering him that many. I kept him pinned behind the baseline and you can't hit an approach from back there. Sometimes he tried, but he had too far to go to reach the net, and I was passing him.

My volleys were charmed, and I spent most of the afternoon finishing off points with them. My deep groundstrokes kept me at the net, and Kenny away.

Straight sets in a French final? I couldn't quite believe it when I completed the 6–4, 6–3, 6–4 victory. Monetarily it meant $7000.

LESSON 12
Forehand and Topspin

It doesn't matter to me whether I hit a forehand or backhand because I reckon I can slap them with equal power and control. But for most people the forehand is the stronger, the stroke used for attacking and pressuring the opponent.

John Newcombe has developed a nice quick-shuffle to run around his backhand in order to smash a forehand return of serve. He showed it off handsomely in winning the 1970 and 1971 Wimbledons. His forehand return is unusually strong, and he uses it whenever he can. If he gets a second serve to the left court, aimed at his backhand, that isn't too deep or fast, he slides to his left quickly and smacks the return down the line. It's a good maneuver, but once you decide to do it—do it. Don't change your mind when the serve crosses the net. You should have your mind made up what you'll do with certain serves before they come to you, and then take that course.

It's pretty obvious when a player decides to hit a ball one way and suddenly changes his mind. He usually botches it. Of course, there are times when the shot coming at you is so good that you're trying bloody hard just to hit it.

In rallies from the baseline my forehand is almost always hit with topspin. It's reasonably easy to put top on the forehand, dropping the racket head below the level of the ball and coming over the ball with a snap of the wrist. With top your stroke will clear the net with plenty to spare, and the topspin will hold the ball in the court. You should work on strengthening your wrist if you intend to use much topspin. The topped forehand seems to be gaining in popularity. I can remember one of the original Australian greats, Jack Crawford, advising against top and recommending a flat forehand. But he conceded that Lew Hoad had something with his topspin. In my day all the good ones, except for Rosewall, are using topspin on the forehand.

It's a nice feeling to hit the hell out of the ball and know it'll go way over the net—and not the backstop as well.

13 THIRTEEN STRAIGHT LOSING POINTS

I HAD a good chance for another $1000 in the doubles. Emmo and I had a relatively easy time moving to the final against the world's No. 1 pair, John Newcombe and Tony Roche.

Emmo is a great accomplice. Five different partners with whom he won the French title six times between 1960 and 1965 will testify to that. I was one of them. I've always marveled at those tremendous reflexes that allow him to make winning volleys time after time on balls that seem destined to go by him. He prowls the net, a panther, intercepting all but the absolutely best hit returns. He can flick the racket behind his back to cut off a ball shooting to his left when he has committed himself the other way. He did this twice during the same point against Chuck McKinley in a crucial Davis Cup match in 1963. A wooden Indian would come to life as Emmo's partner.

Since he'd lost in the singles, in the fourth round to Zeljko Franulovic, Emmo was especially keen in the doubles.

There was no reason why we shouldn't have repeated our victory of 1961, and we would have if I hadn't screwed up like an all-time hacker.

The ending of that final was such an abrupt reversal that I was completely blank on it until Newcombe brought it up a few weeks later.

"We really zapped you in Paris, Rocket, just when you had us, didn't we?" John was saying.

"I guess so, but I don't remember much about it."

"No wonder," Newc said. "It was enough to send anybody into a trance. I don't wonder that you've tried to blot it out of your mind. We won thirteen points so fast that you and Emmo didn't know where you were. Thirteen straight points. Never been in on anything like that myself."

It began to come back to me. Newc and Tony led two sets to one, but we won the fourth set, got an early service break in the fifth and were moving right along to the championship. It was good tennis with phenomenal volleying, good overheads, and every point a struggle.

At 4–3 for us the serve came to me and we won the first three points for 40–0. That should have been that, to put us in excellent position, either with a chance to break and finish it, or for Emmo to wind it up on his serve.

We never got another point.

I don't know what the odds on that would be, but a million-to-one is close enough. Certainly the odds on my holding serve at 40–0 were very long. I mean my name is Rod Laver, isn't it? I wasn't so sure when it was over.

Those are the situations that drive us all mad, or at least to several beers more than we'd planned on after a match. It was pretty clear how I blew it, and anybody can do it. You don't need Newcombe and Roche on the other side of the net, either. It was a beautiful case of ignoring all the musts. You must get your first serve into play. I didn't put a single first serve in the court from 40–0. I succumbed to the great temptation of thinking 40–0 was the same thing as game. It's very close, but you still have to get that last point. I was thinking automatic 5–3, and I never got the next point. Nothing is automatic. Instead of spinning that first serve in at three-quarter speed, where all the pressure would have been on Newc and Roche to make good returns, I turned off my brain. I remember now I was going for big first serves, finish off the game with a bang. Looks splendid. Be a hero.

And I got just a trifle casual. You have to get into the net right behind your serve, but I wasn't snappy at all at 40–0, thinking one of those triple-game points would fall by itself.

With my second serve to look at constantly, Newc and Roche got a little edge. They could move up and hit with more confidence. Sometimes the pressure shifts subtly, sometimes dramatically. When they got to deuce, Newc and Roche knew they had a real chance. They were off the hook. They knew it . . . I knew it. I got fumbly. When that happened, so did Emmo. Hysteria was in season. Yes, even for players as experienced as us. With the match even at 4–4, Newc and Tony doubled their concentration, while I was still kicking myself mentally about that last game.

As the thought, "Forty-love, you idiot!" flashed over and over in my brain, they were taking us apart. There is just no use in replaying a game like that, until later—as I'm doing now—so you won't make the same mistake again. You've got to make yourself forget it and just say, "Okay, next point." One point at a time is the way you've got to discipline yourself.

It's a lesson everybody has to learn. It cost me a huge championship plus money, but I think it helped the rest of the year. I wasn't that careless again in a big one.

You can bet that Newc and Tony got their first serves in and were right up to that net. In a few minutes it was over. Thirteen straight points, just because I overlooked the first commandment of doubles. Put your first serve into play taking something off the ball to make sure. Forget that flat boomer and put spin on the ball. A man should cut his throat if he is as forgetful of the commandment as I was. If he doesn't his partner probably will cut it for him. Fortunately Emmo was as dazed by the turnabout as I was—and there wasn't a knife in the dressing room.

LESSON 13
Doubles

Although I can take credit for almost singlehandedly losing that French Doubles, my doubles record hasn't been too bad. I did win the French with Emmo in 1961, the Australian three straight years with Bob Mark between 1959 and 1961, the Italian with Dr. John Fraser (Neale's brother) in 1962, and Wimbledon with Emmo in 1971.

I've made my money and my name on singles, and, like most players, that's my first consideration. But my greatest enjoyment has come from doubles because the action is so much faster with all the reflex volleying and the spectacular rallies during which you might attack and retreat several times before a point is won.

Doubles is an entirely different game from singles, and usually more exciting to watch. Despite this fact tournament emphasis has been on singles. But I suspect that tennis would make a better impression on American TV if some doubles matches were covered.

Of course, doubles is the usual game for the vast majority of non-tournament types in clubs and on public courts. A few like the old French Davis Cup hero, Jean Borotra, continue playing singles into their seventies. "Never give the game up—never!" is Jean's cry. But doubles is a less strenuous way to keep on with the game till doomsday, and no reason you shouldn't. Frequently the older you get, the better doubles you play because it is a game of guile and control in which the sluggers can be baffled and browbeaten. An embarrassing example of that for Lew Hoad, 22, and Neale Fraser, 23, occurred in the Wimbledon final of 1957 when they were thoroughly outmaneuvered and beaten by Gar Mulloy, 42, and Budge Patty, 33.

It happens all the time, an older, less powerful team who understand the principles of doubles slickering a couple of youths who might be considerably superior in singles.

You don't need a big serve in doubles. It might, in fact be a handicap, since a cannonball doesn't give you as much time to get to the net. Better a spin serve that you can count on hitting into the court the first time all the time—as I didn't in Paris.

You aren't going to lose often if you and your partner keep the first serve going in, and moving it around to prevent your foes from zeroing in on it.

The volley is the shot on which most doubles points end, but probably more important is the return of serve. Sureness is preferable to speed as you try to keep the server off balance. A soft chip at his feet, a lob over his partner's head, even a lob to the server will keep them guessing. An occasional blast directly at the net man or down his alley will keep him honest, particularly if he shows signs of being the roving kind. Most often you will want to shorten your swing, just meeting the ball to make certain of a sure, low return.

The ideal in doubles is for you and your partner to get to the net and dominate, both when you're serving and returning. It doesn't always work that way. In winning the decisive match in the Federation Cup of 1969 (the worldwide women's team competition corresponding to the Davis Cup), Nancy Richey and Peaches Bartkowicz of the United States upset Margaret Smith Court and Judy Tegart Dalton of Australia. Hardly anybody who watched could believe it. Nancy and Peaches never advanced to the net. Incredibly Peaches stayed on the baseline even when Nancy served.

The theory is that you can't beat a pair of strong volleyers like Margaret and Judy that way. Ninety-nine times out of a hundred, the theory is right. The exception comes when you can lob as well as Nancy and Peaches did that day. The overhead is the most tiring shot to hit, and Margaret and Judy were forced to swing at scores of lobs. They broke down—most players will.

Unusual formations and tactics can drive your opponents up the backstop. I remember vividly the job Americans Ham Richardson and Alex Olmedo did on Neale Fraser—an excellent doubles player— during the Davis Cup final of 1958 at Brisbane. Fraser, in the left court (as Mal Anderson's partner), had been returning brilliantly against the Americans. He was grooved with his troublesome crosscourt return to the server. So they took this return away from Neale by stationing the net man directly in front of the server. The Americans call it the "Australian formation" while we call it the "tandem formation." Whatever, it made Fraser crumble.

With the net man in the way of his normal crosscourt return he had to go down the line, and he couldn't adapt himself to a new return. Naturally the server had to adapt, too, moving to his right to fill the hole vacated by his net man instead of charging ahead as usual. Neither Richardson nor Olmedo had any trouble adjusting as server. They were quick enough to deal with whatever weak returns Fraser could make in the new direction.

When his partner is serving, the net man must be a threat to "poach"—that is, move along the net quickly to intercept the normal crosscourt return. Sometimes a good team will poach all the time. Unless you and your partner are fast and well-mated this isn't a good idea. But you must poach once in a while just to let the enemy know that you aren't going to act like a statue and let them have half the court in which to hit their returns freely. You have to impose a mental hazard, making them wonder when you'll move.

This mental hazard weighed heavily on Aussies Hoad and Rosewall in the 1954 Davis Cup final when the Yanks Tony Trabert and Vic Seixas beat them in the decisive doubles match. Each time the Americans served, the net man turned his back to his opponents and made a hand signal to his partner, the server—like a catcher signaling a pitcher in baseball. The signal told the server whether the net man would cross in an attempt to poach. Often it was a bluff and the net man stayed put, but the signal system was a gimmick that disconcerted Hoad and Rosewall.

One of the rarest of disrupting ploys was pulled by the late Rafe Osuna, a marvelously swift and clever doubles player. In the U.S. National Doubles of 1966, Osuna was paired with Ronnie Barnes in the quarterfinals against Wimbledon champions Newcombe and Roche, heavy favorites. When Barnes served, Osuna straddled the center line, crouching low, so that Ronnie's serve could clear him. I've never heard of this, before or since, the net man exactly in the center of the court, ready to dart either way to cut off the return. Rafe had the Aussies mystified, and he and Barnes, decidedly the weaker team, came close to winning the match in the fifth set. Only somebody who can anticipate and move as rapidly as Osuna could get away with that in the big league, but it is a neat concentration-shaker to file away for possible use.

As a left-hander I've always played the left court. I feel that a lefty in the right court is at a disadvantage in trying to return crosscourt a serve wide to his backhand. Some players feel, however, that with a lefty in the right court (and a right-hander in the left) you'll have more volleying strength, since both forehands will be down the middle where most shots are hit in doubles. Also you have the court better covered for overheads, since you tend to smash better on your forehand side.

I've preferred the left side because I've been more comfortable there, and I've been lucky in recent years to have Emmo, a great right-court player, as my partner. That's the main thing: lining up the way you and your partner feel the surest.

And, of course, you want a partner you feel sure and easy with. There's no point to playing doubles with somebody you don't get along with (although I've noticed that in mixed doubles, getting along as roommates and courtmates may be two entirely different things. An otherwise happily married couple may turn a mixed doubles partnership into a scene from *Who's Afraid of Virginia Woolf?*)

You should have a "think-nothing-of-it-old-pal" air about you when your accomplice flubs a routine overhead on the big point. It isn't going to help your mood, his confidence, or the team's chances if you act injured by his mistakes. Compatibility and cool are the essence.

It should be understood that anytime either of you has a chance to make a point by picking off a ball that might have gone through to the other—do it. But make the point. This isn't hogging. It's just good sense to make the decisive move when you see the chance, particularly to hammer a forehand or shallow overhead. Teamwork and consistency win doubles matches. When your partner lunges in front of you to pounce for the kill, your move is to fill the hole he vacated.

If you can keep the ball low, your opponents will have to hit up to you, and you'll be able to put away a lot of balls. That's what you're after, ideally, the chance to murder a shoulder-high volley.

Until you have that opening, concentrate throughout on The Guiding Principle: keep the ball in play, avoiding temptation to overpower. Any ball hit over the net with care is worth two blasts that may well land in the bush.

14 PARADISE REGAINED— WIMBLEDON

WITH THE French mine, the Slam became as real as that baby kicking in Mary's belly. The chances on this baby weren't nearly as favorable as Mary's. There were still two excellent chances for it to miscarry—Wimbledon and Forest Hills. But now it was definitely alive. When you win both the Australian and the French, then it's established you're shooting for the moon.

It was a fantastic coincidence that both my babies were programmed to make it on the same day. Mary's obstetrician calculated that she would give birth on September 7, the day scheduled for the final of the U.S. Open at Forest Hills. It didn't work out that way. Rick was nineteen days late, and I decided I'd never take an obstetrician's prediction too seriously again. Dr. Bob Woodruff is a fine guy. He did a wonderful job, but I don't want to go to the race track with him.

After the Australian, I had no particular Slam feeling, other than wanting it and knowing it was possible. Winning the Australian isn't that big a thing. It has the weakest field, and it's too early in the year to base anything on. But the French is altogether different. You've conquered the most demanding tournament physically, mastered the only clay test in the Slam and you're halfway home.

161

In all tennis history five men and two women have won the Australian and French in succession to go into Wimbledon with a Slam alive and and quivering; Margaret Smith Court did it three times before her Slam and went no farther, Emmo twice. Jack Crawford in 1933 and Lew Hoad in 1956 went around three turns before fading at the Forest Hills finish. Don Budge, Maureen Connolly, Mrs. Court, and I held up all the way.

The pressures of Wimbledon and Forest Hills are different during a Slam, and it's hard to say which is more severe. Wimbledon pressure has to do with the event itself. This is the world championship, a sports event that everybody pays attention to. For two weeks of the year Wimbledon is a big story on all the world's sports pages, even in cities where tennis has little or no importance. There is no such thing at Wimbledon as an insignificant match because wherever you play, even on the most remote court, people will fill the spectator areas, whether there be grandstands or merely standing room.

The actor on Broadway, the singer at La Scala, the dancer at the Bolshoi Theatre understand what the tennis player at Wimbledon feels. So does the golfer at the Masters, the football player in the Super Bowl, and the baseball player in the World Series. It isn't the money. The connoisseurs are here. We play for ourselves, and we perform and play because it's in us and we must. We would do it whether or not anyone bothered to watch us. But we also play to be seen, to gain attention, to please and impress others. That's an important part of it. My love for tennis goes to my depths, but when the time comes that I can't play the Centre Court at Wimbledon, something vital will have gone out of that love.

The connoisseurs are the fans who pay to get in and the critics of the press, radio, and television who don't. At Wimbledon they're the keenest in the world. We can feel the expertise of these people, even though they're the quietest spectators and the least intrusive critics.

No reporters are permitted in the dressing rooms or the players' dining room and lounge, so we have a privacy that doesn't exist elsewhere. We need it more because in London, as no place else, a tennis player is a celebrity. I could walk the streets of any American city for days without being recognized, but it couldn't happen in London. Tennis is so widely exposed in the press and on TV that even the minor players have followings. When the limousines carrying the players pull into the grounds, there's always a mob at the dressing room entrance anxious to gawk at whoever's arriving and to ask for autographs. Fortunately the English are orderly and polite. Nobody tries to tear your clothes off or pound you on the back.

Limousine service is one of the features of Wimbledon that makes you feel like an extraordinary somebody. I doubt that any other sporting event takes such good and special care of its participants. You feel like a potentate when a limousine pulls up at your lodging every day to take you to the courts. It also takes you home, if you wish. This service is standard for every one of the nearly 300 players, for the duration of the tournament.

England is the only country with what you could call a "tennis press," as America has a baseball press and Australia a cricket press. The writers concentrate on the game, and know what they're talking about—a good deal of the time. They write well, with grace, humor, and bite, too. David Gray of the *Guardian*, Lance Tingay of the *Telegraph*, Rex Bellamy of *The Times*, Peter Wilson of the *Mirror*, Frank Rostron of *The Express*, John Barrett of *The Financial Times*, and John Ballantine of *The Sunday Times* have millions of readers. I wonder if they ever tighten up at the typewriter during Wimbledon. Do they take the choke on a big match, and stress the wrong aspects? Or try too hard and come up with botched prose? Do they strain and fail?

Peter Wilson, until his recent retirement, was probably the most widely read sportswriter in the world, a columnist covering every big sporting event. Boxing is one of his great loves, but he wouldn't leave home in 1969 to cover the Joe Frazier–Jerry Quarry heavyweight title fight in New York the first day of Wimbledon. It was the first heavyweight championship he'd missed in about thirty years, and boxing is very strong in England, too. But Peter wouldn't forsake Wimbledon even for a chance to play king-for-a-day in the Sultan of Kuwait's harem.

The British public is a captive audience for Wimbledon. There's little else on TV during the fortnight—live during the day, and a review of play in the evening. For many years both existing channels carried the tennis so there was absolutely nothing else to look at except the opposite wall. Regardless, tickets are nearly impossible to get, and people line up for standing room and sleep all night outside the gate for a chance at some general admission tickets. Scalpers do a big business. Attendance doesn't vary much. They can't stuff many more than 315,000 bodies into the place over twelve days of play. In the days before television, people would buy tickets that entitled them merely to be on the grounds without a seat for any of the climactic matches on Centre Court or Court No. 1. They could keep track of the matches inside by watching the scoreboards. At least they got the feel of the place.

That's part of the phenomenon of Wimbledon.

Wimbledon.

That's all you have to say. Everybody gets the idea. It's not really the name of the tournament, although by this time it might as well be. Actually this world championship, regarded as the English championship, has been called the Lawn Tennis Championship Meeting since it began in 1877. It could be called The Tournament, and everybody would understand.

The name Wimbledon comes from the London suburb where the All England Lawn Tennis and Croquet Club has its grounds. They are magnificent grounds, big league by any standard, dominated by a stadium that is Centre Court. When Centre Court is full, which is always, 15,000 spectators are there, 3000 of them standing. They've been standing sometimes six and seven hours, packed like a cattle car.

"When they faints, they faints standing up," an usher told me. "Somebody calls out to tell us there's been a fainting, otherwise we'd never know, and somehow we push through and get the person."

Nobody minds. You bring your lunch and enter the standing areas at noon. It stays light well into the evening in England, so that you might still be wedged into that fresh-air hole of Calcutta watching tennis at 9:15 P.M.

Faintings are not passed off casually at Wimbledon. Statistics are compiled and are announced every year by St. John Ambulance Brigade, the medical unit in attendance, and in 1969 the crowds obliged by setting an all-time Wimbledon fainting record. No fewer than 1700 passed out during the twelve days.

A Grand Swoon, wouldn't you say, old chap? St. John Ambulance gave that figure to the press as proudly as a football press agent trumpeting a scoring record. One customer out of every 190 was treated to St. John smelling salts.

I have never keeled over at Wimbledon, but when I consider what a fashionable place it is to faint, and the efficiency of the care, I shall never fear when feeling queasy there.

Court No. 1, a fine stadium on its own, holds 6500, and smaller grandstands are positioned at Courts No. 2 and 3. At the other twelve courts, it's a standing, jamming proposition, again, with herds pressing against the fences that enclose the courts. During the first week when all the courts are in use, the crowds are over 30,000 daily, and surely they could sell 50,000 seats in Centre Court if they were available.

Considering the incredible success of Wimbledon, the men like Herman David, who run the place, emerged as extremely principled blokes in their determination to stage an open Wimbledon in 1968 in opposition to the wishes of the International Lawn Tennis Federation. Wimbledon sells out regardless of the quality of the tennis. The British love it and the game so much they'd turn out to watch Ma and Pa Kettle play mixed doubles against the champions of Spearfish, South Dakota.

But Wimbledon stood for the best, and insisted on being the best in more than name. Only the prestige of Wimbledon could break the status quo and force open tennis into existence in 1968. I really never thought I'd see it in my day as a player, and I was resigned to exclusion.

Our professional game was bumbling along, the money was good, and though we were always discussing and arguing open tennis, we weren't expecting it. There was no point in moaning about our exclusion; we'd chosen our way of life. We'd had the prestige part of tennis as amateurs. Now we were away from it but able to earn a decent living anyway.

So we bounced around on our one-nighters. We traveled to remote places like Khartoum, La Paz, and Reston, Virginia. There was never any time off to adjust to the changes in time zones after a long flight. That's still a problem, combatting the punchiness you feel after flying, say, from New York to London. I've found that taking a brisk workout as soon as possible after I land—instead of going directly to bed—helps clear the fuzziness quicker. Either a practice session or a run. This could apply to anybody.

We'd play occasional eight and twelve-man tournaments in the summer in the U.S. Reston, a suburb of Washington, D.C., doesn't sound remote, but when we played there in 1965 they were just building the place. Our tournament was part of the promotion for this brand-new city, and everything was disorganized. You needed a guide to find the court. The area was so dusty we thought we were coming down with silicosis, and there were no dressing rooms. We dressed in our cars and showered some other time.

I thought about a lot of these times in my ragtag life when we heard that we'd be going back to Wimbledon like pardoned men. The time in Khartoum in 1965 when they'd been having serious rioting and there were soldiers and machine guns everywhere. We were scared to death, and we'd gone there for $1000—to be split among four of us. We'd go anywhere for almost anything in those days. Because of the trouble there had been no newspapers or radio, no way of publicizing the matches. But the promoter wasn't giving up. He and a couple of his friends got on the phone and started calling people. It started a chain reaction, and there were about 1000 people there for the matches. We couldn't believe it. We started in the late afternoon on grass courts and played until dark at six. Then everybody walked to a nearby cement court that was lighted and we resumed and played until the bug curfew. After a while the lights attracted so many insects that it was impossible to go on, and that's where the matches ended. The crowd realized this was a natural conclusion, and went away quietly and happy, having enjoyed some good tennis.

La Paz was interesting, but I don't want to go back. Not to play tennis. In that altitude—something like 12,000 feet—the balls fly like pigeons and if you play hard you're liable to get a nosebleed. We played a four-man tournament, and first prize was a $600 watch. I laugh when I think how we killed ourselves to win a watch, blood streaming down our faces and the balls zooming everywhere.

Nobody but the spectators knew we were in Bolivia playing on top of a mountain. Personal pride pushed us, that's all. Everywhere. I tried as hard at La Paz and amidst all those bugs in Khartoum as I ever did at Wimbledon or Paris. They may have amounted to nothing more than exhibitions, but I seldom saw a pro give less than his best unless he was sick or injured. I'm certain I never saw anybody tank a match, or take it easy to make the other guy feel better. There were occasions, against the weaker players—we called them the donkeys—that I could practice certain shots, try to work on my weaknesses. That was possible and helpful—and could get me beat once in a while.

One of the things I experimented with was lobbing through the rafters. This isn't a tactic you'll find in any tennis text, and it may never come in handy again with the game growing up for us pros. But in the gypsy days, when we played in all sorts of odd buildings, low beams weren't infrequent, and you had to be able to adjust. I soon found out in pro tennis that you were dead without a good lob—by far the most underrated shot in the game. And you had to be able to lob over and through the rafters many nights. Pancho Segura was the leading practicioner of rafter-lobbing. His lobs always found their way through mazes of rafters and beams. I got pretty good at it and one night in Utica I beat Gimeno with a beaut that wandered among the girders as though directed by radar.

You had to be able to laugh it off, even when you didn't get paid, or when the conditions were so ridiculous that a rhinoceros wouldn't have gone onto the court. The word was around about tennis pros: "Put up the money and they'll play barefoot on broken glass."

It was absolutely true. Gypsies don't make demands regarding playing conditions. We'd play if we suspected the money wasn't forthcoming. You can look at a crowd—or a noncrowd—and guess what's happening. But we liked to play tennis. It never seemed like a chore to me.

Maybe I thought about the perfect grass, the adulation and the limousines at Wimbledon as I inspected an armory in Utica for openings in the ceiling supports. But that was my life then.

These hardships we pros shared made us proud of our skills and perseverance. They were good for us. I think they helped our games, made us more determined. The five-year exile from Wimbledon and the rest of the places at the top made me appreciate open tennis more than the younger players who've moved right into it as a matter of course. They never had to risk their necks playing in a crummy ice rink like the one in Altringham, England, where Hoad and I almost broke our necks on the slick portable floor. Condensation dripped from the ceiling making the footing horrible. Neither one of us could do much. They should have taken up the flooring and given us skates. The score went to 20–20 and I did the splits going for a shot. Snap! I felt something go. A tendon? No—my jockstrap. With a face that matched my hair I called time and trotted to the dressing room for a replacement. "Emergency," I blurted to the umpire as the spectators guffawed. We had to quit at 27–27, the longest set I ever played, because we could hardly stand.

And there was another English rink in Nottingham where Frank Sedgman hit more passing shots by me than I'd ever seen. I was passing him pretty well, too. We suddenly got the idea the court might be too big. It was—a yard wider than regulation, and two feet longer. Somebody painted the lines wrong, and there was nothing to do but settle down at the baseline. No use rushing the net with all that extra room to cover.

The first pro match I played in the U.S., at Boston Garden, didn't do anything to help my state of mind. Instead of spreading the canvas court on the basketball floor, or the ice, as is the practice in large arenas, they put it on a rough floor of planking that covered the ice. Another mistake. You might as well ask Minnesota Fats to shoot pool on a lumpy table.

That was the beginning of my first winter in America—my first real winter. I'd seen snow only once before, briefly during a tournament in New York the previous winter. This winter of 1963 there was to be no escaping it. One hopeful aspect of my pro debut in America was that I was playing big Barry MacKay. It was nice to get away from a menu of Hoad and Rosewall. It was like taking my head out of the cement mixer for a night, but I soon found out Barry could be worse on a court like that. He had one of the biggest serves going, and trying to return it on that bumpy court was like trying to swat jackrabbits with a broom. "Jesus," I thought, "so this is the pro tennis tour?"

Another beating. It took me a long time to get even, and by the time I did I was just pleased to be alive. That U.S. tour was sixty matches in eighty days. It seemed like around the world in eighty days. There were six of us—Rosewall, Gimeno, MacKay, Luis Ayala, Butch Buchholz, and me—and a couple of station wagons. We were on the run every minute, grabbing hotdogs, getting to bed about three every morning, driving, driving, driving.

One night in upper New York State, cold as a witch's mitt, snow all over the roads, we were on our way to Albany. The road was like grease. As we slid and swerved, I said to myself, "What am I doing here?"

The money was all right, but what was I doing freezing and skidding on my way to Albany when I could have been getting on nicely as an amateur, playing in Jamaica that week.

Of course, everybody has his doubts about his job once in a while. As I began to play better, I felt better. I wound up the tour second to Rosewall, and I collected more than $50,000 for the year, so I was sure I'd make my guarantee.

It was $110,000 over three years, although the word "guarantee" is a bit dreamy. All through 1962 the pros were after me to sign on with them. There weren't promoters backing the operation as Lamar Hunt does now. The players themselves were trying to hold pro tennis together, and they weren't doing very well—but how could they? They were trying to play and do everything else too.

They all talked to me about turning pro, but mostly Hoad and Rosewall, since they knew me better than the rest. They started with a $75,000 offer for three years, and I said to come back after Forest Hills. Then I'd won my first Slam, and they knew they had to go higher: $85,000. I decided I wanted six figures, and finally we settled on $110,000. This was after I'd turned down a separate offer from Pancho Gonzales of a $50,000 minimum and $100,000 maximum for a one year head-to-head tour. Pancho and I would have cut up the gate, and no doubt I could have made the maximum with the old champion coming out of retirement to face the Grand-Slammer. He had the biggest name, but I didn't know how I could face my Aussie friends if I did that, and I wasn't too keen on Pancho. I felt surer of a long-term contract with men I knew.

It was all on trust, actually, this figure of $110,000. There was nothing in escrow, no millionaire or experienced promoter to back it up. I was to get 25 percent of the gate on nights I won and 20 percent otherwise. Hoad and Rosewall pledged themselves to make up the difference if I didn't reach $110,000 in three years. They didn't have to, I'm glad to say, because I made $150,000 my first three years. I'm sure Lew and Kenny would have tried, but it was still a pretty shaky contract, and I doubt I'd have held them to it.

A financial gamble, maybe, but I wanted to get off on my own, and not have to haggle with every tournament as I did as an amateur. Even though I had earned a nice living as an amateur, I just wasn't a man to bargain and haggle over expense money like some of the fellows. I'm sure that several not as good as I extracted more money, and good luck to them. The most I ever asked for—and got—was $1000 to play the National Indoors in New York in 1962. I thought I was being exorbitant, and purposely so, because I didn't want to leave home in February.

When they complied, I reluctantly made the trip, and saw snow for the first time.

I hope it doesn't sound egotistical to say that in addition to trying to secure my own future, I was doing something for the future of professional tennis as well. The boys were desperate to get me. They needed new blood badly, a new face, the amateur with the big reputation. They hadn't signed one in a long time. Their most recent converts had been Ayala, who wasn't a big name, and MacKay, Alex Olmedo, Buchholz, and Gimeno, who were just beginning to make names when they signed pro contracts. No top star had turned pro in three years. Gonzales hung out in one of his innumerable retirements, and the last tremendous name to sign on had been Hoad in 1957. They really needed me if there was going to be any kind of pro tennis at all, and that's why they were willing to give me such a large cut of the action. I'll admit that 25 percent of zero isn't always rewarding, but many nights the take was all right.

After five years like that, I could take any kind of playing conditions. Butch Buchholz, who'd been an outcast longer than I, felt the same. At the beginning of 1968 when Lamar Hunt began a badly organized tour with rookies Roger Taylor, John Newcombe, Tony Roche, and Niki Pilic, almost everybody was miserable but Butch, the old hand.

"As long as the building doesn't blow up, nothing can shake me," Butch said. "I'm a veteran of the Texas death march. My first year as a pro, 1961, somebody—and it must have been a fugitive from the Texas Rangers—scheduled us throughout the state on a tour that meant about five hundred miles a day driving. We were in towns that nobody has heard of yet, playing the worst buildings and courts, for short money. Every night I wanted to quit and go home, try to get reinstated as an amateur. I was only twenty. But I was a pro and I stuck it out. These kids now don't know what a tough tour is like."

They are less likely to know, and perhaps the opportunity is gone—if opportunity is the word. As the game booms a complete circuit of opens in the leading cities has sprouted and the sport is becoming genuinely a big league one. I guess I'll never play Nottingham again, or Khartoum, or Accra, or La Paz. The kids who miss out on this seasoning just can't know the sensation of deliverance running through us old pros when we walked through the Doherty Gate into Wimbledon again on June 24, 1968, a part of the act once more. Newcombe, Roche, Pilic, Taylor, had never been away. They were amateurs in 1967, pros in 1968. They couldn't know the elation of being recognized as respectable men again.

LESSON 14
Court Conditions and Surfaces

The singles court is 78 by 27 feet, and that doesn't change, although on occasion I have played pro tour matches on courts that have been improperly laid out. But within that 78 by 27 you can find yourself in entirely different atmospheres.

I don't know how many different types of surface I've played on, from antbed—the first I tried at home—to a downtown thoroughfare in St. Louis where we played an exhibition in 1964 for a lunch hour crowd of shoppers. I've played on the bumpy deck of an aircraft carrier, on cement courts so glossy you thought they were mirrors, on grass that scrawny Masai cattle wouldn't have. My first years as a roaming pro, playing one-night stands, we stretched our canvas over any fairly level base—ice, boards, concrete—and that canvas was a quick, new, traumatic experience.

I learned to shorten my backswing, make it compact, which you must do on fast surfaces. No glorious windups like the kind I used to have for my forehand. On uncertain grass I'd use hardly any backswing at all, poising the racket as I would for a volley, waiting until the last instant to see which way the ball would jump and then slash at it.

One of the fastest courts I've played was at the Seventh Regiment Armory in New York where the National Indoors used to be located. Polished wood was the footing, and the lighting wouldn't have done a cave justice. That ball would shoot through like a Japanese express train in the dark. Never mind the backswing. Just probe and hope.

On these fast surfaces, just try to meet the ball on return of serve; block it. The pace of your opponent's shot and the ball rocketing off the court will be sufficient without trying to add any more yourself. And think about getting to the net fast. You can't stand back on a fast court and let the ball bounce. If you don't become a volleyer in speedy circumstances you may as well take up chess.

Wind will change the situation within the 78 by 27 rectangle, too.

173

Sometimes you think you'd be better off trading in your racket for a sailboat. Use more spin so you can control the ball, and a lower toss on serve so that the ball doesn't blow off course unnecessarily. Remember you can hit hard against the wind but a bare tap may be enough with the wind. Test your shots carefully before the match starts, and on a tricky windy day warm up from both sides of the court.

Not many people relish playing in the wind or under less than ideal conditions. But don't let yourself go sour. Conditions are the same for you and your opponent. He's bothered, too. Maybe more so—there's a good chance of that. He may not know as much as you do about making bad conditions work to your advantage: things like going to net as often as you can get there—even when receiving serve—if you've a strong wind at your back that will slow up his passing shots and make his lobs fall short.

Act like you love it. This is your kind of day and court. You grew up playing on furrowed fields in hailstorms, right? Isn't it glorious just being out here and working up a good sweat?

You can drive an opponent crazy by refusing to let anything bother you when obviously the situation is a mess.

How to Play Championship Tennis in Pictures

ALL PHOTOS BY RUSS ADAMS

I do fifty double knee jumps every day

Because I'm short I'm not going to knock anybody dead with my serve. I fire an occasional ace, but the cannonball treatment isn't my style. Nevertheless, I couldn't be a winner without an effective serve, one that is consistent and accurate. The importance of getting the first serve into play cannot be overemphasized. You've got two enemies: your opponent and the net. The latter is more dangerous and causes you more trouble. Concentrate on getting the serve over the net. Don't worry about serving long. Better to take a chance on that than to cut it too fine and serve into the net. I almost never hit a flat serve. A spin serve is surer. Take plenty of time. The game goes at your pace when you're serving. A common mistake is not watching the ball right up to the point of impact. It's stupid not to—and yet this is something I have to continually remind myself. But when you're serving you have time to think the whole thing through—and it's the only stroke where this is possible. Do it unrushed in your own good sweet time.

Throwing the ball high enough is vital—just above the height of your swing, so that when you're reaching up you have to wait just a fraction of a second for it to come down. It's a disadvantage to throw too high or too low. For a small fellow, like myself, the worst thing is to throw too low. In the service motion the most important part, to my mind, is the elbow bending and the head of the racket dropping all the way down the middle of the back (the backscratcher position).

179

One of the longest sets I've played was the 34-game duel against Fred Stolle in the second set of the third round of the 1969 Australian. It took me a long time to solve Fred's serve, one of the finest in the game. There's nothing fancy, no unnecessary motion, pumping or arm-swinging. He throws the ball up, brings the racket all the way back to the back-scratcher position as the ball reaches the height on the toss. Then he comes right over it, following through and on up to the net. Fred's serve was instrumental in his winning the German and American singles titles in 1966 and helping Australia take the Davis Cup in 1964 through 1966.

No rest for the wicked character across the net who wants to beat me. That's my philosophy, and it's why I hit the ball on the rise so he'll have less chance to get himself ready. As soon as I know I'm going to be hitting a forehand, I get that racket back—preparation—and I've turned my right shoulder to the net (your left shoulder if you're right-handed). You don't always have time for the pure approach to strokes, and the nicety of turning the entire side-on to the net. Plenty of times you're straight away, but there's always time to bend your knees and keep your eye fastened to that ball. No matter how you stroke or who you are, if you glue your eye to the ball right up to the instant of contact with the strings, you're going to do some good. I'm using good old topspin here, my usual on a groundstroke from the baseline, taking the ball low, before it's had a chance to come up much, rolling over it and finishing with the high follow-through. By lifting the ball higher with this stroke you come up with a topspin lob—very damaging when you pitch it over the head of the man at the net because it literally sprints away from him.

Andres Gimeno says that as a boy he could handle a forehand better than a fork—and he liked to eat very much. It has always been his strong shot, and if the ball is high, as in this case, he goes up on his toes to get right up there with it. He is less side-on to the net than recommended in the manuals, but he gets results, which is the main thing. He prepares side-on, but his shoulders come around to face the net. He's using topspin, and the whip carries the racket over his shoulder at the completion of his swing.

There's more topspin in the game than ever before, the players realizing they can hit the ball extremely hard without too much danger of the shot carrying beyond the baseline. The margin of error is smaller because the topped ball clears the net by a comfortable distance. Topspin also makes the shot difficult to handle for the volleyer. But left-handers seldom hit a topspin backhand. I'm glad I learned it early because it's been a bread-and-butter stroke. As I prepare, my left shoulder is well around—my back practically to the net—and my right foot is a pivot, turning somewhat toward the net. The racket starts low (along with my shoulder) and finishes high as I come over the ball. I cock my wrist—that is, lay it back—as I prepare, and then snap it over the ball on impact. That snap and rolling the racket over the ball produce the topspin. I have to hit the ball in front of me, and contact the bottom side first on the way up. The ball doesn't find its way to precise spots like Rosewall's accurate flat-slice backhand, but it stays in the court, and that's the basic idea, isn't it?

188

That doomsday stroking machine, Kenny Rosewall, has made me witness this backhand too many times. There may have been better—Don Budge's perhaps—but I haven't seen them. Kenny's preparation is meticulous. He gets the racket back in plenty of time as he moves for the ball. (Prepare! Prepare! Please!) The essence of it is getting his right shoulder well around to the ball, and down. Kenny's racket is slightly open as he puts a bit of slice on the ball. His eyes never leave that ball. His weight shifts from back foot to front at the moment he hits the ball, and his follow-through is straight to the net. Rosewall has knocked this shot past me so frequently that the least he could have done was pose for free for these photos. Which he did.

190

The thought of volleying makes some players want to head for the golf course. They approach the net as though it were the Berlin Wall. Sharp reflexes are chiefly what's needed, and I guess you inherit those. But any reflexes can be pepped up by just standing there and letting somebody hammer shots at you—softly at first. Some wonderful volleys have been made in self-defense. Actually, this is one of the great-fun parts of tennis. You miss a lot in your doubles if you don't venture to the net where the points are made. Just remember there's hardly any backswing—that's one of my problems—and you try to keep your wrist lower than the head of the racket, no matter how low the volley. Keep the racket out in front of you and punch briskly. There isn't much follow-through, but don't let the racket head drop once you've connected. If you lock your eye onto that ball all the way, volleying should be easier than anything else.

191

192

There are times when I feel good about observing the marvelous backhand
volley of Roy Emerson, doubles partner supreme. What a weapon to have
on my side. But from this angle—head-on—it can only mean grief unless I
get lucky. The idea is to punch the ball, with the racket out in front of your
body and the head of it above your wrist—a firm wrist. Not much backswing, the shorter the better. Emmo's weight is coming forward, and he locks
his wrist at impact. The desired result is an absolute winner or a deep volley
that will set up a winner on the next one.

Shots at your feet are trouble, whether in a cowboy movie or on a tennis court. I'm a connoisseur of both art forms, and the answer to both problems is: you do the best you can—adapting quickly. When the villain in a Western shoots at your feet, you dance; when that villain across the net does likewise, you half-volley. Bend your knees and stay low. Get your racket back early, but not too far back—the backswing is short. Try to meet the ball with your weight moving forward. Anybody as insistent about getting to the net as I am will face this situation often. If you can't perfect a half-volley, maybe you can come up with a few engaging dance steps to amuse the gallery as the ball goes by.

196

My finish to the 1969 Wimbledon was an overhead smash of a Newcombe lob, and that's what this shot always should be: the finisher. I find I can hit the ball harder if I get into the air, thus throwing my body entirely behind the shot. I get ready side-on to the net and use my right arm (my nonracket arm) as a guide. As I line up the ball the racket drops back into the back-scratching position, as with the serve. Then I go up and—let's hope—pow! An overhead takes better timing than any other shot, and a lot of practice, but it's worth it to be able to end a point with one blast. Don't let the ball bounce unless the lob is tremendously high or it's so windy that hitting the ball in the air is tricky. By letting the ball bounce you're only giving your opponent more time to regain position.

15 RESPECTABILITY IS A CLUB TIE

THOSE OF us who had won titles at Wimbledon were pretty obvious. We were permitted to wear the club tie again, the garish purple and green stripes of the All England Club.

It may be difficult for someone outside of tennis to believe, but a man was actually stripped of his membership when he became a pro. It is a Wimbledon custom, a nice and generous one, that a man or woman who wins a title in the Championships becomes an honorary member with club privileges and the right to wear the club colors.

But soon after that evil day when I signed a pro contract, I had the same experience as other pros before me. A letter arrived from the All England Club revoking my membership, instructing me that I must not wear the tie. I suppose if I'd lived in England, a representative of the club would have visited me, probably somebody looking like C. Aubrey Smith, to slap my face, cut off the tie, and rebuke me for dishonorable conduct.

I know it's laughable, but it also served to reinforce the fact that pro was a dirty word in tennis, and that we had, in fact, lost our citizenship in a supposedly decent world.

Miraculously, as if by papal decree, we were legitimized again when Wimbledon decided to join the seventh decade of the twentieth century. Club ties sprouted like the first crocuses of spring on the many great players who reappeared for that historic first open Wimbledon. Frank Sedgman, who was forty and

199

making a sentimental journey to play the tournament he won in 1952, had his tie on. So did Hoad, who was thirty-four and had won in 1956–57; and Don Budge, fifty-two, the original Grand Slammer, returned to enter the senior doubles for men over forty-five. Pancho Segura had no club necktie. He'd played only two Wimbledons back in 1946–7 before turning pro, but it wouldn't have seemed right to open up the world championship without Segoo. He was forty-seven, but he put his name in the record book by playing in the longest set in Wimbledon annals. For three hours Segoo delighted the crowd with his shotmaking and theatrics as he and Alex Olmedo downed the South Africans Gordon Forbes and Abe Segal, 32–30, 5–7, 6–4, 6–4. "I waited a long time for this day, so I had to stay on the court for a while to make up for those lost years," Segoo laughed. Everybody was glad he'd made it.

The fans were sorry when it was obvious that Gonzales and Hoad were seeded too high, could be beaten by lesser names, younger and better conditioned opponents. Alex Metreveli, the Russian who wore down eighth-seeded Gonzales, was nearly as dazed by his feat as old Pancho. "I read about him as a child," said Alex. "Gonzales is the one tennis player whose name is known all over my country." Did we have to hear that from a Russian, too?

There won't be a Wimbledon again like that in 1968. It was a reunion, an amnesty ceremony with all the pros coming out from their holes to glow once again in the sunshine of the All England Club's forgiving smile. Many of them were out of shape, playing on memories. Others, Andres Gimeno for one, were so nervous that they couldn't do a thing. Andres, seeded No. 3, fell to the Wolfman, the hairy Ray Moore in the upset of the tournament. From the first day the amateurs had great fun punching holes in the pros' reputations. The pros didn't know quite how to perform in respectable company, and I was the only one to uphold my seed, No. 1. Tony Roche, a pro rookie who'd never been away from Wimbledon, was seeded No. 15, and he was my final-round opponent.

Amateurs Arthur Ashe and Clark Graebner got to the semifinals, although as I've said they were amateur in label only. Still it made for a wild, unpredictable tournament from the moment that Niki Pilic, seeded 16th, was beaten in the first round by a lightly considered American, Herbie Fitz Gibbon. Fitz Gibbon was reasonably amateur, while Pilic had been a quarterfinalist in 1967, his last year as an amateur. In playing American college tennis in the Northeast for Princeton, Herbie knew how to act in the wind. It was blowing a gale that day, and poor Pilic was outdoors for practically the first time of the year. Traveling with the pros and playing entirely in arenas, he'd forgotten the existence of wind.

Just before the end the tall Yugoslav cried out in English, "Why we have to play in such weather this tennis—why?"

Outside of college players, fewer and fewer amateurs will appear in future Wimbledons. The professional tennis player is established. In 1968 the pros were in a minority, and although they won most of the titles, they briefly lost face in their many beatings by alleged amateurs. Then, as prize money grew, professionalism became thoroughly acceptable. It wouldn't have done so if Wimbledon hadn't stood up for progress and the game's integrity in 1968. We were back in the public eye. Wimbledon was open. We were permitted to visit the Lourdes of London and lose our leprosy.

Strangely, and amusingly, it was a bloke with almost no knowledge of tennis who became one of the tournament game's saviors by practically forcing opens into being. Without a frightening push from Dave Dixon of New Orleans—a man all but forgotten —Wimbledon probably wouldn't have been so determined to open up in 1968.

Dixon's sport is golf. He plays well enough to have qualified for the National Amateur. In 1967 he began taking a closer interest in other sports. As chairman of a proposed domed stadium for New Orleans he was looking into any sport or activity that would keep the building busy. Football and baseball were obvious, but those wouldn't come close to filling the schedule of a year-round sporting palace.

"What about tennis?" Dave wondered. "Was there such a

thing as a pro tennis circuit?" Like almost anybody else in the world at that time, he couldn't be sure. He had vague recollections of occasional odd paragraphs at the bottom of sports pages—tucked in among the truss ads—relating to pro tennis. Wasn't Pancho Gonzales still alive? Hadn't he seen something about Australians named Laver and Rosewall? He asked his secretary to check up on it, and then he went on to something else.

Sometime later the secretary had discovered our flimsy organization, the International Professional Tennis Association, and learned of a tournament we were playing in Binghamton, New York. Dixon was going to be in New York City that week, so he decided to run up to Binghamton over the weekend and see for himself.

Nobody was ever hooked faster than Dave Dixon. "Where have these guys been? They're fantastic athletes," was his reaction. "And nobody knows about them. I got to Binghamton, and hardly anybody in the city could tell me where the tournament was. No posters, no publicity. Finally we found them hidden out at a private club, and we sat on uncomfortable wooden bleachers to watch."

Abruptly, Dixon was transformed from landlord to promoter. Instead of trying to fit tennis into the prospective stadium, he sought to fit himself into the tennis business and begin marketing the game, convinced that by modernizing it could be a smash.

He went home to convince his friend Lamar Hunt of Dallas that tennis could join the pro sports boom, and they became partners. Off Dave flew to London, where we were playing, to offer us contracts with World Championship Tennis. We would receive guarantees against prize money to play in tournaments that WCT promoted.

At the same time George MacCall, the U.S. Davis Cup captain from 1965 through 1967, was forming his National Tennis League, and made us roughly the same proposition. Because it was obvious that Dixon, although a pleasant and smooth individual, didn't know his backside from a backhand, most of us signed with MacCall. We were wary of the novice. Dixon did grab three of our group—Butch Buchholz, Dennis Ralston, and Pierre Barthes—and he was undismayed.

Since he couldn't get the best pros, he would land the best amateurs. His idea wasn't new, but his approach and his ammunition were. Dave was backed with Lamar Hunt's money, which flows no less reassuringly than Texas oil. The guarantees he offered John Newcombe, Tony Roche, Cliff Drysdale, Roger Taylor, and Niki Pilic weren't based on wishes and good intentions as mine had been in 1963. The money was there, ranging from Wimbledon champ Newcombe's $50,000-per-year on down. Since MacCall had signed Roy Emerson, the amateur game within a month lost six of its top ten.

Amateurs had defected before, but never in such a rush of quantity and quality.

Newcombe, Pilic, and Taylor had been Wimbledon semifinalists in 1967. The men at the head of English tennis knew they had been offering a diluted world championship at Wimbledon, but the future loomed as ridiculous. They had been anxious to force open tennis, and now Dave Dixon's raid made it imperative.

Dave didn't last long in tennis, no more than a few months, not even until the first open Wimbledon at which he should have been introduced from Centre Court.

He bubbled with radical ideas. His troupe used the controversial VASSS (Van Alen Streamlined Scoring System) and wore different-colored shirts, either measure enough to send coronaries rippling through tennis' old guard. These are innovations that may yet be accepted. His principal difficulty was not tampering with tradition but failing to administer his first tour efficiently. World Championship Tennis lost nearly $100,000 in three months, and Hunt bought Dixon out and sent him to the sidelines. Hunt has reorganized and done well since, multiplying the size of his roster considerably.

Wherever you are, Dave Dixon, I and the rest of the pros owe you our thanks.

LESSON 15
Court Manners and Etiquette

Sportsmanship is the essence of the game, and yet you don't want to be too good a sport. Or what I call a false sportsman.

I will give you a couple of examples. In 1966 at Forest Hills, Clark Graebner, the American, and Jan Leschly, the Dane, were in the fifth set of an exciting semifinal. Leschly hit a ball that sailed over the baseline, apparently Graebner's point at a time when every point was golden. But Graebner said no. He called to the umpire that his racket had ticked the ball. Nobody noticed, nobody heard, but Clark knew it wasn't his point, and he wouldn't take it. In such a case the umpire accepts the player's refusal of the point and awards it to his opponent. Graebner won the match anyway, so maybe being a good sport pays off.

Now, in 1967 I was up against Andres Gimeno in the final of the U.S. Pro Championship in Boston. On set point for me in the second set, I knocked a ball just wide of the sideline. That should have made it deuce and kept Andres alive. Instead the linesman signaled that the ball had hit the line. Point, game, and set to Laver. Gimeno fussed. I asked the umpire to check with the linesman to make sure. I didn't want the point that way. I made it clear that I hoped the linesman would change his mind. He wouldn't.

I thought of a similar instance three years before on the same court. I was playing Pancho Gonzales for the title and I hit a winner on an important point. The linesman called it out. Pancho wanted that point badly, but not on a bad call. He pointed to the spot where the ball had landed six inches inside the baseline, but he couldn't convince the linesman. In such situations players benefitting from outrageous calls have been known to throw the next point or the next game to demonstrate their so-called sportsmanship.

Did I? Did Pancho? Not on your life. Once we had registered disapproval and asked the linesman to reconsider (they can change their calls, you know), we brushed that point out of our minds. On to the next point. In a tournament match you must play the calls, as we say—accept what comes. There will be bad calls when humans are involved, but I think the supposedly noble gesture of giving away a point is a grandstand play. Further it's an out-and-out insult to the officials who are unpaid volunteers graciously giving their time and effort to aid in the presentation of a tournament.

In a match without linesmen and umpire, you're on the honor system. Make your calls quickly and fairly. If there's any doubt, give your opponent the benefit of that doubt. Don't let your opponent take advantage of you. If he's serving before you're ready, tell him politely. You don't have to get into a screaming match about quick-serving as Gonzales and I once did.

In a club match you can be pretty casual, but if your opponent cramps or injures himself and wants to resume three hours later, you may have to remind him about the play-is-continuous rule. You're not being a bastard by expecting a default if your opponent can't continue after a brief rest. Fitness is part of the game, and if a player breaks down physically, then he's the loser.

This rule is stretched badly, even at the top level. At the Philadelphia Indoor in 1970 Butch Buchholz was going at John Newcombe in a quarterfinal. One of Butch's shots skipped off the net and struck Newcombe in the eye. Newcombe was carted off to the dressing room for examination and treatment. Long delay. Buchholz thought he was being a good sport by not demanding his rights: a default. By the time they returned to the court Butch had gone cold, and he was in a mental stew about whether he should have insisted on the victory. He lost. It cost him money that night and possibly the $10,000 first prize.

Butch was wrong in not speaking up. The officials were wrong in allowing the delay. Newcombe was a bigger name than Buchholz. Everybody felt sympathetic, but it should have been Newc's tough luck, a break of the game.

It happens all the time, but don't accept it in a tournament. The rule says nothing about extenuating circumstances, only that play must be continuous.

Like Graebner, in that match with Leschly, you are expected to call infractions against yourself such as touching the net, double-hitting (a "carry"), or hitting the ball when it is "not up" (having bounced twice).

If you suspect someone of giving you the business consistently on bad calls, you can refuse to play him again. Or break his rackets over your knee. I never resort to the latter because I weigh only 147, and hardly anybody I play with is smaller.

16 A SHAKY BEGINNING

As a boy my particular idol was Lew Hoad. Lew didn't invent topspin by any means, or the all-out approach of hitting hard for winners in every situation. But from what I can learn, nobody in the game ever had stronger wrists and was quite so menacing with topspin off both backhand and forehand. I wanted to hit the ball that way, and Charlie Hollis encouraged me.

I got a great thrill from staying with the Hoads on a visit to Sydney for a junior tournament. Lew's parents often put up young players who came to town. He wasn't at home. His folks told me he was overseas playing Wimbledon, the greatest tournament in the world. It was then that Wimbledon began to register with me and the feeling began growing that I had to go there, to play there.

It would be a while yet, four years. The place was overwhelming when I first saw it in 1956. I wasn't too nervous, though, because I didn't expect to do much. Orlando Sirola, the giant Italian, saw that I didn't. It was David and Goliath in reverse as the big fellow, who stood fifteen inches over me at six feet seven, stoned me. He seemed to be serving out of a tree. The first set went to deuce, 5–5, and when he'd beaten me, 7–5, 6–4, 6–2, I didn't feel bad. I knew I'd be back, although not as quickly as I thought. I spent the 1957 season in the Australian Army, and couldn't go away from the country until 1958.

207

That year I started to find out about Wimbledon nerves. I won my first two rounds and earned my competitive introduction to that shrine called Centre Court, against Jaroslav Drobny, one of England's favorites. In 1954, Drob, a Czechoslovakian refugee, had won the title at the unlikely age of thirty-two, interfering in the American-Australian postwar rule. He wasn't given much chance to become champion after he lost the 1949 and 1952 finals, so when he came through in 1954 against Rosewall, the British rejoiced.

To me he looked like a brewer who'd been drinking the profits, a jolly fellow deceptive in appearance because he had surgical touch and control with his left hand.

It was an ordeal. First, I was worried about making an idiot of myself bowing. Unless you're Japanese or hang out with royalty, you probably don't know any more about bowing form than I did. But, you see, when you walk onto Centre Court it's customary that you and your opponent turn toward the royal box, which is behind the near baseline, stop and bow. The women curtsy. I didn't know a bow from a curtsy, but you know how terrified you can feel if you think you're going to foul up in front of 15,000 people.

If you blow the bow, there's nothing they can do to you. Nobody gets their head taken off for that sort of thing anymore. But it's something I worried about. I suppose I should give you a few hints on bowing in case you ever get as far as Centre Court. The main thing is not to bend too far, because you might fall on your face, which would be a bad show. A quick dip will do it, with something of a smile. The people watching know it's not your line, but I didn't know they knew.

Frankly, I don't remember my first bow, but by this time it's second nature. I was so nervous, my throat was dry and my hands were shaking. Then I looked at Drobny. Out of shape, I thought. His appearance should have given me confidence, except my hands wouldn't stop shaking. Everywhere I looked there were people, 15,000 of them. Half the population of Rockhampton. And they were all looking at me, expecting me to put up some sort of opposition, not waste their time.

Well, if you can't play well, play fast. It was fast. Drob served hard and flat and chipped the ball here and there so I was always bowing—to him—bending and reaching and never coming up with much. He'd been around, a slick old bloke who, as a teen-ager two decades earlier, had played against Budge in Europe during Don's Slam year. It was 6–1, 6–1 so fast that all I wanted to do was stay bowed and count the grassblades. But nobody had thrown a rock. It was only a tennis match. As I thought about that, I didn't feel weak any more. I was all right and I played a respectable third set, 6–4.

I wasn't going to lose many more matches here: Just 2 out of the next 42.

The next year, 1959, I would be in the final, losing to Alex Olmedo, and in 1960 in the final again, losing to Neale Fraser. I won in 1961–62 and then the opens of 1968–69.

In 1967 Wimbledon staged a pro tournament which I won, a test to see how the professionals might be accepted treading the sacred sod. The grass did not turn brown when touched by the outcasts' feet, nor did our presence precipitate a rerun of the Great Plague. We had played pro tournaments in London, of course, indoors at Wembley Pool every year. But crashing Wimbledon meant that we might be on the verge of the absolution which we received the following year.

Wimbledon is a tournament with a split personality, a vast garden party with hardened professional athletes in its midst breaking their humps for cash and recognition while the aficionados smell the flowers and eat strawberries and cream.

It began during the Victorian era, in 1877, as an amusement of upper-class sportsmen, a pitter-patter athletic diversion on the croquet lawns with all the proper touches. Tennis doesn't stop for tea, in the fashion of cricket, but nobody fails to stop some time for their tea. A tea garden expressly for that purpose is located outside of Centre Court where the famous strawberries and cream are sold as well, along with a concession to the present day: Wimpyburgers. Aside from the hamburgers and the limousines, you might think you were walking into the nineteenth century as you enter the grounds. When you glance toward the royal box you expect to catch a glimpse of Victoria herself. That's one feeling Wimbledon gives you—an endless perpetuation of 1877.

Endless, maybe, but not mindless. Though the place is thick with tradition, there is life and vigor within the unchanging layer of stuffiness. Wimbledon, through its stature, made open tennis a reality. And Wimbledon is the paragon of operating efficiency. When it is stated that play will begin at two—they mean precisely. In 1968, when heavy rains stacked up the first week's program, it seemed reasonable to open play earlier on a couple of days, but deviating from the two P.M. starting time nearly took a special session of Parliament. After a long meeting of the management committee it was finally decided that it might be all right—as an emergency measure—to begin at one. Precisely.

Rigid custom and social frivolity are one side of Wimbledon. The other side—what it's all about to me, and I think most people—is the contests of athletes. Winning is everything, and Wimbledon is where we make our reputations. I suppose the crowds would still come if Wimbledon hadn't admitted us in 1968, and the tennis remained restricted and inferior. That's what tradition can do for an event. Now that the tennis is the ultimate, the finest ever played, the crowds can't increase much. There's only so much room. But the satisfaction of winning now is incomparable. The competition has never been so fierce. Money has something to do with it, but Wimbledon is one event we'd all play for nothing. First prize then—$7200—was far from the biggest purse. The competitive atmosphere was, of course, what we pros had to get back into. There was just no way to change the public's feeling that our tour matches were meaningless exhibitions. Never mind the injuries and the agonies that went into those matches. We left one place and traveled to another so quickly that nobody ever knew. To the public, particularly the American public—for some reason I've never worked out—we were trained seals putting on a marvelous, well-drilled act. Of course, the English have always taken their tennis more seriously than anyone else. They feel the anguish and the drama of Wimbledon. To them any bloke who goes through a couple of rounds of the tournament becomes a hero, and the public soon knows all about him.

Wimbledon is as much the women's as the men's, and this is the only place where they enjoy complete equality—except, of course, for the money. The British appreciate women's tennis, and at least twice I've been overshadowed by the female champion: in 1961 when Ann Mortimer subdued national heroine Chris Truman in the first all-English final in forty-seven years, and in 1969 when Ann Haydon Jones, another English-woman, broke the three-year reign of Californian Billie Jean King.

Dressed by couturier Teddy Tinling—who has made tennis dresses as handsome as ball gowns—some of the girls are indeed much better to look at than my finest topspin backhand. Despite their charm and chic, the girls are as combative as we men. Maybe more so, which is why I believe that they should quit at about age twenty-five. After that a woman should be home rais-ing babies, not lobs. At first it's a nice lark for a girl—travel and sport, good exercise and experience. But they seem to grow hard and too serious about tennis after college age when it becomes a profession.

They handle it better if they marry. Margaret Smith Court, the strong Australian, played more relaxed tennis after twenty-five when she married, and kept winning big titles. Another Australian, Gail Sherriff Chanfreau, brought her husband, the French player Jean Baptiste Chanfreau, financial as well as emo-tional support. They play the same tournaments, and Gail, who stands higher in the women's game than her roommate does in the men's, usually wins more prize money.

Of all the extraordinary female costumes at Wimbledon, the most direct and beguiling was that worn by an American model Pat Stewart in 1959. Her panties were not gold lamé, like the ones belonging to Karol Fageros that were prudishly ruled off in 1958 by Wimbledon officials. Nor were they as lacy as the famed underwear of Gussie Moran.

On Pat's cotton bottom was embroidered her phone number,

revealed every time she served. It was there until her fiancé found out and objected.

Pat, who modeled girdles when she wasn't playing, seems to have the right outlook. "That's the way the strap snaps," she shrugs off a defeat. She played well enough to be ranked No. 20 in 1962 in America, but she believes, "my most important numbers are my own: 36-26-37. I'll take those to No. 1 in tennis any day." So would her admirers.

Because of Wimbledon's fervor for tennis, there is also an aspect alien to tennis in America—although not to other sports. Wimbledon is the only tournament I know that is followed by bookmakers, who make a gambling line. There's a price on a large number of players. In 1969 I went off at 7 to 4. You put up 7 pounds to win 4, but even at that price I suppose quite a few shillings were made on me. Can you imagine trying to get a bet down on Forest Hills?

Then there are the scalpers who hang around the main gate— touts, or spivs, they're called in England. Ticket scalping is unheard of in American tennis. The demand isn't there yet. Scalping isn't against the law in England, although a tout can be pinched for blocking the sidewalk if he becomes annoying.

The top priced ticket at Wimbledon, $3.80, might be scalped for as high as $50, depending on the attraction. There's an old guy named Dick Wymark, the dean of the scalpers. He's over seventy and has been working Wimbledon since just before World War I, from his "office," a shady spot in the parking lot. Dick hands out business cards and can get you a seat for anything, maybe even at the Queen's left for tea. If he knows you, or you've been recommended, he'll mail you tickets and trust you to send him a check. "He's an honorable rogue" is the word around Wimbledon on Dick.

Opening day of the 1969 Wimbledon was rained out. First time that's happened in maybe forty years. Sometimes the place is a bloody rain forest during a tournament, but it never gets rained out. There's an elaborate system of tarpaulins, and when you feel a drop, the tarps come billowing. Play is often delayed, but the day is long in London. It stays light enough for tennis until about nine thirty, so you reckon that if you're scheduled you're going to play. Part of your match anyway.

But that first day they never got started, so I was set back twenty-four hours in playing the first match on Centre Court against the Italian Nicki Pietrangeli. Nicki has always been a master on clay, but he doesn't have much heart for the grass game, and he's getting older and less interested. The match was fast. Too fast perhaps. I wanted to spend more time on Centre.

It didn't seem to matter whether I knew much about the Centre Court or not when I played Premjit Lall in the second round. We were out on Court 4, which is right across from Centre. No grandstand. Spectators stand in the aisles between the courts. The stuffed aisles alongside Court 4 looked like a run on a shaky bank. People were jammed against the fence six or seven deep, and the ones in the last row, pinned against the fences of adjoining courts had no chance of seeing anything. But they could hear the umpire calling the score. Once in a while they could see a racket above the mob if Prem or I went up for an overhead smash. "Laver's getting beat by an Indian" was the word that ran round the grounds.

"That's what's wrong with tennis," a friend of mine said later. He had come all the way from California to see his first Wimbledon, and had good seats for Centre Court. But when "Laver's getting beat!" flashed on the grapevine that operates at every tournament, he couldn't get near Court 4. No more than a couple of hundred people out of the crowd of 30,000 that afternoon could clearly see what was happening. "If they knew what they were doing," said my friend, "they would have put your match with Lall on the Centre when it became obvious you were fighting for your life. That's where the TV is. You have to let everyone in on it if Laver is going to lose."

As far as promoting tennis in America goes, he may have something. Golf has learned that the TV cameras must be where the greatest interest is. Is Arnold Palmer in trouble on the sixteenth green? We'd better look in. If Laver is collapsing on a remote court, we'll find him a better place to come apart, if we can't get the cameras to his court. Move him into the big arena.

It would never happen at Wimbledon. "Just wouldn't do, old chap," they'd tell you. But it's worth considering for American tournaments.

Well, there I was, with my racket feeling like an old frying pan in my hand. Premjit Lall and I go back a long way together. He is a nice-looking, tall fellow, soft-spoken, a university man from Calcutta where he sometimes works as a cement salesman. Fortunately for me, some of his better cement lodged in his right elbow at a critical stage of the third set.

In 1959, the first year of Davis Cup for both of us, our countries met in Boston in the semifinal match to determine the final-round opponent for the U.S., which held the Cup. Both Neale Fraser and I beat Prem in singles, although his teammate Ramanathan Krishnan made it an exciting match by knocking me off on the opening day.

I've never lost to him, but he was clearly outplaying me as he won the first two sets. Prem is the kind of player who always makes a good showing but hardly ever can sustain good play long enough to swing a really big win or take a tournament. I kept waiting for something to go wrong with his game, and when it didn't I began to worry.

There wasn't any crispness in my volleys, and I tend to get more nervous in a match that I'm supposed to win easily. I think anybody does. You get behind and you try to make up the points too fast. This is when you should slow yourself down, and try to think about a few essentials. Watch the ball. Make sure your serve toss is high enough. Don't get helter-skelter. The pressure is all on you, but if you can just slow down—like a basketball team taking time out—then maybe you can win a few points and get the pressure shifted to the other fellow.

Prem didn't seem to be feeling any pressure though. We went to 2–2 in the third. He held for 3–2 and I won my serve for 3–3.

It was right here that I restated a very important truth about tennis to myself:

You can only lose a tennis match.

That's all.

That's the worst that can happen to you out there, and it's

happened to everybody . . . Tilden, Budge, Laver, everybody. They ate as well the next day; the sun came up; they laughed again. It's good to remind yourself of this every once in a while. I don't think anybody who played a game ever wanted to win more than I do, but losing isn't the end of the world. They don't hang you by your thumbs from the backstop or revoke your passport. They don't even deny you your daily grog.

By this I don't mean that you resign yourself to defeat as an unavoidable fact of life, and say, oh, well, tomorrow's another day. Hell no. But whenever I tell myself that all that can happen is losing, I also make sure that if I must lose it will be in my own way, the way I know best—hitting out. I'm not going to grope and puddle around and hope the other fellow comes apart. I'm going to whack the ball. I'm not very demonstrative but sometimes I shout at myself, "Hit the bloody ball!" I've got to get it through my thick head that it's the only way for me. With my topspin I can bang away without worrying about the ball carrying too far.

If I was going to lose to Premjit Lall, I was going to go out with everything blazing. Up to that moment I had been gripped by a certain fear of losing, but after I'd gotten myself straight on that, the fear disappeared. I began hitting the ball better and stayed close to Prem in that game, 30–30. I felt I'd get him there for the break, but he hit a good forehand down the line that sent me into the corner on the enclosure and I had to lob. I'd been lobbing short all through the match, and I didn't alter my pattern here. He had an easy ball at the net, but the cement settled in his elbow. He knocked the ball past me and beyond the baseline. I had the ad, then the game with a good backhand, and I never stopped. That service break began a run of 15 games, as I won 3–6, 4–6, 6–3, 6–0, 6–0.

Since I was hitting again, and not pressing, I think I would have got him anyway. But one shot can change it all. Had he made good on that smash and held his serve, I'd still have been in a shaky position serving at 3–4 and two sets down.

LESSON 16
The Crisp Volley

A good punch in the nose—that's the volley. A short, stiff jab with almost no backswing. You're blocking the ball, not stroking it.

The wrist is firm and below the racket when you punch, and you use the pace from your opponent's shot—if it's a good shot. Occasionally when a shot sits there weakly to be volleyed away you have to supply a little of your own power.

By keeping your eye on the ball intently and blocking it you can become a pretty good volleyer and a terror at an ordinary level. There is more to it than that as you progress. You will want to bevel the racket slightly so that you are hitting slightly under the ball to create a slice or underspin. This gives you more control.

Then there's footwork, without which you can't become a really fine volleyer. As you jab with your racket you're also taking a jab step into the ball. A right-hander steps in with his left foot for a forehand volley and with his right foot for a backhand. This insures that you're hitting the ball out front where a good volley must be hit.

That step is going to put more impact into your punch so that the volleys will gain length and fly to the corners and the baseline. Remember: you don't need backswing to give you depth. Meeting the ball out front with your body moving behind that jab step will do it.

To take the step you have to be side-on to the net. Not always possible in a fast match. Frequently you'll be caught head-on to the net. Then you pivot at the hips, like a baseball catcher who has to rush a throw to second base from his haunches.

"Wrong-footing" is a favorite tactic of Kenny Rosewall, and it's a good one for the volleyer once he feels he has control of the stroke. Wrong-footing is hitting to the place your opponent has just vacated, or will vacate to cover the next logical shot. He's gone to his left corner, say, to return your shot and then he dashes to his right to cover the wide opening. You wrong-foot him by volleying right back to that left corner, and if your timing is right he can't change directions to go back for the ball. But if you aren't accurate it will backfire because you may hit the ball right back at the fellow, not behind him.

Rosewall likes to do this especially with his backhand. You hit a crosscourt shot and he'll get his backhand volley on it, and rather than place it in the open corner he'll come straight back at you with the angle, and this beats an awful lot of good players. If they can spin around and get to the ball they won't do much with it and Kenny has a setup on the next shot.

When the ball is below the level of the net you're going to have to bend to get down to it. The ideal is still to keep the wrist below the racket. This will help you keep your volleys low, even the defensive volleys. If you don't bend and stay low you're going to pop your volleys up, and that's when the other guy gives you a punch in the nose with his volley.

17 A MAN NAMED GONZALES

WHILE I was getting started on my eighth Wimbledon, a good deal more attention was being devoted to Pancho Gonzales' third. It's always been Pancho grabbing the headlines, for as long as I've been a pro, and I suppose it always will be Pancho. He shows no signs of giving out, even though he periodically "retires." It was when he came out of one of those retirements in 1964 that I first began encountering him and his unpleasantness. When my son Rick was born, Mary asked me if I minded his crying. "I'm used to it," I said. "I've been listening to Pancho for five years."

I suppose I'll miss it when he's not around, but that'll be awhile. He's a grandfather now and he'll still be playing when he's a great-grandfather. I don't think he'd be in it if we were still gypsy pros. Open tennis gave him a new zest for the game, put him back in the great showcases like Wimbledon. As Pancho aged and mellowed, I don't think losing took so much out of him.

When I first played him in a pro tournament at College Park, Maryland, he was a very savage man. Toey at best. We Australians would say, "bit of a toey (edgy) bloke, Pancho," which was meant as understatement. He seemed to hate the rest of us, and himself as well when he lost. It absolutely killed him to lose. He fought you for everything, intimidated everybody in the place if he could—opponent, linesmen and umpires, ball-boys, spectators. Pancho has the air that says he's champion.

218

I remember sensing that in 1957 when I saw him first against Rosewall in a pro match at home. I never dreamed I'd be playing him. I was a teen-ager and he was getting near thirty.

If anything he's more regal today. When we're playing each other the contrast is almost comical. Me with my bowlegs and 49,000 freckles, a little guy chasing about. Him with his dark forbidding face, crowned by the black hair tinged with gray, tall, graceful, gliding. The anger, the threat of an explosion, is always near the surface. He is still capable of calling a linesman an idiot, of irresponsibly pitching his racket so that it could split a bystander's skull, of trying to strangle a photographer whose clicking irks him.

Gonzales is the master gamesman, a badgerer and moaner. Yet his legs have stayed stronger than the vitriol content in his system. He couldn't play the nearly forty-week schedule I covered in 1969, but he's able to prepare himself mentally and physically for the prime occasions, and he seems to be enjoying it more. Winning a big tournament is supposed to be beyond Pancho now, but didn't he beat Peter Curtis, Newcombe, Rosewall, Stan Smith, and Ashe in succession to win $12,500 and the Howard Hughes Open at Las Vegas at the close of 1969? Regardless of his capacity to conquer, there are dramas within a tournament that he will create and dominate.

One of those was his first round Wimbledon match against Charlie Pasarell, a twenty-five-year-old who had been the No. 1 player of the U.S. in 1967 and can beat anybody. He had Pancho beat when night came, stopping them, Charlie ahead by two sets. They had played the longest singles set in Wimbledon history, Charlie winning 24–22 and Pancho thought that was enough, insufficient light. Pancho has always worried more about seeing the ball than getting to it and hitting it. No light is ever good enough for him.

Mike Gibson, the Wimbledon referee, told Pancho to get on with it, he wasn't calling play off yet. "I realize it's difficult for the older man, but I must treat them as equals," Gibson said.

The Old Wolf howled, but Gibson wouldn't relent. The second set went to Charlie fast. Pancho gave up on it, and the gallery got on him for not trying and for bickering. Not the right spirit, old boy. And they booed him. Yes, a Wimbledon crowd booed Pancho Gonzales. My God, you wouldn't think they'd boo Hitler in that place. The boo may be a part of sport, but not at Wimbledon. Yet they gave it to Pancho.

I've played there some days when I would have welcomed a shout, a boo, even a smoker's cough. It can be so quiet on that Centre Court that you wonder if the world has ended and nobody's bothered to tell you. But that first day closed riotously with Pancho stalking off the court steaming, enveloped in a massive scolding.

He was back the next day, though, to win three straight sets and the match. Pasarell had seven match points on Pancho but couldn't grab one of them, and there was the old man putting together eleven straight points at the end to complete a magnificent five-set triumph. It took them 112 games, Wimbledon's longest match and the second longest singles ever played.

This time Pancho strode from Centre behind a broad grin and applause that lasted for a half-minute. That's a lot of clapping for a British gallery.

Pancho has known the kind of applause none of the rest of us will ever get. He's just more appealing, and this seems to increase as he ages. He gets more sympathy. This makes it difficult to play against him. Tony Roche found that out in 1968 when Pancho upset him at Forest Hills. The crowd was almost hostile to Tony, and they urged Pancho on with shouts and furious applause.

He's a loner, and never made any attempt to be anything but antagonistic in my first days as a pro. He even sued me once, and that's still the most unsettling thing that ever happened to me.

In 1963, trying to put some semblance of order in the professional game, we players formed an organization called the IPTA—International Professional Tennis Association. We made a rule that nobody could play the tournaments unless he was a member. It seemed reasonable to us, and Pancho was the only one who refused to join. Pancho always goes his own way. He insisted we had to let him play any time he wanted, and we refused.

Suddenly I was subpoenaed. So were Buchholz, Rosewall, Gimeno, and the others. Pancho was suing us for $250,000 for violation of antitrust laws. I'd never heard of antitrust. My respect for Pancho dropped to nil, although it didn't have far to drop. Here he was, slapping a suit on somebody trying to form a sound organization to help the game.

Maybe he was right, in a way, saying that we shouldn't keep him out of tournaments. But the point was it wouldn't have cost him much to join, and it was a time when pro tennis players needed solidarity to accomplish anything. They still do, but the situation isn't as precarious.

There I was in the wrong kind of court. Topspin wouldn't help me with that judge in Los Angeles, and I had to play it straight. I was a nervous wreck on the witness stand. You get so confused trying to remember things that happened long before and seemed of no importance at the time. When I now think of pressure in court, it's that trial—not Wimbledon. It took two days and cost us $7000 in legal fees. We didn't have to pay Pancho any money, but he won, getting the right to negotiate his own deals with any tournament.

In a free enterprise system, he had a point, but there were times that he got paid and the rest of us didn't and that wasn't good for us or the game. But then the game was Gonzales, as much as we hated to acknowledge it.

We knew he was mean and tough, but getting handed a subpoena one afternoon at the Los Angeles Tennis Club was a chilling thing. It happens to a lot of people, and I guess you can get sued by colleagues and even friends. But it was spooky being sued by a fellow player. Even if you didn't like him, you'd been through a lot together. And that sum of $250,000, it hit me tremendously. Where were we going to get $250,000 if Pancho won? I might work the next twenty years for my end. I suppose everybody who gets sued experiences that first moment of sweat and fear.

I could understand some of Pancho's bitterness because he

felt he'd been taken advantage of in early financial dealings. He played a head-to-head tour against Tony Trabert in 1955–56 and made only about $15,000 while Trabert, the loser, had a contract that earned him around $100,000. Pancho wanted to make his own arrangements independent of any group, and he's still enough of a drawing card to deal for himself and demand guarantees exclusive of prize money at some tournaments.

It has been a Gonzales characteristic that when he got mad he played better. If something bothered him and he began to rage—look out. This is unusual. Almost invariably the man who loses his temper loses his composure, his concentration, and his game crumbles. Not Pancho.

I hardly ever lose my temper, and almost never in a match. Nobody would put up with that sort of thing when I was a boy in Australia. Neither Charlie Hollis nor my folks would stand for any outbursts, which they considered poor sportsmanship. They also taught me that a show of temper is a great help to your opponent because it lets him know that you're disturbed and your confidence is letting down. That's generally true, except with Pancho.

Pancho would like you to lose your temper. He wants to break down your concentration with his own fuming and fussing. That's what a lot of it is about. Most of us are used to it now, and we accept it as part of the game. We still don't like it because no matter how ready we are for an explosion, we're apprehensive that the delay and his mad scene will pierce our concentration. That's the danger. While Pancho is screaming at a linesman or threatening to punch a spectator who's made a noise, you're standing there trying to put it all out of your mind, hoping your rhythm hasn't been destroyed. Another reason for his fuming is to stall and gain a time-out for himself to rest. (Everybody has stalled at one time or another, though few as theatrically as Pancho. My method of taking a break is to "accidentally" step on one of my shoes in such a way that it comes off. Then I have a few moments to make necessary adjustments.)

Most of the time you can't do anything but stand there and wait till the storm has passed. Sometimes you're the object of the storm. Either way, Pancho has made me damned mad. That was his intention, of course, but we both found out something: I also play better when I'm mad. I don't care for the feeling, and it has happened only against Gonzales.

Once in New York, at the Seventh Regiment Armory he accused me of quick-serving him. This was in the third set.

"Goddamn it, you served before I was ready," he screeched. "You've been doing it all afternoon!"

"Why have you waited till now to say anything?" I yelled, surprised to hear myself barking right back at him.

He had his racket upraised, as though he were Sitting Bull protecting the hunting ground from the white man. It wasn't a tomahawk, just a tennis racket but with Pancho enraged, would he know the difference? I wondered later if anybody had ever been scalped with a tennis racket.

"Do what you want, Pancho," I continued to yell. "You'll never upset me." My bristles were up. I got hostile and it helped. I finished off that set and won the fourth and the match, 6–1.

We've had other run-ins. Once outside of Melbourne we were screaming at each other about something or other, and the crowd was shocked because nobody'd ever heard me say a word on court. Not long ago in Bogota we were playing our hearts out in a match that meant $100 difference to the winner. In the dressing room afterward he accused me of poor sportsmanship. I nearly fell over. This sounded like the Arabs accusing the Israelis of ganging up on them. "I've really given up on you, Pancho, after a statement like that," I growled.

We began shouting, and Dennis Ralston and Fred Stolle, who were in the room, took a look at each other and got out fast. They thought it was going to be a fight. I didn't know what would happen, but I was tired of all his crap.

I certainly didn't want to fight him, though. When I was a teen-ager in Brisbane, I spent my lunch hours at Snowy Hill's Gym, trying to build myself up. I'd hit the bags and do much of the same training the boxers did. "Discourage that kid," I remember hearing one of the hangers-on advise Snowy. "A

scrawny mug with his awful coordination will get himself killed."
I couldn't punch then, and I doubt if I can now, very effectively,
but I thought I might get a chance to try. But Pancho and I
just yelled, and we finished the day playing gin rummy together.

It's just as well nothing happened. I've seen Pancho punch
steel lockers after losing a match, and tear up dressing rooms.

Pancho will never be one of the boys, but he's getting looser
and more friendly. He can be very charming—women have
known that for years. I don't think Richard Burton, Errol Flynn,
or Giovanni Casanova ever did any better with the sheilas than
Pancho.

I think his coolness toward the rest of us was partly a natural
aloofness and partly a design to set us on edge and stoke himself up. It helped him to think he disliked us, to build up a
hate for us—to think of us as the enemy. I can see how that
could work once in a while—for a big game in a team sport or
for a fight. But when you're playing somebody night after night,
only a Pancho could keep it up.

I'd heard all about him from Hoad and Rosewall and the
others. But I was brought up to regard everybody as a good guy.
I was anxious to meet Pancho and get along with him. He didn't
want to say hello. The first time I played him I beat him. He
was madder than a wet hen, so mad I thought he wasn't going
to shake hands. He just brushed my hand with his and stormed
off.

We played for the second time shortly after that at White
Plains, New York. I won the first set, 6–0, and I'll wager that
hasn't happened to Pancho more than a few times. I was ahead
3–1 in the second, a best-of-three match, and I figured the old
boy was really over the hill.

That's the first time I made that mistake. Pancho not only
beat me but he came back from two sets down to take Rosewall
in the final.

A Philadelphia columnist, Jim Barniak, has lamented: "Laver
doesn't have charisma. If you asked him what charisma was he'd
think you were referring to the Romanian junior champion."
Please, Mr. Barniak, everybody knows the Romanian junior

champ is Marcu, not Charisma. Charisma won ten years ago.

I know I don't have it. Pancho does. I understand that, and I'm glad he does. With it Pancho has helped to hold the game together. Pancho's personality puts people in the seats.

When he comes to town, a newspaperman can write about tantrums, sex appeal, flamboyance—and occasionally tennis.

I appreciate him more now, he amuses me. There's depth to the man I didn't recognize before, and a generosity in advising younger players.

But when he's out there on court he's still Pancho the bastard. I didn't mind Pancho having his show, and I expect this verdict of history: that 1969 was as much his Wimbledon as mine. I might have won the title, but I never was involved in a match as incredible as his triumph over Pasarell. Pancho always finds a way to upstage you.

Playing Against Familiar Opponents

I guess it can look rehearsed when Kenny Rosewall and I play each other. We've gone through it so often that there simply isn't anything new we can introduce by way of a surprise. Maybe if he started missing his backhands I'd be surprised—and pleased.

Principally what I have to do is just play my own game, and try to play it better than he plays his. I've got to jump on a short ball and get to the net. If I get lulled into rallying from the baseline with him I'm going to get killed.

It isn't likely that you'll run into somebody as often as I do Rosewall, and possibly there is something extra you can do to vary your pattern if you're having trouble with a certain opponent. You know each other very well, but is there a shot you haven't used that you can work on privately and spring on this guy—a drop shot, a lob, a chipped return? Something he's never seen from you that will complicate his estimate of you?

Try to analyze the pattern of your matches with this fellow. What is he murdering you with? Net rushing? Have you been lobbing enough? Or have you been trying too hard to hit perfect passing shots? Would blasts right at him, or soft shots at his feet be a different counter? Have you been trying to run him from one side to the other without much success—if so, how would he respond to a few drop shots to draw him in, followed by lobs?

If you think over your previous matches carefully, I'm pretty sure you'll see the need and place for something a little different.

But if you've been beating the guy, or playing him satisfactorily, well just keeping playing your game and enjoying it.

18 A FEW WORDS FROM MARY LAVER

MARY AND I were amused by an old friend from Boston named Jerome Scheuer, who was over for his first Wimbledon at the age of eighty. Jerry is a stern-looking, white-haired gentleman, bent over, and always turned out immaculately in suit and tie whatever the weather. I've been seeing him at tournaments ever since I started coming to America, and most of us had the vague idea he invented tennis. He knows as much about the game, the techniques, and the players as anybody I've encountered. He knows our styles better than we do ourselves. Maybe that isn't unusual, because there are a lot of good players who haven't any idea what they're doing except hitting the ball. When you become acquainted with him you realize that Jerry has a fine sense of humor—except about one thing: the greatest player of all time. That was Bill Tilden. Jerry has watched all the greats, and known most of them, as a buff since 1905, when he fancied a bloke named Harold Hackett (one of America's most successful doubles players). We go through the argument at least once a year, and Jerry won't budge on the subject of Tilden being the best. Neither will Allison Danzig, who was one of the supreme tennis writers during forty-five years with *The New York Times*.

227

"But, Jerry," Andres Gimeno will yip, "all modern athletes are better. Equipment is better. Competition is wider, conditions are tougher. The schedule is longer. They used to win with groundstrokes on grass. You can't do that no more."

"Tilden would pass any of you big servers and volleyers," Scheuer answers. "You never saw groundstrokes like his. He'd outvolley you, too, and whenever he needed an ace he'd serve it. On certain days Don Budge may have been as good, but Tilden uniformly was the best."

It's been thirty years since Budge's prime. Although he doesn't think anyone has come along to rival Budge, much less Tilden, Jerry still savors the game, and he thinks I play well. I'm grateful for that. He also regards tennis players as artists.

Sometimes when I question what I'm doing, spending my life chasing a little white ball around—wondering if there's really any point to it—I feel better thinking of Jerry. I suppose at one time or another everybody has doubts about his occupation being worthwhile and his contributions to mankind.

Jerry scoffs at that. "Why, the pleasure you give people who watch is immeasurable. You can't imagine the service you render through entertainment. You do wonders for me, not to mention the young you inspire to take up this healthful game."

I like that.

Jan Leschly, the Dane, has a nice way of saying things too. After I beat him in the third round, I said, "Hard luck, Jan."

He replied, "No, it was good to be out here, to be part of it." Jan's a lovely guy, a rarity, an excellent player whose greatest joy isn't winning but playing. Maybe it's something uniquely Danish. Torben Ulrich, fit and happy and finally turned professional at the age of forty, has that outlook. "Pancho gives great happiness," Torben said after losing the enchanting five-setter those antiques put on at Forest Hills. "It is good to watch the master." Jan and Torben try hard, but they realize that after all it's just a game.

Premjit Lall was good for me. That match showed me I wasn't concentrating fully. Wimbledon is a very tricky place because it lasts two weeks. So does the French, but there isn't as much importance attached to it. When you get to Wimbledon you want to go all out on every point. That's the feeling you have, but there's a danger of burning yourself out too early. There's a delicate balance between killing yourself and playing well enough to win. You have to save something for the long pull, pace yourself, build up for the tough ones. But what's the use of careful pacing if you lose to a Lall in the second round? You've got plenty left for next week, but you're spending next week on the practice court.

Once I won my first set from Lall, the rest of the match was relatively easy, but I became aware that it wasn't enough just to show up. I had to concentrate thoroughly and hit the shots.

Having Mary with me at the Dolphin Square helped immensely. We'd go out for dinner once in a while with a few friends, to a place we like called the Ponte Vecchio on the old Brompton Road. It's a gathering spot for pros when we're in London. But if we didn't feel like leaving the flat, she'd fix a steak and we'd watch television. Not the tennis, though, which comes on every night in partial replay of the day's big matches. I don't like to watch much tennis. I don't want to have it on my mind all the time. Sometimes a reporter would come over for a few minutes, but I discourage that during a big tournament. When I'm not actually playing, I try to guard my time. I want to rest, and spend it with Mary if she's around. I don't like distractions, unless I create them myself to keep my mind off the tournament. Too many players lose matches by mulling them over beforehand.

Mary has observed me closer than anybody. She knows me better than I do, and I'm going to let her take over here for a few paragraphs to give her impressions:

"It was interesting the way Rod and I never talked about the Grand Slam in 1969. We knew he was going for this thing, that he had a goal, and it was good for his game to have a goal. It wasn't superstition, but we just didn't talk about it.

"I don't think athletes do dwell on something like this. That's the sportswriters' job. Each tournament is an individual matter, that's the way Rod feels. There was no sense lumping them together in his mind. Play them one at a time, to use the cliché.

"It's always amazed me how loose and easygoing he is, particularly when the pressure builds. I thought he might show nerves a bit in 1968, the first time back at Wimbledon, and he had every reason to with all that went wrong. He had the bad wrist—eventually developing into the bad elbow—and half-way through the tournament his right foot became infected, the infection spreading up the leg.

"Nobody knew. That's the Aussie code—never let on. He was strapping his wrist before every match, but never in the dressing room where the word would get around. It wasn't only the show-must-go-on bit. He didn't want to give anybody he played a lift from knowing he wasn't completely right.

"So just before he was to play we'd go to a phone booth on the grounds and crowd inside while I wrapped the wrist. It looked like we were trying to revive the booth-stuffing fad of the late 1950s. The way we sneaked around to avoid being noticed we seemed like spies making a contact.

"The foot problem came from a blister. We were lucky that Dr. Norm Rudy, a friend from Los Angeles, was staying at the Dolphin Square, too. He came to our room in the middle of the night, lanced the blister and took care of everything. Rod was playing the next day.

"During a tournament as important as Wimbledon, you may share a bedroom and most of the day with Rod, but he's not really with you. I mean his mind is somewhere else. He gets quiet. He'll converse some, but never remembers what he's said. Most people think of him as a quiet person anyway, but this lapse into near silence was new for me when he took me to tournaments after we were married. Rod and I hit it off right away when we met, and we always have a million things to say to each other. I had to get used to the quietness of tournament time.

"But I don't mean he gets moody. Nothing can upset him. He's got the happiest attitude I've ever seen, the ideal temperament for what he's doing. He actually thrives on all the travel.

He wants to have his day filled with things to do, unlike Pancho Gonzales, for instance, who wants to be left alone. Some players get overloaded with business commitments. On the surface Rod looks like one of them, always going here and there for commercial appearances and appointments. But the more things he does, and the tighter his schedule becomes, the faster his mind works on whatever he's doing.

"He doesn't like to just sit and think. He never worries about a match, or thinks much about it until just a few minutes before he goes onto the court. Then he wants to be by himself and go over his plans and preparation.

"Until then I doubt that it even crosses his mind who he's playing. Yet somewhere down there, below the consciousness, something is getting him revved up and is fixing his attention on the job without making him fluttery. I think that's what's going on when he's so detached: the automatic buildup within.

"Keeping busy is his way of consciously avoiding thinking too much about the day's match. He does the shopping when we're on the road, and the laundry and other errands. He has his favorite markets in London, and often at Dolphin Square he'll do the cooking. He had to in 1969 because I pulled a stomach muscle trying to open a stubborn window and was on the casualty list myself for a few days.

"That doesn't mean he's another Escoffier. He's an Australian —steak and eggs three times a day wouldn't seem odd to him. At least he fixes those well.

"Wimbledon in 1969 presented a folksy portrait of the champion that nobody saw but me. The Rocket bustling between his pots and pans, soaking his elbow with the hydroculator one minute and checking on the dinner the next . . . scooping up the soiled tennis clothes for a run to the laundromat . . . jollying up the pregnant wife and asking if the kid has kicked lately. The hero of Centre Court was also a behind-the-scenes domestic dynamo.

"Sometimes we'll take the limousine service to Wimbledon that's furnished to all the players. More often Rod will drive himself. I like the limousines. Rod drives the way he plays tennis: he keeps things spinning. They're hairy rides, but he knows London and he prides himself on taking a different route to the tournament every time we make the forty-five-minute drive. That's another of his little routines to put his mind on something else.

"People ask me about his ravaged fingernails that he's chewed nearly to the elbow. They think he must be awfully nervous. That's the only outward sign, and it's diminishing. I've put him on a diet of thumbs. Chew those and let the other eight grow up normally. He says he's chewing less and enjoying it more.

"But what he seems to be worrying about is somebody else. His heaviest chewing is done while he's watching a match. Or television, or a movie. *Butch Cassidy* came close to giving him the look of Venus de Milo. He loves cowboy flicks and must have seen *Butch* twenty times. If he's watching a Western on TV, I can hear his chomping over the gunfire.

"He had no business winning the U.S. Pro tournament in Boston right after Wimbledon. I was mad at him. He was due a mild slump; he'd come off grass to a very slow synthetic fiber court in the space of a couple of days. But nothing can discourage him more than momentarily.

"The worst thing that can happen to a tennis player is to lose his zest for the game. From what I've seen this is rather common. They get tired of playing so much. Or the traveling. They want to spend more time with families that are growing up. Maybe they're getting older and losing more.

"We hear a fellow say, 'You won't see me next year.' Then he'll be back on the circuit because it's still the only way he knows to make such a good living.

"I don't want that to happen to Rod. I don't see any sign of it, but if he gets tired of tennis I want him to quit. We've tried to manage his money so that he won't feel economic pressure or think he has to play to pay the mortgage. If he wants to get out, he'll be able to.

"But I don't see a man who loves it like Rod leaving for quite a while. It's life to him.

"If the pressure was a little heavier than usual in 1969 because of the Slam, the baby helped counteract it. Rod was really excited about becoming a father. He wanted a boy and got what he wanted: Rick Rodney Laver. He thinks Paris was the hardest work of the Slam year—but that's only because he wasn't the one who had Rick.

"He delivered the Slam, and I delivered the heir. Neither of us could have improved on our performances and we didn't try. Rod decided not to enter the Australian Open in 1970 because the money was so low. One night he said, 'Guess I won't be trying for a repeat this year, Mary.'

" 'Well, dear, neither will I,' I replied.

"We didn't want to be ostentatious."

The Care and Feeding of a Tennis Player

Mary said it all in that chapter.

19 THE THIRD LEG OF THE SLAM: WIMBLEDON

ALTHOUGH ARTHUR ASHE had the reputation and publicity, twenty-two-year-old Stan Smith was the best American of 1969. His dedication could keep him up there for a long time. He, Cliff Richey, and Marty Riessen were the only Americans to beat me during the year, and Stan pushed me harder than anybody else at Wimbledon. Maybe after beating him in straight sets in Paris I allowed my mind to wander in the third set of this match. I won the first two and I might have finished it in three, but Stan wouldn't let me.

He kept coming at me with more determination than ever. At six feet four inches he's nearly as tall as the Italian Orlando Sirola, my first Wimbledon opponent back in 1956. But Stan is a lot more agile and competitive. As a boy in Pasadena, with his size 13 feet, he was so clumsy he was turned down as a ballboy for the U.S.-Mexico Davis Cup match of 1963. Six years later, a star graduate of a self-imposed conditioning program, he was making me look like a ballboy in the third, fourth, and fifth sets.

He began attacking on return of serve as well as on his own booming serve that came out of the sky. He seemed to get to the net in one stride, towering there with bleached head like the

Matterhorn. His reach left no openings for passing shots, and lobs had to be dead perfect to clear him. When he won the third set his confidence began climbing, and I could tell he now felt he could beat me. You shouldn't let a Stan Smith get into that mood.

He won the fourth set by simply outhitting me. I wasn't playing badly. My game was grooved now, and I had only brief, insignificant letdowns the rest of the way. But Stan had the scent of fricasseed Laver, and he kept coming to win his serve for 1–0 in the fifth and take the next two points to pin me at 0–30. That was a very uncomfortable set. Although I didn't lose my serve, I was behind in every service game.

Backhands pulled me out of it, plus very concentrated serving. I made sure to get the first ball into play. A couple of spinning backhands into the corners got me the service break, and I held for 3–1.

Smith became only more determined. A service break like that in the fifth set will usually make a young, relatively inexperienced player feel the weight of the situation, make it easier for him to rationalize and accept the impending "good loss," as it's called. Not Stan. He never stopped thinking he could win. He's strong and he kept the power coming, his flat volleys zinging across the grass. Usually I counter power well and break it down, but Stan kept me too rushed.

Each time I served I was lucky to escape, but at 5–3, when I was serving for the match, he looked certain to pull even, cornering me at 0–40. He had three chances to break. I had to serve a little better, get to the net an instant quicker, volley a shade deeper. When I left the court after doing just that to win five successive points, I thought if he had broken me it probably would have been my downfall. Stan was so tough and unrelenting when behind that a break would have put wings on his confidence. I don't think I could have fended him off.

Smith left the court dejected, but also knowing that he had it in him to beat me. It makes life that much harder when another good player has that revelation. I'm in the business of thwarting and breaking confidence, not building it. It's built in

Stan now, and will take some flogging. The next time we played, four months later, he did beat me.

In America's first open, at Forest Hills in 1968, the prize money was $100,000 and first prize for men's singles was $14,000. Frankly, the thought of all that money petrified me. I kept thinking about how recently we pros had been pleased to play a week-long tournament for $8000 total. Now they were going to pay the winner $14,000, the biggest pot ever for a tennis player.

I could never get with it. I haven't felt like that before or since, yet it seemed to be a foregone conclusion to everyone else that I'd win. I kept thinking the tenseness would leave me, but it didn't. My elbow bothered me a little, but that's not why Cliff Drysdale beat me in the fourth round. After all, I led two sets to one, and then he mopped me up, 6–1, 6–1. I could hardly put a serve in the court, and Cliff just knocked the ball by me with his tricky, baseball-swing backhand. Drysdale isn't the first two-hander, but he's the best of a current group that includes Frew McMillan of South Africa, Mike Belkin of Canada, Jim McManus, Jimmy Connors, Harold Solomon, and Chris Evert of the U.S., and Ismail El Shafei of Egypt. Of course, Pancho Segura was the king of the two-fisted swingers.

A right-hander, Drysdale uses his two-hander for the backhand. Some feel it's his weaker side, but I wonder. The strength of it is you can't pick it. You don't know where he's going to go with it. I was still having trouble solving him two weeks before Wimbledon when Cliff beat me in the West of England Open at Bristol. Bristol and the London Grass Court Open at Queen's Club are the prime tune-ups for Wimbledon, and I don't take the results very seriously. I use them to reaccustom myself to grass, a surface the pros don't see much of, and to get ready for the big one.

But when Drysdale beat me at Bristol he must have felt he had my number. I hadn't expected to play him in 1969 at Wimbledon because he needed to get by Roy Emerson. The porch off the players' lounge overlooked their court, and periodically I strolled out to check the score. It was a hard match, but as I suspected, Emmo took control and was serving for the victory at 7–6 in the fifth set. I left because Emmo never lets anybody out of that hole. Later I was surprised to hear that Drysdale did get out, and here he was in the quarterfinals with me.

Also in the quarters on our side were Arthur Ashe and Bob Lutz. If Pancho Gonzales hadn't established himself as Wimbledon's most startling performer, the honor would have gone to Lutz, a brash, carefree Southern Californian whose third-round victory over Ken Rosewall left the gallery uncertain of their feelings. Rosewall is a darling of the English. They—and he—greatly regret that Wimbledon is the only really big title to elude him. Kenny had trained himself fine for this one, and it appeared to be the last time he'd be capable of going all the way. Then Lutz, a twenty-two-year-old, stepped off a plane and into his first money tournament, and bashed fourth-seeded Rosewall in four sets.

In his last match as an amateur, Lutz had been beaten by somebody named Mike Estep in the National Intercollegiates at Princeton. "I got bored playing college kids," Lutz alibied that defeat. "But how can you get bored playing Ken Rosewall, when there's money on the line?"

I understood. Normally an upset by a bright new face is well received, but it was hard to enjoy the demise of Rosewall. Lutz might have the greatest potential of any of the good young Americans, but he also has great talent for the dolce vita and may not spare enough time for tennis or be as diligent as his doubles partner, Stan Smith.

The other half of the draw had narrowed to Tony Roche, whom I beat in the 1968 final, and Clark Graebner; John Newcombe and the Dutchman Okker.

I wasn't thinking about any of them. Actually when a tournament like Wimbledon begins I don't pay attention to the draw, trying to figure who I'll meet as the tournament moves along. My feeling is I have to win seven matches. I have to be ready for seven good efforts. But now that it was Drysdale I felt that the championship hinged on this match. His is a strange style that bothers me, and although, except for Lutz, Cliff was the least formidable of the survivors, he might indeed know the way to beat me, as he claimed the summer before at Forest Hills.

Cliff's a smoothy, tall and slim, a good-looking South African who could talk a Kreuger Park lion into becoming a vegetarian. After his big victory over me at Forest Hills, he described to the press how he had directed his shots at certain patches of grass on the court that were greener, thus slicker, so that I had more trouble coping with the skid. I don't think anybody is that accurate, and I don't know if it works anyway. The reason I lost was I served so miserably. But it was his hour, deservedly, and his theories gave the journalists a nice new twist.

There was no doubt that his style bothered me, and I decided I'd better do something to throw him off. You can't keep playing the same pattern against a man who's been beating you. My plan was to vary my net rushing. Sometimes I'd stay back when I served, which is almost unheard of in championship men's tennis on grass. This threw him off. His short, angled returns had been landing around my feet and were difficult to volley or half-volley. By staying back, I could move in on them easily and take the net with a strong approach shot. I began to attack against his serve, which isn't too strong, and put him on the defensive right away. I was wary of him and keen, and he didn't react quickly enough to my new tactics. I got the jump and beat him in the day's fastest match, 6–4, 6–2, 6–3.

The unexpected may throw your opponent way off. The simplest shot can bring the most astounding error if it's a shot he's not looking for. Drysdale couldn't believe it whenever I stayed back on my serve. He had the whole court to return to, and frequently missed it altogether.

Jaroslav Drobny risked all—and collected—with the unexpected shot on the biggest point of his life: match point in the 1954 Wimbledon final against Rosewall. Drobny led two sets to one and 8–7 in the fourth, his serve, but Kenny was wearing him down, killing him with passing shots off that rapier backhand. They went to deuce, and Drob got the ad. One more point. One more assault. If Drob had enough left he'd put it into one last charge, wouldn't he? He went to the baseline, and Kenny set himself to return the buzzing left-handed serve beyond Drob's net-rushing reach. But there was no buzzing serve, and no assault of the net. Drob just patted a soft one to Kenny's backhand and stood there and watched. For an instant Rosewall was startled. He'd begun his swing. He tried to change it to compensate, couldn't, and he knocked the ball meekly into the net.

It was almost insulting. But it was the unexpected in spades— and it worked.

LESSON 19

The Backhand and Topspin

One of the great mental blocks in tennis that shouldn't be there is the backhand. How many people do you hear moaning about their backhand? And avoiding the opportunity to hit it whenever they can?

Usually you learn the forehand first. I think you should start out with the backhand, and stop listening to those who say it's a hard shot.

Why should it be? It's the most natural shot there is—just letting your arm roll out to its full length. Try to think of it that way: unwinding.

Have you been ducking your backhand when you practice? That's what practice is for, you know, to work on the things you don't do well— not to keep tuning up your assets.

Not many players have a topspin backhand. The wrist has to be very strong, even specially built up. I strengthened mine by squeezing tennis balls and lifting pulley weights. I recommend that because in lifting weights you're even using the motion of turning the wrist over. A topspin backhand is nifty for me, Arthur, and a few others. It helps us make a nice living, but it isn't a must by any means.

I'd say that 90 percent of the world's backhands are slices. Anybody who tells you he's hitting a pure flat backhand isn't entirely correct, I'll wager. He's getting under the ball a shade anyway, slicing it a bit.

No reason why it shouldn't be that way. Slice keeps the ball low, helps you control the stroke, and is a good approach shot.

But I think you should experiment with your game. If you think you can topspin a ball—try it. If you want to really hit the ball hard on the backhand, you'll have to consider topspin. It's the only way, then.

At any level of play you have to get that lead shoulder all the way around—right shoulder for a right-hander. Get the shoulder around,

241

hit the ball in front of the front foot, and let your arm unwind, and you've got it.

Repeat after me: the backhand is a cinch. Look at it that way, and you'll see I'm right.

20 THREE DOWN AND ONE TO GO

WE WERE in the second week now, with the singles well spaced to allow a day's rest after each. Within five days of the opening week I played four matches. All that remained in the last four days were the semifinal with Arthur Ashe and the final with John Newcombe.

The impact of Arthur Ashe on tennis is incredible. Probably the best thing that happened to the game in 1968 was that I didn't win the U.S. Open at Forest Hills and he did.

He had the right combination to make the world, especially America, notice: he was black, he was American, he was exciting —a big hitter—he was articulate and he knew his way around. He was new and different, and tennis needed that. His picture was on the cover of *Life* Magazine, his face and voice on nationwide TV programs, and suddenly the public was fully conscious of a tennis player. No American had won at Forest Hills in thirteen years, and no black man had ever won a major championship. Arthur at once was an athletic-political figure, a champion considered a spokesman for blacks.

It was, and is, an awesome role. Sometimes Arthur seems to act as though the world is on his shoulders. But the fact is that pressures on him from all sides must be terrific. I can't imagine how it would be to walk in his shoes. I'm pretty much content to hit tennis balls and mind my family. If that's all there was—

and it's plenty for me—on Arthur's mind, he might have caught up with me by now. I don't think he ever will, though, because he's going in so many different directions. This is what it must be to be a sensitive, concerned Negro celebrity in America today. Perhaps Arthur would have a better chance to fulfill his tennis potential if there were other blacks playing. He wouldn't be the only one. He wouldn't have to be all things. I imagine in baseball, basketball, and football the abundance of blacks makes it easier for all of them. Some are militant, some complacent, some confused, some sure of themselves. I don't know much about the problem, but in other sports you have a range of behavior and feeling among the blacks, just as you do among whites.

With Arthur, he's the one. Would Jackie Robinson have done so well if no other blacks had moved into baseball soon after his lead? I don't know. But every time I'm impatient with Arthur for seeming to squander his tennis talent, or not working hard enough on his game, I tell myself that I can't really fit into his sneakers.

Arthur's 1968 Forest Hills luster had tarnished and he was playing abominably. If you were an Ashe follower at Wimbledon you had wall-to-stomach-wall ulcers by the time he came onto Centre with me for the semis. He'd lost the first two sets in the first round to an obscure South African, Terry Ryan, and twice the tiny Englishman, Graham Stilwell, had a chance to serve out their match in the fifth set.

But Wimbledon is the chance to make everything all right forever for a tennis player. Arthur had the firepower on that fast grass to blow me off the court and keep right on going to the world title. He was very capable of two hot matches now. He's like me—high for Wimbledon—and his best tennis burst forth in that first set, far above anything I had imagined for him. He played that set as well as a man can play. I was doing all right, but Arthur was knocking fireballs everywhere, and Centre Court was roaring.

I thought, if he keeps this up it's all over. There's not much to do about it except hope that he cools. Arthur's history tells you he's streaky and won't keep it up forever, but that isn't very comforting with balls shooting by. I was certain he couldn't maintain the pace for five sets, but the way he was going three might have been enough.

Arthur flies at the ball, and thrashes at it all-out. He's best on the backhand, and I started to pour my serve onto his forehand in the second set. The backhand had been burning me too much. His forehand was all right, too, but it wasn't so unbearable. The ball was staying in play and I began to whack a few winners, too.

I was feeling the kind of pressure I like, the challenge of a very good player in a very important match. I don't know exactly why I respond so well in this kind of situation. I just play with feeling—if I feel the ball can be hit I just hit the damn thing.

We were bombing each other, taking great swipes like fighters throwing Sunday punches. Arthur had prepared carefully, practicing against three left-handers—Jim McManus, Torben Ulrich, and Niki Pilic—so that left-handed spin would be no mystery whatsoever.

But if you can't reach the ball it doesn't matter which way it's spinning. I needed to hit a few beyond Arthur's reach to edge my way into the match. He was hammering everything he could get to, but I connected with three beauts that outran those long legs of his to take his serve and go ahead 4-2 in the second set.

For the first time I had the feeling that I was doing more than just hanging on. Before Arthur could check this surge I'd won six straight games and led 2-0 in the third.

Then he hit a few that ran from me like greyhounds—three magnificent backhands that broke my serve. We were both serving extremely well, and I was serving more aces than usual. We stayed neck-and-neck to 7-all.

I held for 8-7, and I could sense that his fine edge was wearing off just a bit. Arthur was having some trouble with his volleying. He doesn't bend his knees enough to get down to the ball, and when his touch goes off a shade it's his volleying that suffers most. I was trying to chip my returns low to make him reach for the volley, and he was reaching as though the ball was a cobra, sort of poking. He wouldn't get down to it, and his volleys were going into the net.

That's the way the third set ended, with him netting a volley, and I'd finally gotten on top of him. Now, I had to keep him down.

The ball was looking as big as a soccer ball to me. That's the way it is when you're dug in and knocking off everything. I had the first game with my serve, and I wanted the second.

I pushed him to 15–40, but he seemed to have the first break-point saved when he moved me out of position in the rear of the court so that he could baby a volley just over the net.

It was a good place for a drop volley because I was so far out of the play, about thirty feet from the ball when it bounced softly on my side of the court. I was running forward when he tapped the ball, figuring it for the logical shot.

The ball began to come down a second time, and nobody in the place thought I could get it. I wasn't thinking about the possibilities, just going for it in a mad dash like somebody trying to catch an egg rolling off a table across the room.

Later, after I'd won, 2–6, 6–2, 9–7, 6–0, Arthur said, "Speed is what Laver beats you with." And Fred Stolle remarked, "The reason Rocket gets balls like that drop volley is he plays every shot in practice just as hard. It's just second nature for him to go after every ball in practice, even the no-chance kind, and not let it bounce more than once. He's made himself want to hit every ball regardless of the circumstances. This attitude transfers to matches. He wasn't that quick as a kid. I think his work on the practice court gave him that extra step."

It had to be extra to get me within a shout of that ball. Moving so fast I wondered if I'd go through the net, I got my racket under the ball just before it touched down again and flicked it over Arthur's head.

He seemed transfixed by my sprint, certain with everyone else that I wouldn't make it. Now it was his turn to run. He pivoted and those giant strides of his got him to the ball, but he didn't have time to hit much of a shot. His backhand was in the net.

It was 2–0 and I wanted 3–0. Then it was 3–0 and I wanted 4–0. I guess this is the killer instinct. Whatever it is, I had no thought of relaxing. I had Arthur down and I was going to pound him. I never have any plan of trying for a love set, but each game I won made me want to win more. I was afraid of Arthur, afraid to let down for an instant until I had that sixth game. When it ended 6–0 I was stunned, but relieved that I'd been able to turn him off by turning myself on.

I was in my sixth straight Wimbledon final. Each time a different opponent: losing to Alex Olmedo in 1959 and Neale Fraser in 1960, beating Chuck McKinley in 1961, Marty Mulligan in 1962 and Tony Roche in 1968.

A couple of Englishmen did as well in the early days of the game. Willis Renshaw won seven titles between 1881 and 1889, and Laurie Doherty was in six finals between 1898 and 1906, winning five. I think I've got a chance to break Renshaw's record of final round appearances and championships. I'll bet on it if I can find a bookmaker to give me the right price. But not too much.

In those old days, in fact until 1922, Wimbledon used the challenge-round system. This meant that the champion didn't have to risk defeat by going through the tournament the following year. He was automatically placed in the final, and the survivor of the tournament challenged the champ for the title. Thus in winning a record six straight times (1881–86) Willis Renshaw played only one match per tournament in the years after he battled through the entire draw in 1881. Fred Perry, champion in 1934–36, had to play through, and it was his streak of 21 straight Wimbledon match wins that stood as a record until I completed the 1969 tournament with 28.

John Newcombe came into the final over Okker and Roche, and he came with the idea that he could beat me. He got that idea two weeks previously a few miles away at Queen's Club when he defeated me in the London Open. Just a trial match in my mind, but in the mind of the man who beats you it must have more meaning. His confidence increases.

Newcombe is muscular, strong, well trained—and also bright. Although he made his name as a slugger, he can be thoughtful and patient, too. He demonstrated this earlier in the season by winning two of the biggest clay court events, the Italian and the British Hard Court.

In 1963 you began hearing of Newcombe as a surprise selection to play for Australia against the U.S. in the Davis Cup final. He was strictly a 19-year-old banger then, the son of a Sydney dentist who wisely cancelled his appointments for a few days after John was selected. Dr. Newcombe felt he'd be too nervous to take up his instruments during the matches, and his patients were grateful for his decision. John lost both his matches, to Dennis Ralston and Chuck McKinley, as the Yanks took the Cup. His game needed refining and he dropped out of sight for a while until he reached the Forest Hills final in 1966 and then became Wimbledon's last amateur champion in 1967.

Now he had a pretty good plan, but I have to admit that once into the Wimbledon final, I never thought I'd lose. Centre Court is where I get the feeling I can beat anybody—Tilden's ghost, Budge thirty years ago, Pancho twenty years ago. Anybody. Bring them in. I don't mean to sound like Cassius Muhammad Ali Clay, but the place makes me feel important, bigger, stronger. I feel very tall walking out there. This atmosphere can bring out the best in a player, or it can ruin him. I've seen excellent players, not fellows you'd call chokers, destroyed by Centre Court nerves. The crowd can destroy a man, too, if they fall in love with his opponent.

When I'm on Centre Court in the final this is what my life has been about, a day I've worked for from the first swats on that antbed court in Langdale. Maybe more people watched me on this day in 1969 than ever watched all the tennis matches ever played before because Tel-Star was carrying it around the world. That's something to think about before you hit a ball—or pick your nose. You make sure your fly is zipped up before you walk into all those living rooms, and your hair is combed when you genuflect toward the royal box.

Centre Court is where I live.

There's no electric chair waiting when you complete the tennis player's last mile, the walk from the dressing room to Centre, only a tall, green umpire's chair dominating the grassy chamber. You will get out of the place alive . . . you think . . . but you're not sure. Sometimes you don't care. A player can feel so mortified that he wishes they'd just turn on the juice and fry him right there. For me it would be death in the cathedral, and not a bad place to pass on.

After I beat him in the 1968 final, Tony Roche sighed, "I just wanted to find a hole out there and crawl in and cover myself up—but there was no place to get away from the Rocket."

Wimbledon nerves are worst before you go on Centre. I've seen blokes change clothes two or three times, check new socks for holes, pace the dressing room floor, do any number of little things that they think may put off the walk to Centre. They're just kidding themselves, of course. When Peter Morgan comes in and says it's time to go, we're always ready. We know there's no deviation from punctuality in that place. We aren't dragged screaming, but sometimes our legs feel like silly putty.

It's always the same when you march out for the final. E. G. Bulley, the locker attendant, carries your rackets and the referee, Mike Gibson, walks along to make sure you don't get lost on the way, which is all of fifteen yards. Above the doorway to the court is that sign: "If you can treat those two impostors . . ." or some bloody thing. [The line, "If you can meet with Triumph and Disaster/And treat those two impostors just the same," from Kipling's poem "If," appears on that signboard as well as a similar one above the marquee entrance to the stadium court at Forest Hills.]

You enter, bow along with your opponent and then begin the warm-up, which in England is called the knock-up. The expression is hilarious to Americans because it means something entirely different in their language.

Contrary to American custom, you are never introduced to

the crowd by the umpire, a public address announcer, or anyone else. The English consider it superfluous, feeling that anybody in Centre who doesn't know Newcombe from Laver should be under surveillance by Scotland Yard.

By this time the court looks like a faded billiard table, the grass scuffed and worn. But it plays like a new billiard table— fast, level, true. After the terrific pounding the courts aren't the handsome lawns we began on two weeks before. But they never betray you. The bounce can still be depended on.

I looked up at Mary, lovely in a bright yellow dress and a matching ribbon in her dark hair. She'd gone into the tank for the Ashe match, but she wouldn't miss this one. When I played Arthur, Mary wasn't feeling well and she stayed at the flat and tried to watch on TV. Her answer to tension is the bathtub. She got so nervous that she took three baths during the match, finishing the afternoon as the super-clean wife of a winner.

Newcombe was at home here, too. Any man who has won Wimbledon feels a kinship for Centre, and John had won there as often as I, considering his three doubles championships.

John knew I liked pace, and he wasn't going to give me any. Good thinking. He wanted to jerk me around, and he did it skillfully. He chipped his returns instead of hitting away in his usual fashion. When I came to the net he tried to lob over me. I spent a lot of time looking at the sky. Hitting repeated overheads can be tiring. Though I won the first set I began to miss my smashes in the second and he took that one.

The crowd liked it. The champion was in danger, and when Newcombe dashed ahead to 4–1 in the third they knew it would be a fight. Wonderful. Exciting finals aren't the rule at Wimbledon. Actually they're rare. It seems true of most tournaments that the close, exciting matches occur everywhere but the final. Not always, fortunately, but too often. If Gonzales and Pasarell's first-rounder had been the final it would have been an all-time sporting occasion. It seldom works out that way.

I was at 1–4, down a break with everybody hoping that the things would get even tougher for me. That was all right. The annoyance at taking Lall too lightly, the concern of getting into a fifth set with Smith, the apprehension about Drysdale, and the fear that Ashe wouldn't come down to earth were behind me. Now I was on my stage, one that I knew and loved, and it was up to me to strut like a proud player and do my act.

My serve, so good at the start of the match, had been going way off in the third set, culminating with a double fault at game point for the break that sent Newcombe ahead, 3-1. That was to be the low point in my serving, although I had no way of knowing.

After Newcombe won his serve for 4-1 he seemed certain to win the set and be in excellent position to go on to the championship. But that was the high point in his serving and within two minutes the momentum was to revert back to me.

I had to hold on to my serve now, and I did in a tight game for 2-4. On the last two swings of that game I was certain my overhead game was in order again. At 30-all Newcombe lifted one of his lobs and I smashed it away for 40-30. Then I stepped to the line and cracked an ace.

That felt fantastic. When my serve is right I know I can do anything.

I was off on one of my streaks, a run of seven games that gave me the third set and a pleasant 2-0 lead in the fourth and what was to be the final set.

To my mind the whole match was a backhand I hit past Newcombe in the seventh game of that third set. Even though my mental outlook had been reinforced by the smash and the ace that held my serve, Newcombe still was ahead 4-2 and serving.

After I won the first point for 0-15, we got into an exchange and he belted a forehand crosscourt wide to my right. As I lunged for it he pressed tight to the net ready to cut off anything. He edged a bit to his left, figuring logically that if I got to the ball all I could do was try and slap it down the line. I got there, barely ("Rocket beats you with his bloody legs, that's what," says Fred Stolle). A down-the-line backhand is my favorite in that situation. Everybody knew it, and I made up my mind I had to go the other way. (Pancho Gonzales has said, "The dangerous thing about Laver is he hits the impossible shot when he's out of position—the time you least expect it.")

That was the time. I sliced like a man delivering a karate chop and sent a low underspinning ball crosscourt. I still don't believe the angle—and neither does Newcombe. The shot was a clear contradiction of everything we'd seen and done. There was no way it could clear the net and still land inside the court, yet it kept fluttering along somehow almost parallel to the net, eluding Newcombe's frantic wave and landing just within the far sideline. You don't plan a shot like that, not unless you're on marijuana, and the only grass I'm partial to is Wimbledon's. I had the general direction in mind and the rest just happened. It was nice to watch.

But Newcombe was shocked. I reckon the shot value was worth a lot more points than just that one to 0–30. There was enough of a crack in his morale for me to pour through. Moments later I had his service game as he double faulted the last point.

Newcombe was faltering and I was doing everything I could to help him. I won my serve quickly, then whacked two good forehands and a backhand to get another break for 5–4.

"Hit the ball," I kept reminding myself, but it was coming instinctively. On set point the only bad bounce of the day saved Newcombe for a second. But I followed my next serve with a stiff backhand volley that gave me the set.

Now I was up 2–1 in sets, and I was determined to get him before he could recover.

He came in with the serve and I swatted a backhand down the line. All John could do was hurl himself after the ball, but it was well past him. He picked himself up and smiled despairingly. Everyone laughed good-naturedly, and a laugh is welcome in that place once in a while.

Two more backhands of mine pinched him at 0–40. Somewhere John found his serve for an instant, and he banged three good ones to pull himself to deuce. He was grunting as he served, tiring I could tell. I was peeved at not getting one of those serves back, then relieved when he missed by an inch with a lob that would have been trouble. My ad. He volleyed my return short, to the service line. For a long second it seemed the scene was frozen as we stood still facing each other at the net for this virtual match point. Which way would I hit the ball? He knew it didn't matter since I almost surely could pass him whichever route I took, but he readied himself for a stab. I waited for the ball to bounce, took it with my backhand, and drove it straight down the line.

One-love for me with serve. I kept right on going to the cup, the check, and the victory party. The score was 6–4, 5–7, 6–4, 6–4. On actual match point I put away a smash of Newcombe's final lob. It was a satisfying ending.

They rolled out the green carpet to protect that hallowed sod from the street shoes of the Duke of Kent who came down to make the presentations.

After Newcombe won his Wimbledon in 1967, he told the Duchess of Kent, then presenting the trophy, that he was going to go out and get drunk. Good, straightforward Aussie talk. Also expensive talk. It takes an awful lot of beer to get an Aussie full.

Fred Stolle likes to illustrate that point with a story concerning a national championship he won with Roy Emerson in the U.S. "We were playing the National Doubles in Boston," says Fred, "and our pattern for that week was alternate sleeping. One of us would party one night while the other stayed home at the hotel. We'd reverse it the next night. One of us rested, we figured, was enough to win the championship.

"It was my night out before the semifinals when we were going to play the top American team, Clark Graebner and Marty Riessen. I was at this bash at a place on Beacon Hill when I got into conversation with a character they call the Baron of Hungary who hangs around the tennis.

"The Baron wanted to make a little wager on the match the next day and asked me how much I liked myself and Emmo. Fivers, I said. 'Baron, I'll give you five-to-one and you can have Riessen and Graebner.' The Baron brightened noticeably. We had the icebox well flanked, and he never let me move a step.

'Have a beer, Fred' was just about the extent of his conversation as the hours went by. He kept reaching in and opening them for me. I kept drinking.

"As we moved through our second case I looked at my watch and it was about two thirty in the morning. 'Baron,' I said, 'I've got to leave, I don't want to be late for the match. It starts at noon, you know.'

"He wasn't in very good shape, but he said, 'Fred, don't you think you ought to let Emmo know about the bet? He ought to realize how important the match is.'

" 'Right you are, Baron.' It struck me then as logical and I picked up the phone and rang Emmo, waking him from a sound sleep. He was not pleased. I believe he called me a bloody idiot while I was explaining the bet.

"I nodded to the Baron in the stands before the match. He looked like he might have a headache, but he seemed pleased about what he thought was a sure thing. I never played better and we killed Riessen and Graebner."

Beer is mother's milk for an Aussie. I don't know whether Newcombe could afford enough of it in his finest amateur hour to follow through on his statement to the Duchess of Kent. But I had won $7200, and that will buy enough lager to do in even an Aussie.

We had some champagne Saturday evening to celebrate in our flat with George MacCall and his wife and my close friends from New Zealand, John McDonald and his wife. I struggled into my dress suit for the Wimbledon ball where I'd have the ceremonial first dance with the women's champion, Ann Jones. It was the first time two left-handers have shared the opening fox trot which was "Fly Me to the Moon." I can't remember which of us led, but we didn't endanger the reputation of Marge and Gower Champion.

The last thing I recall about the evening was sitting in a discotheque called Raffles with the music and the beer flowing nicely. I was grinning a lot, and Aretha Franklin was wailing, "R-e-s-p-e-c-t . . ." Pat Stolle, Fred's wife, was talking with Mary about naming our baby.

"Well," Pat was saying, "I think Forest would be quite good if it's a boy. Since the baby is supposed to be born during Forest Hills, it would be a nice remembrance, wouldn't it?"

Mary didn't think so.

Nor did she like the proposal of Slamma for a girl. Or Slammer for a boy. She didn't seem to care for the tennis motif, and I assured her we wouldn't name the kid Drop Shot because we already had a dog by that name.

Everything began to run together. I forgot about Newcombe, the Slam, Forest Laver, Aretha Franklin, dancing with Ann Jones . . . and I woke up much later that morning in the bathtub, my tuxedo still on. I'd never been so well dressed for the tub.

At about 7:00 A.M., Mary tells me, the phone rang. It was a call from a newspaperman in Australia who wanted to talk to me about my victory.

"This is Mrs. Laver," she said.

"Well," said the reporter, "is your husband available now?"

"Uh," she mumbled, thinking of the body in the bath, "Rod's out." She didn't want to lie and she didn't want to tell the truth. I think that was a pretty good answer.

"Gone out at this hour?" the fellow persisted. "When will he be back?"

"In about five hours. Why don't you try him then."

The next time he rang I was ready to chat. I'd found my head behind the tub where it had rolled, and screwed it back on.

LESSON 20
Returning Serve

Make up your mind on this: you're going to get that serve back over the net. Consistent returning puts pressure on the server. Usually you'll just block the first serve, since your opponent will probably have some pace on the ball.

Move in for the second serve and give that a good swat. Most people play too far back to return serve. You want to try to take the ball on the rise, and maybe you'll find yourself standing inside the baseline to do this. Try it.

Pancho Segura, one of the cleverest guys to play the game, used to move up to take the second serve, like most players, but frequently he would delay that move until his opponent was into the service motion. "Maybe my move will distract him and he'll double fault," was Pancho's reasoning.

Prepare.

May I repeat: prepare. Get that racket back as soon as you know whether the ball's coming to your forehand or backhand. Too many players are late in preparing to make the stroke and getting the racket back. Remind yourself to prepare as your opponent makes his service toss.

Even a broken-down-looking return gives the server a problem. Once you've put the ball over the net you've got an even chance of winning the point. Try to keep the ball low, especially against an opponent who follows his serve to the net. Use a lob occasionally against a net rusher. It will startle him.

Don't overhit. Nothing picks up your opponent more than ripping returns of serve—that slap harmlessly into the net.

Get that return over the net. Any way. Or go stand in the corner.

21 THE SPOILS OF VICTORY

MONDAY I was fine and loose. I took care of a few business appointments before taking a cab to the airport with Mary. Business was better. Mark McCormack had been among the first to shake hands with me after my victory over Newcombe.

"This will do a lot for those contracts we talked about," Mark said. And it has. I never had any idea how the name Rod Laver could be exploited, but Mark McCormack, as business agent, has been making fortunes for sports page names since he began guiding one of the better known—Arnold Palmer. I'm his first fling at tennis—a reluctant one. Having him and his aides, Jay Lafave and Dick Alford, minding my affairs has meant a lot to my game, giving me a free mind and saving time so that my primary consideration can be playing. Endorsements do take a certain amount of time in appearances, conferences, and posing for promotional photos. I'm not the free man I once was. But with Mark's International Management, Inc., handling the business, I'm not burdened with the approach and negotiations to obtain the best deal. Frequently I was chiseled before IMI took over. I can't sell myself as well as somebody else can. That's not my line. Mary and I were going crazy trying to answer business mail, keep track of endorsements, and merchandise myself in the best manner. As a trained accountant, she's a great help, but still it was impossible to look after it all and really know what was best.

I realized this early in the game. Even though tennis hasn't always presented a new, booming market as it does now, there were certain commercial opportunities for the leading players, and I was taking advantage of every one I could. Some were for incredibly low money, considering what McCormack has done for me, but I took them all, figuring everything was gravy. I had no grasp of the possibilities, but I knew I had to get an agent of some sort. Every successful athlete reaches that point.

McCormack, a young Cleveland lawyer, is the first name you think of in this line. He made his name handling the affairs of golfers Arnold Palmer, Jack Nicklaus, and Gary Player. Now he also has as clients at least a dozen more name golfers and other sporting celebrities like Jean-Claude Killy of skiing, Jackie Stewart of auto racing, Paul Warfield of football, John Havlicek of basketball, Stan Mikita of hockey, and Brooks Robinson of baseball.

I thought he might like a tennis player as well, and I wrote him a letter about it in 1966. Mark replied negatively. There weren't enough opportunities to sell a tennis player to make it worth his while. That was more than a personal disappointment to me. It indicated that tennis was still in the backwater.

In 1968 I tried again. Tennis was now open, we pros were sprung from Siberia, and McCormack showed some interest. He sent Jay Lafave to talk to me. At about three o'clock one September morning in P. J. Clarke's saloon in New York (after I'd been beaten in the U.S. Open), Jay and I hammered out a tentative deal. Later I signed.

I was an experiment for International Management, their first tennis player. But, of course, I brought my $90,000 contract with National Tennis League into the deal, and that was a good start to build on.

Mark's management has worked fabulously for me. Before he stepped into my affairs my nonplaying income was under $25,000 a year. For 1969 it just about doubled, and the probability is that winning the Grand Slam will eventually be worth several hundred thousand dollars in endorsements.

In reorganizing my business life, McCormack gave notice to

the firms holding contracts with me that they would have to do a lot better when those contracts expired. He began looking for similar firms that might be interested in me when the time came to re-negotiate my contracts, and he found altogether new endorsements like a clothing line for Puritan, a tennis camp at the Mt. Washington Hotel in Bretton Woods, New Hampshire, the contract for this book, a movie—nearly twenty associations.

A bright example of how things changed was shoes. I had signed in 1966 with a small New England manufacturer who produced a line of Rod Laver tennis shoes. My deal was $1,000 plus 2.5 percent royalties. It was a bad deal and the shoe was inadequately promoted. I was getting royalty checks periodically for $7.80 or $25—figures like that. Beer money. When that contract was up, McCormack placed me with the German firm Adidas, an arrangement that meant many times more.

Racket endorsements bring in more than $50,000 a year, and that is only for specific areas of the world. For instance, I endorse a Chemold metal racket for the United States of America, a Dunlop wooden racket for Australia, and a Donnay wooden racket for Europe. In addition, Rod Laver Co., an export firm, buys rackets from Chemold and Donnay and markets them separately in other countries.

Although metal rackets were starting to sell extremely well as many of the players switched from wood, I wasn't anxious to go mod. For one thing I had a contract with Dunlop, who didn't get into metal until later in the rush. More important, I was comfortable with wood (with which I won the Slam), feeling it was better for my game.

Clark Graebner, Gene Scott, and Billie Jean King, turning to Wilson's steel racket, started the metal frames on their way in 1967. Changing over to steel abruptly at midseason, the three of them had great success in the American Nationals at Forest Hills, and flashed the message of the gleaming steelies across the country on TV.

Billie Jean won the women's title, Clark got to the men's final. More implausible was the caper of Scott, a lawyer and weekend player, who reached the semis and credited his steel racket. "The steelie helped me serve better and hit the ball harder with less effort, so I could keep up with the guys who were playing regularly and were sharper and in better condition," Scott said. He predicted, "Wood will be obsolete in ten years; wooden rackets will go the way of wooden golf clubs." Later Pancho Gonzales switched to Spalding's aluminum, and his regeneration, whether due to the racket or not, had to be a recommendation.

The rush to metal was on. Sales spurted.

The established sporting goods firms all put out their own models, and some new companies got into the tennis racket business. One of the newcomers was Chemold in New York

It isn't quite true to say that I would endorse and play with a beer bottle if the price was right, although one of the first tennis professionals, Tom Pettit of the Newport Casino, actually swung a champagne bottle so deftly that he could beat a number of club players armed with rackets. Pettit, incidentally, played in the first open match, an exhibition he lost to the American champion Dick Sears, at Newport in 1882.

No, I wouldn't have given up wood for aluminum just for money. However, the money was so attractive that I couldn't be stubborn in my conviction that wood remained superior. Some of those defectors, including Billie Jean King, returned to wood, feeling that touch and control with the old rackets meant more than the zip they got from steel. I said hesitantly that I would try the aluminum, as did Tony Roche, and would use it only if after a trial I believed it could improve my game. I wanted to be sure I had at least the same touch, and that I could serve better with less energy used.

I did concede that the latter would probably be true, but without touch I would feel like Andrew Wyeth using a gummy brush. I think most athletes care about what they endorse. They want it to be a quality product. I do. But endorsing, say, clothing and a racket are two different things. A pair of tennis shorts may make you look better, thus feel better, but I doubt that they will affect your game. But a racket is a special thing to me, and if I use it and recommend it I want to feel it's the best possible weapon for a tennis player. That's the way I felt about Chemold, although there were bugs at first as there have been in all the metal frames. I used it for quite a while, including my 13-win run dominating the Tennis Champions Classic and earning me $160,-000 early in 1971. But for me (perhaps not for you) aluminum never quite gave one the "feel" I got from wood, so I gave it up and reverted to wood. There was an escape provision in my contract.

That's what I mean about the efficiency of the McCormack organization. Other tennis players who followed me to Mark include John Newcombe, Roger Taylor, Margaret Court, and Evonne Goolagong.

Never did Mark, Jay Lafave, or Dick Alford talk about what a Grand Slam could do for me commercially. I guess they were afraid to jinx me. But I could tell they were thinking about it as soon as I won the Australian. After Wimbledon they were as excited as I was. They're nice guys, and I consider them friends, but a percentage of Laver on the verge of achieving the Grand Slam will tend to increase the excitement.

LESSON 21
Equipment

Without a racket you're up the creek without a paddle. This is your tool and you should choose it carefully. There's a lot of psychology involved in racket selection, I'll grant you—color scheme, catchy names (The Grand Slam), endorsement (Rod Laver Personal Model).

There are any number of styles and models with which you can play a comparable game. The most important thing in racket selection is feel. You want a racket that fits into your hand comfortably and isn't too heavy, particularly in the head. A head-heavy racket can lead to sore elbow. The weight will probably be between 13 and 15 ounces and the grip between 4½ and 5 inches around.

Lighter rackets with slimmer handles are especially recommended for women. If anything, I think the normal tendency is toward a racket that is slightly too heavy and too big around the handle. My own grip is 4⅝ inches and the weight is 14 ounces. Wood or metal is a matter of personal preference. As I've said before, the metal rackets are whippier and probably put less strain on a player over a long haul. Wood tends to be favored by the "touch" players, but I'm talking about a good deal more touch than average player possesses.

I travel too much to keep a racket in a press, which would add to the weight of my gear. And I don't keep rackets long enough to worry about warping. Probably a press is a good idea for players who don't use a racket for a long period of time, perhaps over the winter. Racket covers will protect the strings during travel.

While I use gut strings, they aren't necessary for the ordinary player, and probably they're a drawback—expensive, more vulnerable to wear and moisture. A good nylon will do just as well for most players. If your racket gets wet you can help preserve the strings by sprinkling talcum powder on them.

Color is going to come in for clothing. Tasteful pastels would seem desirable. More so for the women. I think they'll have matching tennis dresses and shoes, and perhaps even Teddy Tinling's prediction will come true. Teddy, the couturier who designed Gussie Moran's lace panties and creates very-high-style outfits for the girls, prophesies that in the coming tennis world of color even the courts will be of varied shades.

"Green is such a crashing bore," says Teddy. "Royal blue is the best color to show off the women. Why not change the shades of the courts along with the clothes?"

Why not? But green still seems to go best with my hair, Teddy.

22 THE BEGINNING OF THE END

THE REST of the summer is something of a mystery to me because I didn't lose a match. Leaving London, I flew to Boston and Mary to Los Angeles, from where we alternately sympathized and sparred at long-distance rates during the U.S. Pro Championship. I've said I expected to lose there and, at the moment, would have welcomed defeat because it would have sent me right home to comfort Mary. But I didn't lose. And I didn't lose in pro tournaments in St. Louis, Binghamton, Ft. Worth, and Baltimore leading up to Forest Hills.

This not only surprised me; in fact it made me slightly edgy. Where was the letdown that you have to have? Except for the U.S. Pro Championship those American tournaments didn't mean that much. A loss or two would have been a relief, and given me some time off. Instead I had to play right through the final each time. Nothing like this had ever happened to me. I know that Suzanne Lenglen and Helen Wills Moody used to go years without losing, and Budge and Tilden had undefeated summers. But nobody is that dominant today. The opposition is tougher. Even in 1969 I got beat fairly frequently—16 times in 122 matches.

Nevertheless I came into New York to finish the Slam with a streak of 23 straight match victories that began with Pietrangeli at Wimbledon. When I walked into the Forest Hills Stadium alongside a young Mexican, Luis Garcia, to launch the U.S.

264

Open, my last defeat was nearly three months behind me—by Newcombe at Queen's.

Two things were on my mind when I arrived at the West Side Tennis Club in the borough of Queens: Mary and the Grand Slam. Mary came first, and this was a concern that hadn't existed in 1962. Then it was just tennis. Possibly the double concern was better for me. In worrying about Mary, I don't think the weight of going for the Slam got to me as it did in 1962. I was older, too, and I'd been through it before.

Mary's presence in my life made me more relaxed. Those tense phone calls between Boston and Los Angeles of July were forgotten, and now our calls buoyed each of us.

There were a couple of vital things I learned from the 1962 ordeal. Censor your newspaper reading. Stay in a quiet, secluded place during the tournament.

Billie Jean King's dad, Bill Moffitt, once gave her the best advice an athlete can get: "Don't read anything that's written about you," he told her. "It will be either overly complimentary or overly critical, and neither will do you any good."

Billie Jean could be glad she didn't read the London paper that suggested she had cancer when she became ill just before Wimbledon of 1968. But so many reporters asked her about it that she found out. She was merely run down, but the newspapers can blow these things up. An athlete is better off not to take the press to heart.

You have to talk to reporters. I like most of them, and they've been good to me. But you don't have to read what they write. They're all looking for a different angle, and that angle could spoil your digestion or your sleep.

Certainly they were going to ask about the Slam and I was going to discuss it. But as long as I didn't see it in black and white I didn't have to build up additional pressure on myself. You can contribute to the pressure yourself.

I did that in 1962 by reading everything that was written, and by being more available to the reporters and well-wishers than I should have. This time I didn't stay in a hotel where I could be tracked down, and I didn't go out much to eat.

Chuck Heston was very helpful. Chuck, who has impersonated Moses, Michelangelo, Andrew Jackson, Ben Hur—and also does a good impersonation of a tennis player when he can escape filming—loaned me his Manhattan apartment on the East River. John McDonald, my friend of many years since I first played in his native New Zealand, kindly came over from London to act as confidant, cook, practice partner, and buffer.

We moved into Heston's spacious, high-ceilinged penthouse with a tape recorder for musical company, a supply of eggs and steak, and settled into a quiet routine, spending as little time as possible at the West Side Club, then only to play or practice. Unlike Wimbledon, there's no privacy for the players, no place to relax away from the press or the crowds. At one time I imagine Forest Hills was a very pleasant place, well out from Manhattan, an enclave of its own. Now Queens is crowded, unattractive. The club is hard to get to through the traffic; parking is impossible. It always amazes me how the English, jammed into that little island, have managed to preserve their greenery so that Wimbledon is such a countrified place within a huge city, while Queens has become a depressing jumble.

Financially the U.S. Open is No. 1. Prize money at Forest Hills added up to $137,000 in 1969, with $16,000 for the winner of the men's singles. In prestige, it's No. 2, behind Wimbledon. But in playing conditions, it's a far-down bush league all its own. The courts are grass, and American grass is for cows and lovers—not tennis players. In fact, American grass courts are so uncertain underfoot that an unwary cow might break a leg strolling from baseline to net. Or starve. There isn't much grass left on an American court by the time a tournament reaches its climax.

Uncertainties of American grass make tennis at Forest Hills comparable to driving the Indianapolis 500 on cobblestones. The 1969 Open, practically ruined by record New York rains, made it clear that grass must be replaced by a level, all-weather surface, perhaps a proven synthetic.

But grass is tradition, and tradition has been the grass-stained enemy of the growth of spectator tennis in America. Because the most important tournaments have been on grass, it is a sad fact that few Americans know how thrilling it is to watch excellent tennis. There isn't much of it in a grass tournament in the States.

When you say that Wimbledon is a grass court tournament and Forest Hills is a grass court tournament—and isn't grass, after all, grass?—you may as well say that Raquel Welch is a woman and Twiggy is a woman, and what's the difference? Wimbledon is so alluring and appealing because it is cuddled and cared for more than King Farouk ever was. No American club has the grass-growing climate or the resources to duplicate Wimbledon. Even so, Wimbledon doesn't produce as exciting tennis as the slower surfaces. But at least at Wimbledon you know where the ball will bounce—and that it will bounce.

Because grass makes for a low, skidding bounce, points are normally over very quickly. An ordinary serve can become impossible when it begins darting this way and that off bad grass, and an ordinary player can keep a good one on the court for hours without either accomplishing very much other than the promotion of tedium. The longest three-set match in history was played at Newport, Rhode Island, on a grass court in 1967. Dick Leach and Dick Dell hung in for more than six hours—spread over two days—to outlast Len Schloss and Tom Mozur, 3–6, 49–47, 22–20: 147 games. Fortunately it wasn't a best-of-five-sets match. It's also fortunate that Leach made a lucky shot on match point, or they might still be playing.

Of the sixteen matches in tennis history reaching or exceeding 100 games, nine were played on American grass, another on British grass at Wimbledon. One was indoors on canvas at Salisbury, Maryland, also a very fast surface, and two were on American cement, just about as fast. The other three were indoors on boards, very fast.

A match like that one at Newport is dreadful. You can imagine where it would drive a television producer who was covering it. Right up the antenna. Though I love tennis I would find it more boring than watching a week of "I Love Lucy."

Of course, that is why tennis didn't succeed very well on TV in America until recently. Limited television coverage was for years mostly devoted to Forest Hills and the National Indoors at

Salisbury, Maryland (on a fast canvas). Frankly, the tennis has been deadly dull serve-and-volley stuff. Wham-bam . . . the point's over. Bad to play; bad to watch.

The theory in America has seemed to be that since Dick Sears—the first champion in 1881—did his thing on grass, it would be a sacrilege to change. Tennis was a warm-up for a tea party in those days, and grass was lovely. It still is for club players. You can play barefoot, luxurious exercise. But when your livelihood depends on it, you feel like Rudy Nureyev trying to dance in a rockgarden.

I hope this isn't taken as a knock at the groundskeepers—Owen Sheridan at Forest Hills, Walter Chambers at Longwood, or Joe Leandra at Newport—all splendid, hardworking men who keep their courts so nice for the members. But labor problems and the climate are insuperable. American grass just won't hold up long beneath a thundering herd of tournament players. All the groundskeepers would be as happy as us pros to roll up the grass and ship it to neighborhoods that need parks.

Grass is becoming deader for athletes than God for atheists. We're joining the plastic world. Writing in *Sports Illustrated*, Dan Jenkins said God goofed when He invented grass instead of Astro-Turf. Jenkins was referring to football fields, but tennis fitted, too, although Astro-Turf has been too fast for tennis. Uni-Turf has been slower and better, but perhaps I'm not a neutral witness. I used to represent the company.

But there is progress. Longwood, where they've been playing tennis for more than ninety years—the home club of sainted Dick Sears—has forsaken grass. At least for major tournaments. When I first visited the place, the members would sue for libel if you maligned their beloved grass-blades. The theme song had been "Nearer My Sod to Thee" since St. Dick's day.

Nevertheless they became sick of people like me ripping through their grass, and in 1969 the rape of the grass-blade took place when the stadium court was dug up to replace real turf with Uni-Turf.

Traumatic, for a few minutes, but now the members have the grass to themselves, as well as six synthetic courts that should last indefinitely and are given over to us workingmen during the U.S. Pro Championships.

But, enough moaning, Laver. I did win, and I would play Forest Hills if the surface were macaroni and cheese. I'm a professional. The money is there along with a big title. I've played much worse conditions for a lot less money, or none at all. If the Minnesota Vikings can mash themselves on glaciers, I can do my job on wretched grass.

You adapt. The game I play at Forest Hills—or on any other American grass—is entirely different from how I play on Wimbledon's firm and true grass. Junk brings results at Forest Hills. I serve my kicker (American twist) a lot more because it will take erratic bounces, whereas at Wimbledon it will stand up too high and I use it only to vary my serving pattern. I chip the ball around a lot, hook and slice, even chop, trying to produce skips and annoying hops to throw off the other fellow. You improvise at Forest Hills.

LESSON 22
Know Yourself

It's fine and dandy to read about how Rod Laver and Ken Rosewall and Pancho Gonzales do it, useful and worthwhile, I hope. There are shots that I may be able to help you with in this book. That's why you're reading it.

Nevertheless there is one overriding fact of the matter when you get into a match: you are you. You have progressed to a certain ability in tennis, and you must be aware of this when you play.

It does no good to try to whack a topspin backhand in a difficult spot if you haven't practiced it, or you are unable to make it work. The fact that I can escape with it doesn't help you. You may be better off lobbing.

What I'm getting at is this: don't try to play beyond yourself. You win tennis matches on the other guy's errors and by keeping the ball going. You're just aiding and abetting the enemy by trying to pull off the impractical or impossible shot in certain situations. If you're pushed wide of the court, you'd better hit down the line or lob rather than trying a slick crosscourt that has only a slight chance of succeeding.

Wait for the opportunity to put your best shots into use, until you have the edge and the chances of success are high. Until then, work for that opening by getting the ball back to your opponent's weaknesses.

Cut down on your mistakes. If you're up against a strong server, don't try to overpower him with your returns. Go all out against his weaknesses, not his strengths.

Take stock of your physical limitations. Don't take unnecessary steps or run for balls on which you have little chance. If you don't have a roaring serve and good volleys, don't play a net rushing game.

Know what you can hit well, and when to use it. A little thought on the matter will tell you.

270

Sometimes you'll be inspired. That's the joy of the game. You'll be hitting away like mad and everything will work. Fine. It's most likely to happen when you start out solidly with the things you can do well, not trying to play above yourself. When you win some points and games that way, your confidence will expand.

Talk to any really good professional player and ask him how he plays me. "Keep the ball in play and let Laver make the mistakes," the guy will say. "Laver does make mistakes."

So, I reckon, will your opponent.

23 THE LAST LEG OF THE SLAM: FOREST HILLS

JOHN MCDONALD was good company. He's a little older than I and played Davis Cup for New Zealand. He could give me good practice, and he squeezed the orange juice and poached the eggs beautifully. We know one another's families and habits, have much in common. He lost in the qualifying round and wasn't concerned about his own game. The common goal was my rest and tennis, and I appreciate his part in my winning. At night we'd watch the telly or listen to tapes—Aretha Franklin, Dave Brubeck, Jose Feliciano. Sometimes we'd have a few Australian friends in, and one evening we threw a birthday party for an Aussie living in New York, Mike Irving. Both he and his wife, Veronica, have become top models in America.

My chief preoccupation was my racket handles. Arnold Palmer fusses with his clubs and shapes them to his own liking, and I do the same with my rackets. I'm always unwinding the leather grips, changing them around and rewinding them, experimenting to get the best feel. I sit around like an old maid with her knitting, the rackets in my lap as I fiddle with the grips. It's a sure sign of staleness for me if I'm not rearranging the grips. Pancho Gonzales is the same, and he also works on his aluminum frame, grinding it down here and there, or drilling holes to change the weight ever so slightly and bring about just the right balance.

In the first three rounds of the Open it seemed as though I—an American resident—was trying to destroy the Good Neighbor policy as I went through Luis Garcia of Mexico and Jaime Pinto-Bravo and Jaime Fillol, both of Chile. I picked up a little Spanish in that stretch of straight-set victories, although I don't think any of the words need repeating. None of the Latins was comfortable on grass, although Fillol gave me a spirited first set. He's a good prospect who could become the leading South American.

Dennis Ralston has been the forgotten man of American tennis. People have tended to think of him, if at all, as over the hill because he goes back so far. He was a Wimbledon champion before I was, winning the doubles with Rafe Osuna, in 1960. But he was only eighteen then. He's but a year older than Arthur Ashe, yet the tendency has been to write him off. Memories of Ralston are mainly of Davis Cup disasters, one of them—a defeat by Brazil's Edison Mandarino—ending his amateur career in 1966. But as a pro he had done quite well, often extending me, notably in my only five-set match of the 1968 Wimbledon.

He usually extends me, but he doesn't beat me. I think this is in the back of both our minds when we play. When we get to the critical point, he's going to crack.

But when he led me two sets to one on a lovely sunny afternoon with the Forest Hills stadium nearly full, that critical point was some ways off. Dennis was playing beautifully, returning my serve damagingly with his good-looking net skimmers.

The crowd of about 10,000 had forgotten all their disappointments with Ralston in the past and were rumbling exuberantly for him. The opportunities for an American crowd to push one of their own to a victory over an Australian have been infrequent at Forest Hills in the past twenty years, and they let Ralston and me hear their approval—of him.

A crowd like that can grind their opponent down. You find yourself getting smaller and smaller if you're not careful to do something to counteract it. When we changed ends of the court

I was toweling off quicker than Dennis at the umpire's chair and moving to position a little sooner. As I walked to the baseline . . . silence. No boos, mind you; nobody throwing anything. But the silence told me that I was in enemy country. Then Ralston would begin his walk to the line and the place spilled over with cheering. I felt like a Communist at a John Birch Society meeting. A little of that and you can really be shaken.

I remembered playing Davis Cup in Mexico in 1959, against Rafe Osuna, and the same thing happened. He was lingering during the change, and letting me walk on first. I got the glares and he got the great morale-lifting explosion. Harry Hopman, our captain, straightened it out quickly. I was not to move until Osuna did. That's what I had to do with Ralston, and later in the semifinals with Ashe.

I'm all for cheers, but I'm going to share them whenever possible. So when Ralston walked out and the cheering started I walked, too, and let it fall on me as well.

As a pro I haven't encountered such nationalism much, although it is strong for Pancho Gonzales, especially in his hometown, Los Angeles, where I've had to time my moves to coincide with his.

Ralston was playing very well, but his game doesn't vary much. He has little flair, and as I started serving better and hitting all my shots better, I knew I'd get him. I won the fourth set without much trouble and he became vulnerable. At 2–3 in the fifth, he could have saved a break point against his serve by making an easy backhand volley. My return was high, and he should have put it away. Instead I think he was trying to make it a shade too good, as you will when you're pressing, and he dumped it into the net. I had the break for 4–2, and I could tell by that hangdog look he gets that he was through. And I was into the quarterfinals. I keep finding out one shot can make the difference, in this case Denny's bad volley at the critical point.

To be fair, Denny turned the tables on me the following year, and I had to revise my estimate of him. That story is told in the Epilogue.

I'm the rainmaker. Forest Hills confirmed it. Everywhere I

went and won, the tournament suffered washouts—Brisbane, Paris, Johannesburg, London, Boston, and now Forest Hills. Within 48 hours, 6½ inches of rain struck New York, a 25-year record there for wetness. In South Africa, where it hadn't rained all year, a three-day deluge interrupted the open, and the agricultural officials wanted to hire me and keep me there. Maybe there's something about my crazy, spinning shots that upsets the atmosphere, but while South African farmers hailed the rain, New Yorkers were less than ecstatic. Sections of the city were flooded, including the West Side Tennis Club, whose antiquated protective facilities did little good. The tarps in the stadium and grandstand were inadequate, and coverings don't exist for the other courts.

Forest Hills became a morass, and the tournament closed down to wait two and a half days for the sun. The coverings are simple canvas laid on the grass. If they're left on very long the grass smothers. At Wimbledon, canvas tents, run up on pulleys and cables, are spread above the court, allowing the grass to breathe. You can play there whenever the rain stops. Admittedly it hardly stopped in New York, but when it did the courts were unplayable.

We played anyway, slopping about like rice farmers and ripping chunks of sod from the courts. Any athlete knows that waiting to play is the worst part. We tried to keep busy during the delay, driving to indoor courts in Englewood, New Jersey, to practice, working out in the New York Athletic Club's gym.

It helped to fill the time, although I got stiff running on an indoor track. The pounding affected my legs after playing on grass, and I hustled myself into a hot bath with epsom salts. This is always the thing, anyway, after a hard workout or match. A good tub. I don't think enough American athletes realize this, especially the ones who don't have whirlpool baths available to them. A weekend player, who may have gone a little too hard, can bring himself back for the next day by moving right from the court to a tub. It does a lot more for you than just a long, hot shower.

When the rain finally stopped, my edge was gone. I could feel it immediately as Roy Emerson won the first set and broke me for a lead in the second. I was always in trouble on my serve as we sloshed about the grandstand court. The balls were soggy and heavy, like hitting cantaloupes.

And there was my old buddy Emmo, my friend and rival for a dozen years, with a good chance to finally ruin a Slam for me. Three times I beat him in finals during the 1962 Slam, completing it with a four-set win here.

I had been so nervous during that 1962 match that I lost the feel of the racket completely. I actually held it wrong and hit a volley straight into the ground once. It was so comical that I laughed myself, and that helped break the tension.

I think I've learned to overcome that kind of panic, although I did suffer it once long enough to lose the match at Madison Square Garden earlier in the year to Cliff Richey.

It's what I call "whisky wrists." Your grips don't feel right and your shots are jerky. You're not necessarily choking, but you're so rattled you don't know where you are. You're rushing, you want to get it all over—yet you're not anxious to lose.

You have to slow yourself down. Take a little more time. Release your grip between points. Put your racket in the other hand for a moment, and let your racket hand relax. Stop yourself before you serve, and get in mind what you want to do. You've probably been snatching at the ball instead of watching it closely and hitting through it. Make sure the first serve goes in, even if you have to take something off it. Placement is more important than speed. When you've been going badly and your opponent is gaining confidence, he's going to step in on your second serve and take advantage of it.

Get the first one in. If the situation is reversed, step in on his second serve. It appears to me that most club players stand too far back to receive the second serve, thus reducing the opponent's disadvantage. Move up on the second ball and you can almost always return well enough to follow your return to the net. If your opponent stands far back to receive, bloop your serve short—catch him off balance.

When you've got those whisky wrists, pause and try to think

about a couple of key things. Keep your eye on the ball. Forget where your opponent is, and try to see the ball hit your racket. And bend your knees. That'll help loosen you up. Take a deep breath.

Tell yourself to hit the ball. I mean by that to hit through it. You can only lose, and that's not the worst thing that can happen.

There weren't going to be any nerves for me the rest of the way. Emmo had the lead, and he might beat me, but I felt confident that if I took special care with my serve and kept hitting through the ball that I'd find my form. I had all through the Slam, and this wasn't any different. Emmo had slowed himself down, too. (After all, he knows as much about what's happening as I do, maybe more.) He realized he couldn't clout those heavy balls the way he likes, so he contented himself with taking the pace off his returns. We were slipping and sliding, but I made up my mind I was going to get to the net quicker to knock off those slow returns before they bounced on my side of the court. You're crazy to let a ball land on a grass court most of the time, and at Forest Hills it's like dropping a baby out of a window: It may bounce nicely, but it isn't likely. My legs have won me as many matches as my strokes or my opponents' mistakes, and they won this one. I was quicker on that wet court than Emmo, who swears there's a duckbilled platypus lurking in my family tree. Maybe so. I must have had webbed feet to pull out the second set. He lost the third, 11–13, it turned out, on a forehand passing shot that we both watched anxiously. Roy thought it was good; I couldn't honestly tell; the linesman shouted, "Out!" You get all the calls when you win a Slam.

Rather than game for him it was deuce. Then I hit a pair of passing forehands that he narrowly missed to take the set.

Now he knew he had to go five sets to win, and that has to take something out of any man, even Roy Emerson, especially on that marsh. He had to climb a slippery mountain, and I've known him so long I could sense something leaving him. He never stopped battling. He doesn't get the feeling he's beaten the way Ralston does. A man with one of the greatest records in tennis history still feels he can win. Yet just a smidgin of something was gone, and it made me that much tougher. Roy is two years older than I and that's beginning to hurt him.

Emmo drags his rear foot when he serves, and he ripped up the baseline area horribly. In cleaning up after himself he built a pile of sod chunks next to the fence that separates the court from the grandstand. Soon he'd dug a trench behind the line, and couldn't find any clear patches to serve from. This bothered his motion because he was catching his drag foot in the trench. But since I don't drag I was able to serve reasonably well in the mess he'd created. I went to 4–1 in the fourth, and he caught me. I served to 5–4 and felt very certain when Emmo lost the first three points and was down 0–40—triple match point. Two of them he brushed off, but on the third I caught him with my first topspin lob of the match. He was coming in, and there was no way he could reverse himself quickly to pursue it in the muck. He didn't turn to look, just kept coming to the net and reached for my hand. My old friend had plagued my every step to make this the hardest match of the tournament, 4–6, 8–6, 13–11, 6–4.

Hitting Through the Ball

One of the finest matches I've ever seen was on my first trip to Forest Hills in 1956: Dick Savitt, the big, strong American against Kenny Rosewall, who was to win the U.S. title. They battled it out fantastically on a bad grass court with groundstrokes. Savitt's were booming, and until he tired he had Rosewall in trouble. I was impressed with the way Savitt hit through the ball, getting his body into it and producing a heavy ball.

He prepared well, getting his racket back in plenty of time as soon as he knew whether he'd be hitting a backhand or forehand. Then he got down to the ball, bending his knees, and when he hit the ball he kept his stroke coming with a long follow-through toward the net.

That's hitting through the ball, as opposed to slapping at it or coming across it. Don't stop the groundstroke on impact, but keep following toward the net.

Stay down as you follow through. By coming up (unbending your knees) too soon you raise your chances of hitting the ball long.

Even if you're not too strong, hitting through the ball will give you more power than you thought you had because you're getting your body into the ball. Savitt still does it, and though he's in his forties he's still tough for any player in the world for a set or two.

I was cheering for Rosewall that day, my countryman, but I had to salute Savitt, who was twenty-nine, semiretired from the circuit then, for making Kenny sweat for five sets. Savitt really showed me something about hitting the ball with pace.

He also showed me the value of firm, decisive thinking. Savitt stayed back most of the time, and as I said, the groundstroking was wonderful. Kenny tried to come in when he thought he could, and he was usually frustrated because it was clear that Savitt made up his mind what to do as he approached the ball. If he decided to hit down the line, he held to this and didn't try to suddenly switch if he sensed that Rosewall had it covered.

You see, you must hit your shot, and not worry about the netman. Savitt had played enough so that he wouldn't be ruffled by the sight of his opponent crowding the net. Frequently, at a lower level, you can shake your opponent into errors by merely hurrying to the net.

Conversely, you mustn't take your eye off the ball in order to pay attention to your opponent. Don't let his movements distract you. Decide quickly what you are going to do with the ball, and then hit that shot as though the other court was empty. You're better off to hit the ball well, regardless of where your opponent is, than trying to switch the direction of your shot at the last instant. Even if he smells out the direction and is there, any opponent will have trouble volleying a ball that you hit through. Rosewall had his problems with Savitt.

24 SEMIFINAL

I BRUSHED my teeth before going out to play Arthur Ashe in the semifinals. This isn't a ritual, but I do it more often than not before a big match. I shave and spend a little more time than usual combing my hair, whitening my shoes and making sure I look my best. Feeling fresh in every way and looking good adds to your general confidence and may help you play a little bit better. It doesn't hurt you. The first good players I knew were Roy Emerson and Mal Anderson, both Queenslanders. I looked up to them, and one thing I noticed was that they were so well groomed when they went out to play. I guess I copied them.

There have been times when tight scheduling made it necessary for me to go immediately from one match to another, with no time in between to change and freshen up. I'd feel grubby and ill at ease, not in the right mood to play. I'm sure that in the heat of a match this is soon forgotten, but if my mood is wrong at the outset, it might cost me a couple of points that I may not get back.

I don't think this is vanity, just a feeling that the right appearance is as much a part of being prepared as good equipment. I'd make a lousy hippie.

Ashe remarked that the first match he ever played at Forest Hills was against me. I didn't remember it, ten years before when he was sixteen and I was a Wimbledon finalist. He had been extremely nervous and recalled the feeling that Forest Hills seemed so huge to him then. I had similar recollections of my introduction to the big league, but it was different for Arthur in that he sensed he was in truly alien territory.

That has changed for him, but in 1959 he must have felt very alone when he edged through the crowd on his way from the clubhouse to the grandstand court to play me. Maybe he felt better when he saw that I wasn't too impressive physically and he could look down on me. The score in 1959 was 6–2, 7–5, 6–2. I guess he got over his nerves after a while and played a good second set.

Newcombe and Roche were in the other semifinal as they had been at Wimbledon. They've been playing each other close for nearly ten years since they were kids in Sydney tournaments; and this time the match would go to Roche in five sets as Newc's serve disintegrated at the climax.

Ashe hadn't won anything since I'd played him at Wimbledon, although his sore elbow was all right again and he had corrected a faulty motion so that he was humming that serve again. It's a tremendous serve, but often that's all there is to Arthur. He's bang-bang, thrash-thrash, and the points come in clusters. Unhappily for him there are too many stretches of clunk-clunk.

But he had been serving beautifully to blow Manolo Santana and Ken Rosewall off the court on the way to the semis. I knew the crowd would be backing him up noisily, and I hoped I could keep him from getting into the match. Frankly I was up for this more than usual because I was annoyed with Arthur. Some of his statements had gotten to me. He kept saying that his generation—Newc, Roche, Tom Okker, and himself—were catching up with the older generation—me—and would soon be passing. I suppose I shouldn't let that generation talk bother me, but after all Arthur isn't a kid. He's only five years younger than I; and despite all his publicity he hasn't accomplished much, aside from his hot spell in 1968 when he won the National Amateur and U.S. Open in succession.

He should have won the first and third sets. Instead I won in straight sets over two days, 8–6, 6–3, 14–12. Darkness closed us down at 12–12 in the third set, and it took me only two games the next day to finish it. When I say he should have won those sets, I mean the opportunity was there for a guy who could fasten his mind on the right approach and lock out everything else. Arthur just doesn't do that—he admits it himself—and until he can he won't be a great player.

He served for the first set at 5–4 and tried to blast me with big first serves. They didn't go in, and he was left with his second which made me feel better. I was determined to make the returns somehow, leaving the pressure of hitting winners to him. I chipped the ball down the middle. I used a middle-approach against Arthur to take away the angles. Let him hit it as hard as he wants, I thought, and we'll see how far it goes. He'll kill you for a while, but he can't keep it up.

Arthur didn't come close to winning his serve for the set. Four games later I broke him with a neat lob—that most useful and too often neglected shot—and had the set, 8–6.

The second went pretty fast and I was feeling good, keeping aware that Arthur can flare up and become a forest fire. He jumped to a 3–0 lead in the third set. I got it back and we hung together as the games on the stadium scoreboard increased and daylight decreased. I thought I had the break in the seventeenth game, but he slashed a good forehand volley past me. In the next, me serving at 8–9, Arthur backed me up and had a set point at 30–40. I steadied myself, leaned on the first serve and knocked it into his backhand corner. He couldn't return it. That got me to deuce, and we stayed even to 12–12 when Mike Gibson, the referee, said "enough for today." It was nearly dark.

It was going to be a battle of nerves to see who cracked first. Arthur couldn't afford to, though, or the match was over. I was in a comfortable spot. If I lost the set I was still up 2 to 1. A another strong argument for a revision of the scoring system. These long deuce sets foul up a tournament and make it more difficult to get the game on television.

Jimmy Van Alen, tennis' blue-blooded Bolshevik from the gilded ghetto of Newport, has been lobbying for a new scoring system—his own VASSS (Van Alen Streamlined Scoring System)—

for years. Jimmy is too radical for my tastes, but at least he's thinking, an act often considered blasphemous in tennis circles.

I think Jimmy's tie-breaker has merit. It is a best-of-nine-point sequence with alternate serves when a set has reached 6–6 in games. We players first decided to try it during the 1970 Philadelphia Indoor Open with a slight change proposed by me. I felt the tie-breaker should be best-of-12 points with equal serves, and if the score became tied at 6 points all, you continue, alternating serves. To win, you must be ahead by two points, as in table tennis when you reach 20–all. This system has received a good deal of approval and is used on the World Championship Tennis tour, at Wimbledon, and in much of Europe, but nobody has ever called it Laver's variation on a theme by Van Alen. Meanwhile Jimmy's plan was adopted in the Open at Forest Hills and his Sudden Death, in one form or another, is here to stay.

Of course in 1969 we were on the conventional scoring at Forest Hills, and Ashe had an overnight reprieve. He still had hopes of winning that third set and carrying me into a fifth. He was the last American in the place, and he was the one to be worried. He looked it. Sleeping can come a bit hard when a match is dangling like that.

I didn't want to hang around the apartment thinking about it. We went out for dinner, had a steak and a couple of beers at the Press Box with some friends. We stayed out till eleven and I felt pleasantly tired when we got home. The beers relaxed me and I went right to sleep. I slept only six hours, but my mind hadn't raced because I was relaxed when I went to bed. I felt rested and ready.

The situation further favored me in that Arthur would be serving first. Seldom is anybody completely warmed up to serve an opening game. That's why I frequently choose to receive when I win the toss before a match begins. You see this all the time with the pros. Let your opponent serve first, and if he's cold or the least bit shaky, you have the chance to break him right away and jar his confidence.

There was no toss now, we just continued the same order of serving, and it happened that Arthur was first. Arthur had good chances, leading 30–15 on his serve, and 15–30 in the next game on mine. Those are very special points, of course—the points that can take you to game point. These points must be played correctly. By that I mean getting the first serve into play, and hitting your strokes surely—not pushing them and not taking chances either. You have to hit firmly so as not to give your opponent anything too good to work with, but you don't go blasting away.

You hear the expressions "big points" and "big games," and certainly some points and games are bigger than others. Depends on the situation. Sometimes 0–40 is tragic, and other times—if you have a good lead in the match—you might not struggle at 0–40 because you might be tired and figure it would take too much energy to squirm out of that hole.

But if the match is close and you're down on your serve 15–40 or 0–40 you're going to have to make sure of that first serve and not throw away any points. On the other hand, if your opponent is way down on his serve, then you can go for the winner and get that break of serve. To me the first point of every game is very important—it seems to decide which way the game will go most of the time. The first game of the second set is extremely vital. You have to really screw in your concentration here. If you've won the first set, it's common to have a letdown as the second begins. If you've lost the first set, you've got to charge back into the match. In an even match the eighth game is very big. If you're serving at 4–3 you play consistently—you must hold. No fancy stuff. If your opponent serves at 3–4, here's where you dig in to break, so that you'll be serving for the set. You must return serve, cut down on your backswing, block the ball back— do anything to keep it in play.

Naturally when you're in a deuce set the same tactics apply. But Arthur didn't serve well when he should have held from 30–15. He double faulted by stepping on the baseline for a foot fault, and it was 30–all. He flubbed easy volleys and within a minute his opportunity to go up 13–12 vanished.

I now had the serve at 13–12, and I made certain the first serve went in. Plenty of spin, medium speed. Even though I got behind 15–30 I held to my philosophy: let him hit winners if he can. It was up to him and he couldn't.

One champion was dead and a new champion was in the final.

More rain. It was Monday, overseen by a bleak sky whose lavender clouds were popping. We were twenty-four hours past the day set for Mary and me to collaborate on a coast-to-coast double. The baby was late. Rain delayed my final. God wasn't cooperating.

LESSON 24
Chipping and the Middle Approach

A chip is not a chop, and a chop isn't seen much anymore, although the old-timers like George Lott (one of the great doubles players) insist that we moderns are overlooking a useful stroke. A chop is just that—a sort of karate chop, a hard straight-down slice. It puts back-spin on the ball and can give lesser players problems if hit well. The last two people I remember using it were Margaret duPont and Shirley Fry when I was just coming up. It seemed to trouble some of their female opponents.

But a chip—there's a shot you need, a gliding kind of slice that is quite a good return against a man who charges the net. This is because the ball skims the net and drops at the net-rusher's feet. It is a softly hit shot, a slice just meeting the ball, sending it sliding nicely crosscourt and making your opponent bend low for the ball. Tough to volley a ball like that. You can direct a chip well, but I don't think there's much accuracy to a chop. (Wallace Johnson, another old-timer who nearly beat Tilden with chops, would disagree.)

To chip, you just meet the ball with the racket beveled below the ball. There's hardly any follow-through. A good return for doubles, of course, when the server is generally always coming to the net.

Now, if your opponent is gobbling up your crosscourt chips, or any crosscourt shots, you can remove that possibility by using the middle theory: hitting the ball down the center of the court. This can disturb a player who likes to hit balls wide to either side of him. If you can keep the ball deep when you hit it down the center, your opponent can't hit down the lines or angle the ball off the way he might with crosscourts.

It's not a bad idea to approach the net behind a shot down the middle, as long as it's deep. You're taking away the angle with this approach.

If the guy keeps beating you to death, you might try lobbing—which is the next lesson.

25 GRAND SLAM

TONY ROCHE and I had come a long way out of the Outback to play for the U.S. Open Championship and the biggest prize in tennis, $16,000.

"You could buy your hometown for sixteen grand and put it in a museum as the Roche birthplace," a reporter said to Tony.

"Might need a bit more," replied Tony, whose background was so much like mine. Tarcutta, the sheep town, wasn't any livelier than Marlborough, the cattle town where I spent my early days. My Dad had been the town butcher for a while, and Tony's Dad still is.

We were sitting around the locker room, talking to the writers because the start of our match was put off by the rain. Didn't look like we'd play that day, but there were 4000 hardy people under umbrellas and ponchos waiting for us in the stadium. Not much of a crowd for a national final, but considering the day, we were pleased that many had come. On the wall behind the couch where Tony and I sat were photos of the men who had won the American championship since 1915 when the tournament broke away from its status as a society diversion in Newport and moved to New York to become a major sporting event. My picture was there, from 1962. Tony wanted to be on that wall, but he would have to wait.

Tony was saying to a reporter, "Laver played me in one of his last amateur matches in 1962 when I was just a kid coming up; I gave him a good go in Melbourne, but he had other things on his mind. The Davis Cup was coming up and he was turning pro. He was a hero of mine, left-handed, you know, and a country boy like me.

"I had been hoping he'd win the Grand Slam. I heard about it on the TV that comes out of Wagga Wagga. Then I read about it a couple of days later. The Sydney papers take a while to get to Tarcutta.

"It's a bit different between us now. I had one chance to stop him, and I might have done it in Brisbane except for a bad call. I'll never forget that one."

No reason why Tony should; neither will I.

For the hundredth or so time we were asked to figure out how our rivalry stood. Tony kept better track of it than I did—probably because he was leading. Overall he was ahead 6 wins to 4. He had a good edge for the year (5–3), but apart from the New Zealand Open, he hadn't beaten me in a big one. Three of his wins had come in small pro tournaments. My wins over him had been in the Australian and Philadelphia Opens.

I talked to Mary on the phone. She felt fine, but was puzzled that the baby hadn't come, saying, "Now, it'll be just my luck to go into labor while your match is on TV."

It didn't happen. I was the only one in the family laboring that afternoon when the rain let up long enough to allow us to get started. The court was greasy, but somehow slow, which favored me because Tony's slice didn't take. Movement was tough, and this was a break for me because Tony decided not to put on spikes. He figured his strained thigh muscles would be jarred by the quick stops you make in spikes, possibly bringing on a cramp.

That first set was one of the strangest I've ever played. I should have won it and deserved to lose it. I got what I deserved and Tony took it 9–7, just took it right away from me after I'd been serving for the set at 5–3. He did it with beautiful backhands. I was sloshing and slipping around, and a couple of times I had asked referee Mike Gibson for permission to put on my spiked shoes. I'd wanted to begin the match in them, but he'd refused. After that game Mike said all right. It meant all the difference to me.

Tony immediately won his serve in four points, but I felt surer on my feet and I knew I'd get going. Especially when I stopped him two points short of the set to keep even at 6–6.

But I wasn't so sure when I lost that first set anyway. I'd had a lot of luck during the year, and I wondered if it had run out at last.

Although I've worn spikes here and there throughout my career, the occasions are so rare during my professional days that they take some getting used to. You consciously change your movements at first. Pick up your feet. No sliding. It's a new sensation until you're reaccustomed to them.

The slight uncertainty of moving in spikes was gone for good in the first game of the second set when I came through with a big serve at the crucial point of the match. With the first set his, and the pressure on me, Tony got me down 30–40 on my serve. One more point and he'd be up a set and a break, a pretty good edge in that mush.

We both knew this was a huge point. He took his time getting ready to return, and I did the same lining up—not overly so, maybe not even noticeable to the crowd, but we had to be right for this one. I was righter. I threw myself into the serve, and sliced it wide to his forehand. It didn't come back. He barely touched it, and I could tell it pained him to miss the opportunity. You don't get too many break-point chances on grass—and he didn't have another.

It wouldn't be apparent for a while, but the match turned upside down right there. I won the game and began hitting harder and harder as I got surer of my footing. Then I won the next and the next—five straight. From that break-point chance in the first game, Tony managed to win only 5 of the last 23 games. He came all apart as I wrapped him up, 7–9, 6–1, 6–2, 6–2. Not even a rain delay of a half-hour at the beginning of the third set could rust my concentration or help him pull his together.

Unlike 1962, I had control of myself all through the final

match of the Slam. I was never dazed as I had been against Emmo seven years before during a brief case of nerves down the stretch.

Serving match game, I opened with an ace. I knew what I was about, and wasn't going to let Tony breathe. It was 40–0 when I did try to end with a grand-slamming flourish on a forehand volley. I blew it. A minor disappointment not to be able to score with a put-away as I had on the championship point at Wimbledon.

It fell to Tony to lose it with a forehand that he hit long. Both of us were glad it was over. Afraid to use spikes, he'd been victimized in sneakers, unable to counteract my better shots, including a number of very good lobs. It was one of my best days with the lob, always a useful shot, but even more damaging that day when running was tough.

Not enough ordinary players realize the value of the lob, and I guess I didn't until I became a seasoned pro. It's much more than a desperation measure. As an amateur, even if the odds were against my making a shot, I'd usually let fly anyway. When I became a pro I couldn't risk throwing away points like that because the opposition was equal or better. This meant I had to be realistic. If my chances of making a shot from a difficult position were doubtful, I found you seldom get hurt with a lob.

But there were no more lobs to be hit. Not one more stroke on a chase that began God knows how many strokes ago in Brisbane when I hit the first serve to a fellow I wouldn't know if he walked into the room, Massimo di Domenico. The others I knew pretty well . . . Andres . . . Arthur . . . Emmo . . . Tony . . . Newc . . . Dennis . . . Kenny . . . Okker . . . Smith.

There were 1005 games in 26 Slam matches, and now it was all over.

I had won 30 straight matches since losing to Newcombe in June, the week before Wimbledon, the longest I'd ever gone without a defeat. Here it was September 9—and no letdown yet. It would come soon, in the second round of the Pacific Southwest Open in Los Angeles, Ray Moore ending the streak at 31. I hardly noticed.

Now the applause was coming through to me as I loped toward the net and Tony. Everything was coming through. My concentration burst, flooding my mind with a hundred things.

How was Mary? I wanted to call and see, and ask if she'd watched the match on TV, and wasn't it wonderful to have made the Slam—and the $16,000? During the phone conversation she would say, "You know, Rod, that's the first time you've mentioned the Slam all year. I'm glad there was something about it in the papers to alert me." Then we laughed.

Yes, I'd have to find a phone, but first there would be the TV interview and the press conference.

I was thinking about the evening ahead, too. John would be inviting people to the victory party. Mustn't overlook anyone, or fail to put in enough beer and champagne. And some food, too.

I'd be on the first plane tomorrow, but we should have a glass or two tonight to reflect on this thing properly. I was very thirsty.

I thought about the party they gave me in Brisbane when I got home after the first Slam. Two-pint mugs were the weapons and they kept loading them endlessly. It's an Aussie custom at those affairs that the guest of honor drains his mug at every toast. For the toasts they go through the alphabet, one toast for every letter—A to Z. They may have got to Z, but I'm still waiting to hear it. Or L for that matter.

I wasn't that thirsty.

Tony and I were at the net and he was holding out his hand. Suddenly I was in the air. What's this? I was leaping the net in the classic fashion. I must have gotten high just thinking about that party in Brisbane.

This wasn't me. I hadn't jumped a net in a dozen years. I thought it a bit show-offish for one thing. I feel humble about beating a man; I don't want to be one of those bloody gloating high-jumpers who can't control his emotions. And possibly I've always been self-conscious, afraid to look the fool as I had that 1957 afternoon in Adelaide after I beat Herbie Flam. I was nineteen, giddy at my first victory over a world class player, an

American Davis Cupper, who ranked No. 4 in the amateur game. I really didn't know where I was that day. In mid leap I caught my foot on the net and went on my face. Flam thought I'd fractured my skull—a minute too late for him—and the giggles came rolling down from the grandstand. I felt like the fighter who takes off his robe to discover he's forgotten his trunks.

Never again, I promised myself. I would be a dignified winner and loser.

But here I was bounding about like a kangaroo with spring fever, making it over the net to shake with Tony. Something inside me had released the built-in restrainers and said the hell with poise.

Where was dignity? Oh, well, where was the check for sixteen grand?

And where was the phone? This would be a very pleasant call to the West Coast. I went through the interviews and then found a pay phone behind the press stand. At that moment I also found out something vital to twentieth-century man: you may have the Grand Slam; you may have just come from a televised appearance in millions of homes; and you may even be clutching $16,000 in your omnipotent left hand. But none of this will get you a dial tone if you don't have a dime.

I had everything I wanted but to hear my wife's voice, and I couldn't have that without ten cents. Sixteen thousand dollars —but not a dime in hand. For the first time all afternoon I panicked. Only for a couple of seconds, until a newspaperman nearby loaned me a dime. He looked at the check and figured I was good for it.

LESSON 25
The Lob and the Answer

In the National Doubles of 1967 at Boston, my usual doubles partner Roy Emerson was in a bad way. (He might have been worse off if I'd been there, but I was a pro by then and he was still an amateur.) The grass courts were mucky, the ball wouldn't bounce; Roy had a bad back, and he was playing with an unfamiliar partner, Ronnie Barnes. "You're going to see more lobs in this match than you've seen in a lifetime," Emmo told a reporter.

And that's the way the tournament went for him: he kept lobbing, and he and Barnes kept winning, until finally Emmo broke down in a 105-game quarterfinal. Because of the low bounce and his back, Emmo couldn't get down to the ball to make the stroke he wanted, so he lifted everything much of the time, and it was pretty effective, even against those topflight players.

This was an odd case, but it is a fact that none of us good players, myself included, use the lob often enough. It can wreak havoc, in singles as well as doubles.

You have the defensive lob and the attacking lob. Kenny Rosewall is probably the most effective with the attacking lob, which is a shot with low trajectory. You're actually wrong-footing the person who's coming to net. He's approaching, and at the last second you hit under the ball and lift it. It doesn't have to be too high, but if you can pitch it just over his head, you'll catch him off balance and he won't be able to do much with it. That opens the court for your next shot. Rosewall still catches me with it, even though I've seen it often. He disguises it so well, and the element of surprise is as important as how well you hit the shot.

Hit the attacking lob over to the backhand side. Nobody handles a high backhand very well, and if the fellow runs around it to hit a proper smash then the court is really opened up.

294

When you're out of position and need time to get straightened around, the defensive lob is the shot: up high, 50 or 60 feet.

Strangely a lot of club players omit the lob from their repertory. They seem to be embarrassed by it, as though it's some sort of soft blooper that isn't quite manly. Rubbish. A lob not only gives you time to get into position, it poses a "think" ball for your opponent. He has time to think too much as that ball rises slowly and then descends on him during a tight match. Nobody hits overheads well for too long if the lobs are deep and well placed.

Fellows like Ion Tiriac and Ilie Nastase, the Romanians, have made themselves one of the world's finest doubles teams by tossing up lob after maddening lob. In doubles you can break down your opponents' teamwork with lobs.

One of the most deadly lobs is the topspin lob, and Spain's Manolo Santana was the first player I ever saw hit this ball well and attack with it. When the ball strikes the court it runs away. It's a difficult shot to make. You cock your wrist, as for other topspin shots, and hit up and over the ball with a snap of the wrist. Try it out in practice, and see if it comes to you. It's terrific if you can get it working. Your opponent will come to realize that he can't afford to let it drop. And a topspinning ball is tougher to hit out of the air, so you have an additional psychological edge if you can perfect this shot.

You can fight lobs with lobs, and see whose patience erodes first. Or you can discourage them with sound smashing. If the lob is extremely high, or it's a windy day and the ball is bobbing, you may want to let the ball bounce before smashing it.

Obviously if you allow the ball to bounce, you're permitting your opponent more time to deal with your smash.

It's best to smash the ball out of the air. Get side on to the net, and hum to yourself that folk tune, "If I had a hammer . . ."

Seriously, that's the stroke you want—hammering a nail into the wall. Not too much backswing. Imagine the ball is a nail at the highest point you can reach. And pound it with a hard, downward stroke. I like to leave my feet to throw my body behind the stroke. That takes good timing. Put away a few smashes and you'll dishearten the lobber. I hope.

EPILOGUE

WHEN YOU have to walk through ankle-deep slush to get from your hotel to the court, you know you're in the wrong place. I knew it even more the next morning when I paid my hotel bill. It was one of those rare occasions that I hadn't made enough playing to cover the bill. I opened the 1970 season on January 23 a loser, dropping a five-set match in New York's Madison Square Garden to Pancho Gonzales. It hurt for a lot of reasons. This was a winner-take-all match for $10,000, and the crowd, 14,700, was the largest I'd ever played for in America. Since I held a 2–1 lead in sets and should have won in the fourth, I couldn't be too pleased, especially losing that way to Pancho. And it was the first five-set match I could remember losing.

Was this a bad omen for the year that lay ahead, a year in which I would lose both my Wimbledon and Forest Hills titles? Some people might think so, but I don't think that way.

There were a couple of bad moments for me in 1970—the fourth-round defeat by Roger Taylor at Wimbledon, and the fourth-round loss to Dennis Ralston at Forest Hills. But I couldn't consider it a bad year. After all I won fourteen tournaments, and nobody else came close to that. My prize money was $201,453, a financial record for the game, raising me to $714,230 for eight years as a pro.

Don't misconstrue my thoughts and believe that I've lost my hunger and have an oh-well feeling about Wimbledon and Forest Hills. Not likely. I mean to have those titles again, so I can

297

pass Roy Emerson's record total of twelve Big Four singles championships.

But there are no regrets. I had a good run at Wimbledon— an unprecedented 31-straight match wins before Roger Taylor caught me. It was a sour afternoon for me, but Roger deserves full credit. He lost the first set and kept plugging. When he had his chances he made the most of them and got better. He kept the pressure on me so that I couldn't recover. At match point I was serving. Clunk-clunk . . . two balls into the net. What a way to go, but it does tell you that it can happen here. You may have even done it yourself, friend.

I hadn't been put out of Wimbledon so early since 1958. "Now we can go out and enjoy ourselves," Mary told the newspapermen. It was a nice chins-up line.

The U.S. Open at Forest Hills was different. I played better than I had against Taylor, but Ralston played what several critics described as "the match of his life."

He won the first two sets. I struggled to win the next two. It was then that I confronted a changed Ralston, a cool character. In other years he folded when he and I reached the crisis. Not this time. Nothing stays the same, I guess, and I've had to revise my estimate of Ralston. I had my opportunities. On a break-point against him in the fifth set I hit a forehand return as well as I can, right on his toes. Miraculously he scooped out a backhand half-volley that won him the point.

That shot was the match, we agreed. In 1969 I doubt that he would have made that shot.

Afterward Denny was pleased but gracious. He didn't gloat, "See! How about that one!" at the several reporters and columnists whose standard line had been: "Ralston doesn't win the big ones." He said some nice things about me that seemed to sum up the 1970 season as well.

"I don't think losing Wimbledon and here means the Rocket has slipped," Denny said. "But I don't think he or anybody else can dominate the world the way he did in 1969. It was improbable that he would win the Grand Slam again. With everybody playing for money and the number of good players increasing, it's a whole new world."

I had no thought of another Slam in 1970, simply because our pro group (Lamar Hunt's World Championship Tennis, which took over the MacCall-Podesta operation) did not enter the Australian or French Open. The deal wasn't right. There were in 1970 what I consider the Top Fifteen tournaments, and they were won by nine different men: Australian (Arthur Ashe); Philadelphia Indoor Open (Laver); U.S. Indoor Open (Ilie Nastase); Dunlop Open, Sydney (Laver); South African Open (Laver); Italian Open (Nastase); French Open (Jan Kodes); Wimbledon (John Newcombe); U.S. Pro (Tony Roche); West German Open (Tom Okker); U.S. Open (Ken Rosewall); Pacific Southwest Open (Laver); Paris Indoor Open (Ashe); Embassy Indoor Open, London (Laver); Stockholm Indoor Open (Stan Smith).

I entered eleven, won six. The variety of winners was good for tennis, and showed how strong the men's field has become. Maybe no man will make a Slam again, but the very fact that some people think it's out of the question makes me want to do it again. I'll try. The Slam goal put a zest and drive into me for 1969 that I'd like to feel again.

While Forest Hills eluded me in 1970, I'm sure everybody was pleased with the outcome: Kenny Rosewall winning his biggest prize at age thirty-five. He played in such a rejuvenated way that it's clear he'll be tough into his forties, like Pancho. And that makes me still just a kid, right?

Another youngster, Roy Emerson, and I got to the doubles final at Forest Hills, and I was sure I'd salvage one title. We were up against Niki Pilic, the Yugoslav, and Pierre Barthes, the Frenchman, who'd never won anything together. They beat us. I guess that figured, the way things had gone at Wimbledon and Forest Hills. I was a little annoyed. I wanted to win something in that place. We walked over to the platform where Charlie Tucker, president of the West Side Tennis Club, was awarding the prizes. First he handed Pilic and Barthes their checks for $1500 apiece and little gold balls, the latter emblematic of a U.S. championship on grass.

Then he handed us the silver balls that the runners-up get, along with checks for $1000. I guess I didn't look too happy, and Emmo looked over at me and gave me one of his golden grins—enhanced by all the gold in his front teeth.

"Well, Rocket," he said, "at least they didn't give us a kick in the ass."

I had to laugh. Emmo was so right. As long as you can swing your racket and play this game, win or lose, you don't have much kick coming.

The kicks aimed at me continued to come, annoyingly, from light-footed Kenny Rosewall. As our rivalry ran into the 1970s and began to get more and more attention, it became known as "The Rod and Kenny Show," and the ending was almost always happy for me. We played a lot of terrific matches, most of them tournament finals, and during 1970–71–72 Kenny managed to win only three of fourteen.

Only? Damn him, two he came through in were only the biggest, financially, that any tennis players have ever been involved in. And they came within six months of each other: the finals of a new competition called the World Championship of Tennis, staged in playrooms selected by promoter Lamar Hunt in his hometown, Dallas.

Big D meant Bigger Dollars than we could imagine: $50,000 to the winner of the first-place match and $20,000 to the runnerup. Eight players came to Dallas for the $100,000 shootout, and both times Rosewall took the fifty grand and ran to Sydney, leaving me feeling mugged and morose.

Near the close of the 1970 season, at Forest Hills, Lamar Hunt, Al Hill, Jr., and Mike Davies—the triumvirate atop World Championship Tennis—announced their new scheme for pro tennis, which would be called the World Championship of Tennis. WCT was ready to pull the game together professionally after many false starts by many promoters, including the most recent by George MacCall with my old outfit, National Tennis League, and Dave

Dixon, Hunt's first partner in WCT. Hunt and his nephew, Hill, had bought out MacCall and hired as executive director Welshman Mike Davies, an ex-British Davis Cupper and colleague of mine during earlier helter-skelter touring days. Little Al Hill (as distinguished from Big Al, his father, a good senior player) had been a regular on the tennis varsity at powerhouse Trinity University in San Antonio, and of course Davies had been in tennis all his life. While Lamar's critics within the hostile International Lawn Tennis Federation kept feeling—and hoping—he'd lose interest in tennis and fade away to his other sporting interests, his zest for our game and WCT increased. He has a house in Dallas that makes Versailles look like a tenement, and working hard on the backyard court he's become a decent hacker. There was a time, when Dixon was floundering with WCT and the game hadn't really hooked Lamar, that he might have backed off and forgotten it. But Lamar's not a quitter, and he's very proud. He was determined to make something of pro tennis, as he did of the American Football League, and to my mind his presence has been the single most important factor in the incredible advance of the game.

In presenting WCT's World Championship of Tennis format, Lamar felt that pro tennis needed a logical progression toward a world championship, a season of clearly defined competitions that would lead to a title playoff embracing the leaders over the season. This wasn't an original idea for tennis. Jack Kramer had devised the Grand Prix, which started in 1970, administered by the ILTF and injecting a good deal of the sponsor's (Pepsi Cola) money into the game. You are awarded points on the basis of your finish in Grand Prix tournaments, and the leading points winners gather for a Masters Playoff which that year was a six-man round robin in Tokyo. Although Stan Smith and I finished the playoff with identical 4–1 records, I was accorded second place because my loss was to him.

The trouble with the Grand Prix was its unwieldiness and inequities. There were too many tournaments, and the value of points varied from tournament to tournament, often incomprehensibly. It was chaotically operated, and clearly it was being used by the anti-Hunt ILTF as a means of trying to drive WCT out of business. The ILTF theory was that if Grand Prix events could provide enough prize money, then players wouldn't be tempted to sign contracts with the enemy, Hunt. Tennis politics is terribly dull, even to the insider, and, frankly, I can't keep up with the maneuvering. Actually only two or three people in the world can and do, and only because they work at it every day—guys like Kramer, the head of the Association of Tennis Players (ATP), the players union formed in 1972 that appears to have strength and permanence; Donald Dell, the player-agent who was the force behind forming the union; Bill Riordan, founder of the American indoor circuit.

To me, the political struggle has come down to professionalism vs. amateurism. The ILTF, a collection of the amateur ruling bodies of each country, has regarded the game as its private property, and resents encroachment by Hunt and other pro promoters. This resentment led to the war of 1971–72, when we once again were banned from Wimbledon in 1972. I don't worry about it. I was sorry to be barred from Wimbledon for a year, but I just keep playing, knowing that the pro grame is getting stronger, and feeling that the archaic concepts of the ILTF can't apply much longer. Amateur organizations cannot control professionals, as the ILTF has tried to do in the first days of open tennis. The sooner the ILTF, with its most powerful members—the USLTA, the LTA of England and the French Federation—realizes this, the happier everyone will be. The business of the ILTF is amateur tennis.

That's more than I want to preach about tennis politics.

Anyway, it was obvious that WCT couldn't promote a meaningful pro circuit while shackled by ILTF regulations and ineptness. Hunt, Hill and Davies decided to set up the World Championship of Tennis entirely apart from the ILTF, manned by 32 players who, ideally, would be the top 32 in the world. A poll of tennis writers around the world selected the 32, with me at No. 1. A few of the 32 chose not to sign with WCT—Stan Smith couldn't because he was serving in the U.S. Army—but the majority did, and the roster was filled by those who came next in the balloting.

WCT scheduled this troupe to play twenty $50,000 tournaments in America and eight other countries around the world. Prize money and points would be awarded uniformly. "We're building an entirely new million-dollar competition, strictly professional, to determine the professional champion of the world," said Lamar. So it was.

We opened in Philadelphia at the Spectrum where John Newcombe beat me in the final for the $10,000 first prize that was standard in the WCT tourneys. Everywhere we went the crowds were gratifyingly large and the publicity splendid. The schedule covered ten months, and we were playing other tournaments, too, like Wimbledon, where I lost in the quarters to a sizzling Tom Gorman. One tournament in the WC of T was rained out, so we had nineteen in all and nine different winners, pretty good balance. Newcombe, Rosewall and I won four apiece, and by the time I beat Arthur Ashe to win the Italian Indoor, the last leg at Bologna in November, I was at the head of the class.

Following me in the standings were Tom Okker, Rosewall, Cliff Drysdale, Ashe, Newcombe, Marty Riessen and Bob Lutz— the eight who qualified for the $100,000 playoff. The first two rounds were played at Houston where I beat Lutz and Ashe, and Kenny stunned Newcombe and wiped out Okker.

Ashe and I had a good four-set match, but it was the same old result: going into the 1973 season, Arthur still hasn't beaten me. The victory was worth $20,000 to me by assuring me of at least second place and raising my prize money for 1971 to a record of $292,717. I had been the first tennis player to earn over $200,000 on the court; if I could beat Kenny I'd be the first over $300,000. Meanwhile, as Arthur and I were shaking hands, the WCT press agent Ron Bookman (now associate publisher of *World Tennis Magazine*) was announcing to the press at Hofheinz Pavilion: "Rod Laver has become the first millionaire in tennis history. With today's win his prize money for nine years as a pro is $1,006,947."

Mary, who'd been sitting in the row in front of the press, turned around and smiled at Bookman: "Ron, would you read those figures again? There's a very nice ring to them."

Bookman obliged, "One - oh - oh - six - nine - four - seven."

It had a lilt to it, all right, and is good for publicity purposes. But the figure hardly makes me a millionaire. I'm sure you're aware of taxes and the fact that it has cost something to live in the years between 1963 and today. I hope this doesn't sound too materialistic—still, those figures let me know I've been successful at what I set out to do.

Nobody would rather deflate a millionaire and steal some of his money than Kenny Rosewall (who crossed the million mark himself during the summer of '72, in his sixteenth professional season).

Neil Armstrong, the moon-tripping astronaut, was among the 8700 spectators in the Dallas Memorial Auditorium. He showed up to present the huge trophy, and I wondered if Armstrong ever got as high in his rocket as Rosewall sometimes does on a tennis court. It was one of those stratospheric days for Kenney as he whipped me, 6–4, 1–6, 7–6, 7–6. As you can tell by the score, I had a good shot at it, losing two tie-breakers. But Kenny was way up emotionally, and he played those tense tie-breakers particularly well, winning them 7–3 and 7–4. I think I lost it in the third set as he served at 3–3. It was a five-deuce game with five break points for me. I played it a little too safe. Maybe $50,000 on a match puts a few more twitches in there and restrains you a little. When he escaped from that game he seemed to get looser, and his backhand and half-volleys got sharper.

He came down long enough to hug the trophy, pocket the check plus a diamond ring that annually goes to the champ, a sports car thrown in by a TV sponsor and a diamond bracelet for his wife, Wilma. I had $20,000 and—if it was possible—added respect for the little nuisance.

Thus ended a season that began with the brightest tournament concept yet for pro tennis as well as an event I called "The Rod Laver Benefit." That's not what Fred Podesta, the promoter, called it, but he might as well have because Laver was the only one who made any money out of it. The "Benefit" was a $210,000 series

of one-night stands across the U.S. actually named the Tennis
Champions Classic. Rosewall and I launched the series at Madison Square Garden in New York, and the idea was that the winner
would take $10,000, the loser nothing, and at the next stop another pro would appear to challenge the winner. I loved it. I don't
think I ever sent Podesta a thank-you note, but, Fred, here's a
capitalized Thank You in print. Thirteen matches I played and
thirteen matches I won, extracting $160,000 of Podesta's $210,000.

Getting myself into fantastic shape before the trek began, I
found myself back in the old days of one-nighters in varying
arenas. I had a good night right away to take care of Rosewall,
and then I had a lineup of guys who weren't quite used to this
sort of bouncing: Newcombe, Roche, Emerson, Ashe, Okker,
Ashe, again, Taylor, Okker again, Ralston and Emerson again.
Eleven matches—$110,000. Like plucking mangos from the trees
at home in Queensland. Nobody was quite sure how Podesta decided who the next opponent would be, but we wound up with a
four-man lineup for a semifinal and final at Madison Square
Garden. I beat Ralston for $15,000 in one semi and Okker took
Emerson in the other. Finally I overwhelmed Tiny Tom, 6–5,
6–2, 6–1 for $35,000 more.

The year had hardly begun and I had won more than any other
player up to that time except Laver. I guess you think I was greedy
in playing out the rest of the season. Only Roche had a real chance
at me, holding a match point in grimy Boston Garden where I'd
made my American pro debut, losing to Barry MacKay eight years
before.

That crowd in Boston told me something: the Tennis Champions Classic was a mistake. Just as when I'd faced MacKay and
pro tennis was a zero, there were about 2000 customers in a building holding 15,000. They looked like the same people, left over
from 1963—the hard core you could expect to show up at any tennis event. Tennis was appealing to a wider audience than that
hard core, but for the one-nighters only the core corps bothered
to stop by. One-nighters were dead, and the Classic couldn't revive them or anything but my savings account. Regardless of the

money involved, the Classic seemed an exhibition. The customers wanted tournaments.

For the fourth straight year I was over $100,000 in prize money for 1972. Barely ($100,200). It was an extraordinary year—for me, for our game—and each year improves on the one before. This may sound strange when you consider that I didn't win a major championship, was excluded from Wimbledon, and for the first time in nearly a decade wasn't generally regarded as the Number 1 player in this world.

Yet it was exhilarating because so many positive things happened: American network TV at last discovered tennis; WCT and the ILTF made peace, and WCT expanded; after numerous failures we formed a players union (the ATP) that could mean as much to tennis as the Professional Golfers Association has meant to their game; Commercial Union, a powerful international insurance company, took over the Grand Prix and seemed likely to provide better direction and stability for that event which now lies outside the WCT season; another insurance company, Aetna in Hartford, Connecticut, took over sponsorship of the World Cup, an annual U.S. vs. Australia team event for pros, which should become one of the great fixtures. And at the end of the year Dr. Omar Farid diagnosed my back trouble that had knocked me out for 3 and a half months after my Forest Hills loss to Cliff Richey, as a spinal inflammation. He prescribed medication that I think will give me new life and four or five more good years. The pill Omar's given me might get me blacklisted at Churchill Downs since it contains butazolydin (allegedly the drug that cost Dancer's Image his Derby triumph in 1968). But I don't want to win the Kentucky Derby, just half a dozen or so tennis tournaments a year.

I'd better not overlook the progress made by the women in 1972, led by the Czarina, Gladys Heldman, head of their union (the Women's International Tennis Federation), and by fiery Billie Jean King. I'm astounded by the money that has poured into their side of the game. Billie Jean made $117,000 in 1971 and $113,200 in 1972. Did I think I'd live long enough to be out-earned by a woman in my line of work? It would have been too preposterous to even think about. The women have done an admirable job in opening up new territories for the game.

The biggest disappointment of my career came in 1972: another defeat by Rosewall in the WC of T final in May. Nevertheless, in retrospect, that has its positive aspects, too. Gene Ward in his column in the *New York Daily News* appraised that three-hour-and-thirty-four-minute installment of "The Rod and Kenny Show" as the greatest tennis match ever played. Takes in a few tennis matches, and, though I'm grateful for that opinion of a writer who has watched top tennis for forty years, I'm not sure I'd agree with Gene. I even feel Kenny and I have played some that were better. But, did anyone else but Kenny and I know?

The occasion, in assigning greatness, is all-important. Don Budge probably played better matches than his five-set epic triumph over Gottfried von Cramm in the Davis Cup semifinal of 1937, but the situation and the stakes, the attention paid by the press and public, set that one above the others.

Well, Kenny and I had never played for so many people. There were 8500 in Moody Coliseum at Dallas, but the crowd I mean were countless millions of livingroom types freeloading at their screens. On that Sunday afternoon, May 14, somebody who did try to count the watchers (a TV ratings maker) stated that our match outdrew the pro basketball playoffs on another channel and the pro hockey playoffs on yet another. The estimate was 21.3 million viewers for "The R & K Show," which ran well over its allotted time on 170 NBC stations.

The greatness of this match was that it had everything: a major title, comebacks by both of us, spectacular shotmaking, tension, heavy money, a steady buildup to an unbelievable finish. I had to save a match point to take myself to a winning position . . . and when the match was on my racket, Kenny snatched it off. Dead on his feet, he somehow won the last four points to take the second tie-breaker, the title, the $50,000 and the other baubles again, 4–6, 6–0, 6–3, 6–7, 7–6.

It was as competitive as a sporting contest can be as we ran miles and hit thousands of shots, and I guess that's what held hordes of viewers who knew nothing about tennis.

I think if one match can be said to have made tennis in America this was it. I know it made me more well known than I could imagine, and I don't think the full impact in promoting the game has been felt. It was a chunk of sporting history, and I was part of it, helped make it. That much makes me glow when I think about it. Then I have to think about those two supernatural Rosewall backhands that beat me—made me a loser by just two points —and I know it was The Disappointment of my career.

In talking to the networks, Barry Frank, the TV agent for WCT, confirmed what he suspected: the pros would have to alter their year to get on camera. The 1971 final had been televised on a limited scale but was lost in November football coverage, just as Forest Hills is swamped by baseball and football in September. If WCT could conclude its year in May, the networks would take a chance. NBC took a package deal of eight live tournaments, and CBS put on a taped series of fifteen tournaments called the CBS Classic, which ran in the spring and summer.

In order to stage a WC of T for 1972, Mike Davies made up a winter-spring schedule of ten tournaments plus the $100,000 playoffs in May. Eight of those were televised. Davies wanted a twenty-tournament basis for deciding which eight would play for the most serious money, as in 1971. To arrange that he stipulated that points for the last ten tournaments of 1971 would count in a 1971– 72 season. When we resumed playing in February we already had a half season on our records. From 1973 on, the WCT season is to be only eleven tournaments in length, from January through May, but there would be two groups of 32, with four to qualify from each group for the playoffs.

I was off to a fine start, winning the first three tournaments, five of the ten, and finishing on top of the points standings once more. Next came Rosewall, Okker, Drysdale, Riessen, Ashe, Lutz and Newcombe. Same faces as 1971 though in different order. After I beat Newc and Riessen, and Kenny took Lutz and Ashe, it was our show once more.

All I can say about that final was it took so many twists that I still can't understand how I lost. Two points. I never came so close and lost. But I had my chances and that's all you can ask. I had the serve at 5 points to 4 in the decisive tie-breaker. The odds had switched dramatically to me. I had to win it. I looked at him and he couldn't stand up. Nobody was going to beat me now, after I'd been down 0–3 in the fifth, after I'd saved four break points in the next game to avoid 0–4, and after I'd zinged an ace on match point against me at 4–5. I couldn't lose it now. I wouldn't.

And I did. Or, rather, he beat me, that bloody thief Rosewall.

It had been a shotmaking feast throughout, for more than 3 and a half hours, but after all the sprints and swings and skids I had him. I can tell you the three swings of mine I regret the most. They came in the tie-breaker with me ahead, 3–1. I jerked him out of position and whacked a forehand down the line that Valery Borzov couldn't have touched. The tape interfered, and the ball dropped back on my side. Just a fraction higher, and it'd been 4–1. Then I double-faulted. Instead of maybe 5–1, it was 3–3.

Never mind, I told myself, and I got two of the next three to 5–4 with serve. Two points to the championship—and my serve. Great. Concentrate. I was going to go for his backhand corner. Yes, don't tell me—I know all about that backhand. But this time I'll slice it wide and clean him out of the court. He just can't move anymore to get back in position.

Surprise. He didn't have to move. Terrific serve . . . only the return was even terrificker, a cross-court angle that I'd never seen even from Kenny. I probed to make the half-volley, reached the ball but couldn't control it. Anything over the net would have got me the point with him sagging so badly, but my half-volley went long. It's 5–5.

One more serve, and I still know I can outlast him, even if he can carry me to 6–6. He's absolutely dead, and I feel great. Another serve to the backhand corner, and this is Kenny's last stab. Zoom, the ball goes down the line and I'm passed with plenty to spare. My edge is gone, just like that.

His serve at 7–6—match point. Can he lift the ball to serve it? Doesn't much matter. I'm glassy over those backhands, and I hardly notice that he's floated a serve over the net. I wave at it with a backhand and tap it into the net. "I can't lose," registers in my mind. "How . . ."

Kenny is so bushed he doesn't make sense in the TV interview. Not so bushed that he doesn't make sure the check for fifty grand is signed by Lamar.

They say he's cold and emotionless, but in the dressing room, Kenny broke down and cried. I wanted to, but I still couldn't believe it. A reporter asked him to think back to 1962 and try to imagine what he thought then that he'd be doing in 1972. "Selling insurance in Sydney, I guess," said Kenny. "Certainly not playing tennis. Certainly not for $50,000 in one afternoon."

Is there any place I can buy a policy insuring me against Kenny Rosewall?

It's our match forever—his win, but our match—and I feel people will keep talking about it. I won't discourage them.

As I finish this up early in 1973, the future of tennis seems unlimited. There are two WCT circuits now plus the Grand Prix and an indoor circuit independent of WCT. The days of scrounging to find eight or ten guys for a pro tournament aren't a decade behind us, yet today there are more than 100 good tournament pros, and the number will increase. Unlike golf, which we hope to emulate in many ways, we're restricted by space limitations. Using an arena with one court, we need a week to play a 32-man tournament, so I expect that shortly there will be several major circuits. In 1963 eight men showed up for that U.S. Pro Championship which went broke at Forest Hills (Rosewall, Laver, Gonzales, Olmedo, Hoad, Trabert, Buchholz, Segura). That was pro tennis. Today? As an illustration of what's happening: in January of 1973 five separate pro circuits (two female) went on the road in the U.S. and Europe to play 56 tournaments for more than $2 million in prize money. And that was only for the first half of the year.

Can you blame me and Emmo, Fred, Kenny and Pancho, Andres Gimeno and Mal Anderson—and the rest of the well-over-thirty gang—for hanging in there and teaching the kids more than an occasional lesson?

Hail, farewell, good luck, and here's fuzz in your eye.

Fuzz in your eye? Right. Don't let that fuzzy ball out of your sight for an instant. Hypnotize it. Stare it down. Watch it right into your strings.

If I leave you with one thought it's this: keep your eye on the ball from the instant it hits the other guy's racket until it hits yours. I don't care what kind of grips or footwork or physical equipment you bring into this game, you're going to hit the ball pretty well if you watch it every second.

Forget form, forget Wimbledon, forget Laver . . . there are three things that will make the game better for anybody, including you, Harold and Hattie Hacker—and Rodney George Laver.

Ready?

1. Watch the ball—nothing else.
2. Bend your knees as you hit.
3. Get your first serve in.

The rest is frosting.

And, oh, yes, if you do lose—and how can you after absorbing all this?—let your comment be that the other guy beat you. That's all. He won. (Probably you beat yourself, but that's beside the sporting point. You may add that you never saw the guy play so unbelievably well, if you can't resist rationalizing a little).

But let it go at that. He won. Nobody in the world really wants to listen to your excuses.

Or mine.

APPENDIXES

The Grand Slams
(World ranking of opponents, when so rated, in parentheses)

Don Budge, of Oakland, Calif., at age 22 in 1938

Australian, at Memorial Drive Courts, Adelaide—
defeated:
Les Hancock, Australia, 6–2, 6–3, 6–4
H. Whillans, Australia, 6–1, 6–0, 6–1
L. A. Schwartz, Australia, 6–4, 6–3, 10–8
Adrian Quist (6), Australia, 5–7, 6–4, 6–1, 6–2
John Bromwich (3), Australia, 6–4, 6–2, 6–1

French, at Roland Garros, Paris—
defeated:
Antoine Gentien, France, 6–1, 6–2, 6–4
Ghaus Mohammed, India, 6–1, 6–1, 5–7, 6–0
Franz Kukuljevic, Yugoslavia, 6–2, 8–6, 2–6, 1–6, 6–1
Bernard Destremeau, France, 6–4, 6–3, 6–4
Josip Pallada, Yugoslavia, 6–2, 6–3, 6–3
Roderich Menzel (7), Czechoslovakia, 6–3, 6–2, 6–4

British, at Wimbledon, London—
defeated:
Kenneth Gandar-Dower, England, 6–2, 6–3, 6–3
Henry Billington, England, 7–5, 6–1, 6–1
George Lyttleton-Rogers, Ireland, 6–0, 7–5, 6–1
Ronald Shayes, England, 6–3, 6–4, 6–1
Franz Cejnar, Czechoslovakia, 6–3, 6–0, 7–5
Henner Henkel, Germany, 6–2, 6–4, 6–0
Henry Austin (2), England, 6–1, 6–0, 6–3

United States, at Forest Hills, New York—
 defeated:
  Welby Van Horn, Los Angeles, 6–0, 6–0, 6–1
  Bob Kamrath, Houston, 6–3, 7–5, 9–7
  Charles Hare, England, 6–3, 6–4, 6–0
  Harry Hopman, Australia, 6–3, 6–1, 6–3
  Sidney Wood (5), New York, 6–3, 6–3, 6–3
  Gene Mako (9), Los Angeles, 6–3, 6–8, 6–2, 6–1

Maureen Connolly, of San Diego, at age 18 in 1953

Australian, at Kooyong, Melbourne—
 defeated:
  C. Boreilli, Australia, 6–0, 6–1
  Mrs. R. W. Baker, Australia, 6–1, 6–0
  P. Southcombe, Australia, 6–0, 6–1
  Mrs. Mary Hawton, Australia, 6–2, 6–1
  Julia Sampson, San Marino, Calif., 6–3, 6–2

French, at Roland Garros, Paris—
 defeated:
  Christiane Mercelis, Belgium, 6–1, 6–3
  Mrs. Raymonde Verber Jones, Annandale, Va., 6–3, 6–1
  Mme. Susan Partridge Chatrier, France, 3–6, 6–2, 6–2
  Mrs. Dorothy Head Knode (6), Forest Hills, N.Y. 6–3, 6–3
  Doris Hart (2), Miami, 6–2, 6–4

British, at Wimbledon, London—
 defeated:
  D. Killian, England, 6–0, 6–0
  J. M. Petchell, England, 6–1, 6–1
  Anne Shilcock, England, 6–0, 6–1
  Erika Vollmer, Germany, 6–3, 6–0
  Shirley Fry (4), Akron, Ohio, 6–1, 6–1
  Doris Hart (2), Miami, 8–6, 7–5

United States, at Forest Hills, New York—
 defeated:
  Jean Fallot, New York, 6–1, 6–0
  Pat Stewart, Indianapolis, 6–3, 6–1
  Althea Gibson, New York, 6–2, 6–3

Shirley Fry (4), Akron, Ohio, 6–1, 6–1
Doris Hart (2), Miami, 6–2, 6–4

Rod Laver, of Rockhampton, Australia, at age 24 in 1962

Australian, at White City, Sydney—
defeated:
Fred Sherriff, Australia, 8–6, 6–4, 6–2
Geoff Pares, Australia, 10–8, 18–16, 7–9, 7–5
Owen Davidson, Australia, 6–4, 9–7, 6–4
Bob Hewitt (8), Australia, 6–1, 4–6, 6–4, 7–5
Roy Emerson (2), Australia, 8–6, 0–6, 6–4, 6–2

French, at Roland Garros, Paris—
defeated:
Michele Pirro, Italy, 6–4, 6–0, 6–2
Tony Pickard, England, 6–2, 9–7, 4–6, 6–1
Sergio Jacobini, Italy, 4–6, 6–3, 7–5, 6–1
Marty Mulligan (7), Australia, 6–4, 3–6, 2–6, 10–8, 6–2
Neale Fraser (4), Australia, 3–6, 6–3, 6–2, 3–6, 7–5
Roy Emerson (2), Australia, 3–6, 2–6, 6–3, 9–7, 6–2

British, at Wimbledon, London—
defeated:
Naresh Kumar, India, 7–5, 6–1, 6–2
Tony Pickard, England, 6–1, 6–2, 6–2
Whitney Reed, Alameda, Calif., 6–4, 6–1, 6–4
Pierre Darmon, France, 6–3, 6–2, 13–11
Manolo Santana (3), Spain, 14–16, 9–7, 6–2, 6–2
Neale Fraser (4), Australia, 10–8, 6–1, 7–5
Marty Mulligan (7), Australia, 6–2, 6–2, 6–1

United States, at Forest Hills, New York—
defeated:
Eleazar Davidman, Israel, 6–3, 6–2, 6–3
Eduardo Zuleta, Ecuador, 6–3, 6–3, 6–1
Bodo Nitsche, Germany, 9–7, 6–1, 6–1
Tonio Palafox, Mexico, 6–1, 6–2, 6–2
Frank Froehling, III, Coral Gables, Fla., 6–3, 13–11, 4–6, 6–3
Rafe Osuna (6), Mexico, 6–1, 6–3, 6–4
Roy Emerson (2), Australia, 6–2, 6–4, 5–7, 6–4

Rod Laver, of Rockhampton, Australia, at age 31 in 1969

Australian, at Milton Courts, Brisbane—
  defeated:
    Massimo di Domenico, Italy, 6–2, 6–3, 6–3
    Roy Emerson (8), Australia, 6–2, 6–3, 3–6, 9–7
    Fred Stolle (7), Australia, 6–4, 18–16, 6–2
    Tony Roche (2), Australia, 7–5, 22–20, 9–11, 1–6, 6–3
    Andres Gimeno, Spain, 6–3, 6–4, 7–5

French, at Roland Garros, Paris—
  defeated:
    Koji Watanabe, Japan, 6–1, 6–1, 6–1
    Dick Crealy, Australia, 3–6, 7–9, 6–2, 6–2, 6–4
    Pietro Marzano, Italy, 6–1, 6–0, 8–6
    Stan Smith (9), Pasadena, Calif., 6–4, 6–2, 6–4
    Andres Gimeno, Spain, 3–6, 6–3, 6–4, 6–3
    Tom Okker (5), Netherlands, 4–6, 6–0, 6–2, 6–4
    Ken Rosewall (6), Australia, 6–4, 6–3, 6–4

British, at Wimbledon, London—
  defeated:
    Nicola Pietrangeli, Italy, 6–1, 6–2, 6–2
    Premjit Lall, India, 3–6, 4–6, 6–3, 6–0, 6–0
    Jan Leschly, Denmark, 6–3, 6–3, 6–3
    Stan Smith (9), Pasadena, Calif., 6–4, 6–2, 7–9, 3–6, 6–3
    Cliff Drysdale, South Africa, 6–4, 6–2, 6–3
    Arthur Ashe (4), Gum Spring, Va., 2–6, 6–2, 9–7, 6–0
    John Newcombe (3), Australia, 6–4, 5–7, 6–4, 6–4

United States, at Forest Hills, New York—
  defeated:
    Luis Garcia, Mexico, 6–2, 6–4, 6–2
    Jaime Pinto-Bravo, Chile, 6–4, 7–5, 6–2
    Jaime Fillol, Chile, 8–6, 6–1, 6–2
    Dennis Ralston, Bakersfield, Calif., 6–4, 4–6, 4–6, 6–2, 6–3
    Roy Emerson (8), Australia, 4–6, 8–6, 13–11, 6–4
    Arthur Ashe (4), Gum Spring, Va., 8–6, 6–3, 14–12
    Tony Roche (2), Australia, 7–9, 6–1, 6–2, 6–2

Margaret Smith Court, of Albury, Australia, at age 28 in 1970

Australian
defeated:
Evonne Goolagong, Australia, 6–3, 6–1
Karen Krantzcke (8), Australia, 6–1, 6–3
Kerry Melville (6), Australia, 6–3, 6–1

French
defeated:
Marijke Schaar-Jansen, Netherlands, 6–1, 6–1
Olga Morozova, Russia, 3–6, 8–6, 6–1
Lesley Hunt, Australia, 6–2, 6–1
Rosemary Casals (3), San Francisco, Calif., 7–5, 6–2
Julie Heldman (7), Houston, Tex., 6–0, 6–2
Helga Niessen (5), West Germany, 6–2, 6–4

British
defeated:
Sue Alexander, Australia, 6–0, 6–1
Maria Guzman, Ecuador, 6–0, 6–1
Vlasta Vopickova, Czechoslovakia, 6–3, 6–3
Helga Niessen (5), West Germany, 6–8, 6–0, 6–0
Rosemary Casals (3), San Francisco, Calif., 6–4, 6–1
Billie Jean King (2), Long Beach, Calif., 14–12, 11–9

United States
defeated:
Pam Austin, Rolling Hills, Calif., 6–1, 6–0
Patti Hogan, La Jolla, Calif., 6–1, 6–1
Pat Faulkner, Australia, 6–0, 6–2
Helen Gourlay, Australia, 6–2, 6–2
Nancy Richey (10), San Angelo, Tex., 6–1, 6–3
Rosemary Casals (3), San Francisco, Calif., 6–2, 2–6, 6–1

APPENDIX B

The Complete Year of Laver's Grand Slam

(* = The four major tournaments that constitute the Slam)

January

Sydney, Australia, New South Wales Open—lost final to Tony Roche,
   6–4, 4–6, 9–7, 12–10
* Brisbane, Australia, *Australian Open*—won final over Andres
   Gimeno, 6–3, 6–4, 7–5

February

Auckland, New Zealand, New Zealand Open—lost final to Roche, 6–1,
   6–4, 4–6, 6–3
Philadelphia, Pa., Philadelphia Indoor Open—won final over Roche,
   7–5, 6–4, 6–4
Orlando, Fla., Orlando Pro event—won final over Ken Rosewall,
   6–3, 6–2
Hollywood, Fla., Burger King Pro Cup—lost final to Roche, 6–3, 9–7,
   6–4
Oakland, Calif., Oakland Pro event—lost final to Roche, 4–6, 6–4, 11–9
Portland, Ore., one-night stand—defeated Pancho Gonzales, 7–5, 6–8,
   8–6

March

Seattle, Wash., one-night stand—defeated Gonzales, 10–8, 6–3
Los Angeles, Calif., Los Angeles Pro event—won final over Marty Ries-
   sen, 6–4, 10–8
New York, Madison Square Garden Open—lost first round to Cliff
   Richey, 6–4, 3–6, 6–3

April

Johannesburg, South Africa, South African Open—won final over Tom Okker, 6–3, 10–8, 6–3

Anaheim, Calif., Anaheim Pro event—won final over Ron Holmberg, 31–16, 31–28 (VASSS scoring)

May

Tokyo, Japan, Japanese Pro Championships—finished third in round-robin tournament, winning third-place match over Butch Buchholz, 5–6, 6–2, 6–5

New York, Madison Square Garden Pro Invitation—won final over Roy Emerson, 6–2, 4–6, 6–1

London, Wembley Pro event—won final over Ken Rosewall, 8–6, 6–0

Amsterdam, Netherlands, Dutch Pro Championships—finished fourth in round-robin tournament, losing third-place match to Roche, 6–3, 3–6, 6–2

June

* Paris, *French Open*—won final over Rosewall, 6–4, 6–3, 6–4

Bristol, England, West of England Open—lost third round to Cliff Drysdale, 4–6, 6–2, 7–5

London, London Open (Queens) —lost semifinal to John Newcombe, 6–4, 6–4

July

* London, *The Lawn Tennis Championships* (Wimbledon)—won final over Newcombe, 6–4, 5–7, 6–4, 6–4

Boston, Mass., U.S. Professional Championships—won final over Newcombe, 7–5, 6–2, 4–6, 6–1

August

St. Louis, Mo., St. Louis Pro event—won final over Fred Stolle, 7–5, 3–6, 7–5

Binghampton, N. Y., Binghampton Pro event—won final over Gonzales, 6–1, 6–2

Ft. Worth, Tex., Colonial Pro Championships—won final over Rosewall, 6–3, 6–2

Baltimore, Md., Baltimore Pro event—won final over Gonzales, 6–3, 3–6, 7–5, 4–6, 8–6

September

* New York, *United States Open* (Forest Hills) —won final over Roche, 7–9, 6–1, 6–1, 6–2

Los Angeles, Pacific Southwest Open—lost second round to Ray Moore, 7–5, 3–6, 6–2 (ending 31-match win streak)

October

Las Vegas, Nev., Howard Hughes Open—lost quarterfinal to Stan Smith, 6–2, 6–4

Cologne, Germany, Spoga Pro Championships—lost first round to Riessen, 6–4, 10–12, 9–7

Hamburg, Germany, one-night stand—lost to Rosewall, 2–6, 7–5, 8–6

November

Barcelona, Spain, Barcelona Pro event—lost final to Gimeno, 2–6, 8–6, 4–6, 6–3, 6–1

London, British Covered Courts (Indoor) Open—won final over Roche, 6–4, 6–1, 6–3

Stockholm, Sweden, Stockholm Indoor Open—lost quarterfinal to Stolle, 7–5, 8–10, 6–4

December

Basel, Switzerland, one-night stand—defeated Emerson, 6–3, 6–8, 6–4, 3–6, 6–2

Madrid, Spain, Madrid Pro event—won final over Roger Taylor, 6–3, 6–2

APPENDIX C
Rod Laver's Sixty-three National Championships

Singles (32)

Wimbledon (British)—1961, 1962, 1968, 1969
United States—1962, 1969
French—1962, 1969
Australian—1960, 1962, 1969
Italian—1962, 1971; Italian Indoor 1971
South African—1969, 1970
West German—1961, 1962
United States Pro—1964, 1966, 1967, 1968, 1969
United States Pro Indoor—1972
French Pro—1968
British Hard Court—1962
British Indoor—1969
Canadian—1970
New Zealand—1961
Venezuelan—1961, 1962
Swiss—1962
Dutch—1962
Norwegian—1962
Irish—1962

Doubles (24)

Wimbledon—1971, with Roy Emerson
Australian—1959, 1960, 1961, with Bob Mark; 1969, with Roy Emerson
French—1961, with Roy Emerson
United States Indoor—1962, with Chuck McKinley
United States Pro—1966, with Butch Buchholz; 1969, with Pancho
    Gonzalez; 1970, with Roy Emerson; 1971, with Roy Emerson
British Indoor—1969, with Roy Emerson

British Hard Court—1961, 1968, with Roy Emerson; 1962, with Jaroslav Drobny
Australian Hard Court—1962, with Bob Hewitt
Italian—1962, with John Fraser
Irish—1962, with John Fraser
Austrian—1961, with Roy Emerson; 1962, with Bob Howe
Swiss—1962, with Roy Emerson
Colombian—1961, with Luis Ayala; 1962, with Roy Emerson
Mexican—1961, with Roy Emerson
New Zealand—1961, with Bob Hewitt
Venezuelan—1962, with Roy Emerson

Mixed Doubles (7)

Wimbledon (British)—1959, 1960, with Darlene Hard
French—1961, with Darlene Hard
Venezuelan—1961, 1962, with Darlene Hard
Colombian—1961, 1962, with Darlene Hard

INDEX

INDEX

[Page numbers in italics indicate pictures.]